The Perennial Philosophy

Series

# World Wisdom
# The Library of Perennial Philosophy

The Library of Perennial Philosophy is dedicated to the exposition of the timeless Truth underlying the diverse religions. This Truth, often referred to as the *Sophia Perennis*—or Perennial Wisdom—finds its expression in the revealed Scriptures as well as the writings of the great sages and the artistic creations of the traditional worlds.

*Wisdom's Journey: Living the Spirit of Islam in the Modern World* appears as one of our selections in the Perennial Philosophy series.

## The Perennial Philosophy Series

In the beginning of the twentieth century, a school of thought arose which has focused on the enunciation and explanation of the Perennial Philosophy. Deeply rooted in the sense of the sacred, the writings of its leading exponents establish an indispensable foundation for understanding the timeless Truth and spiritual practices which live in the heart of all religions. Some of these titles are companion volumes to the Treasures of the World's Religions series, which allows a comparison of the writings of the great sages of the past with the perennialist authors of our time.

Cover: Detail from the dome of the Sheikh Lotfollah Mosque, Isfahan

# WISDOM'S JOURNEY

## Living the Spirit of Islam in the Modern World

*by*

John Herlihy

Wisdom's Journey: Living the Spirit of Islam in the Modern World



Library of Congress Cataloging-in-Publication Data

Herlihy, John.
Wisdom's journey : living the spirit of Islam in the modern world / by John Herlihy.
p. cm. -- (The library of perennial philosophy)
Includes index.
ISBN 978-1-933316-64-2 (pbk. : alk. paper) 1. Herlihy, John. 2. Muslim converts from Christianity--Biography 3. Muslims--Conduct of life. I. Title. II. Series.
BP170.5.H47A3 2009
297.5'7--dc22

2008047948

Printed on acid-free paper in the United States of America.

For information address World Wisdom, Inc.
P.O. Box 2682, Bloomington, Indiana 47402-2682
www.worldwisdom.com

# CONTENTS

In the Name of God, Most Merciful, Most Compassionate

# PROLOGUE

## Through the Lattice of the Soul

> When I behold the heavens, the work of your fingers, the moon and the stars which you set in place, what is man that you should be mindful of him? (Psalms VIII:3-4)

If by some magic wand we could retrace our steps through the mirage of time spanning a half century, we would find once again a small boy walking on his way to school. Perhaps only God knows how a distant memory is retained and kept alive like a snapshot from the past through the course of a long and varied life, but I remember making my way on foot to school through a forest of sycamores when I suddenly had a strange inspiration that has stayed with me through the years as a phantom wish. It struck me with the force of an inevitable truth that I wanted to write a book. Of course I had no idea what I could possibly write about; but children don't worry unduly about details and tend to follow the inspiration of their dreams without concern for the unknown. The challenge to use words big enough and the desire to express my thoughts clearly enough to fill a book entered my mind and remained there as a sacred vow down through the years. Whether the words that follow are big enough and my thoughts clear enough will be left for the reader to decide. For my part, I have now fulfilled that childhood vow by writing this book.

A work such as this not only has a story to relate and a message to convey; it also endeavors to deal with the subject of the spiritual life of the soul in a meaningful way that can relate to the aspirations and hopes of the people of our time. This simple aim would have posed no special problem to people of earlier centuries who were more accustomed to religious sentiments and more attuned to the spiritual life of their time. In today's highly charged world, however, reason and intelligence are no longer partners with inner feeling and sacred intuition. Spiritual experience has taken on a questionable nature in the minds of many innocent people, who would otherwise express the natural instincts of their faith in God if it weren't for the overwhelmingly secular and worldly environment that now pervades every aspect of modern life. Therefore, a few initial comments may anticipate and resolve some preconceptions and prejudices concerning the themes developed in this work.

We begin with a provocative question, one that hovers like a phantom deep within our being and haunts modern-day souls with its perennial quality. What is man? And alternatively: who is man that someone should care, much less the Supreme Being who created us? We begin with this important question because it lies sequestered within our minds and hearts as a remembrance of all that we are not and all that lies beyond our reach in a world that does not explain itself. We have only to look at the forces and subtleties of nature that surround us and the profound mysteries that break upon the shores of our consciousness to reveal the unanswered question that lies at the heart of universal mystery. If we pursue this mystery down into the depths of a seashell or up to the bird whose miracle of flight defies the laws of gravity, we can hear a whispered revelation that will make itself known through the latticework of the soul where the mystery remains, as elusive as the wind in the trees and as inscrutable as the image of the sphinx.

No doubt many people turn toward religion and the life of spirituality that it offers the aspiring soul in an attempt to answer this powerful question, one that shadows us like the footsteps of time and that never gives up its mystery unless we crawl over the edge of ourselves and scratch beyond the surface of the world to reveal the essence of what lies beneath. In this sense, I am not the exception to the rule but the norm, desperate to arrive at an answer that makes sense, and hoping to find the essence of a truth to live one's life by. We live now in an eclectic world, a global world, and even the disinterested person will encounter people and have experiences that will lead him in directions that were perhaps not available to people of earlier generations and time periods.

Within these pages, the narrative of an evolving spirituality takes its definition and shape from the outward expression of the Religion of Islam. The book's thematic line, and its very substance, sinks its roots into the traditional knowledge contained within the framework of Islam's main sources of knowledge, namely Revelation, Nature, and Man, revelation being an expression of the Mind of God, Nature being the created manifestation of God, and Man being the human reflection of the Spirit of God. A revealed scripture conveys the absolute Word of God, representing a communication that has descended from the Divinity to guide, heal, and ultimately lead mankind to the light of the truth. "Mankind, there hath come to you an instruction from your Lord and a healing for the (diseases) in your hearts, and for the believers, a guidance and a Mercy" (10:57). Nature and Man as sources of knowledge are stated clearly in the Quran: "Soon We shall show them Our signs on the horizons of the earth and within their own souls, until it becomes clear to them that this is the Truth" (41:53). Mother Nature, whose inner messages reach from the depths of the human soul to the outer limits of the horizon, contains within its order of physical magnitude a balance and harmony through its signs and symbols that humanity cannot live without. Finally, Man himself—known as *insan* in Quranic Arabic—is the human revelation and thus a source of knowledge by virtue of the divine imprint stamped on his being, making him a creature *in divinis* and thus a true reflection of the Divinity. The more he comes to understand himself not only as *Homo sapiens* but also as *Homo spiritualis*, the more he becomes the sacred mirror reflecting the light of a truth that verifies all knowledge. Muhammad, upon him blessings and peace,[1] once said: "He who knows himself, knows God."

Over 30 years have now passed by since I embraced the Religion of Islam and became a Muslim. Before my conversion, I thought myself the master of my own destiny. Fortunately however, as I will soon relate, the circumstances of my life forced this view to collapse through the sheer weight of its own absurdity. Life's truth finally overwhelmed my own personal lie. I began to realize that there must be something more than the petty self-centeredness of the individual ego, something more than merely human intelligence, something more to human life than its expression as a chance encounter followed by

[1] As a gesture of reverence and respect, Muslims the world over, in both the spoken and written word, extend their *salaams* to the Prophet in this manner.

its termination in death. One day, as unexpected as life itself, I was exposed to the basic profession of faith in Islam which proclaims the unity of God and asserts that Muhammad is God's messenger to mankind. Once the essential elements of the religion were explained, I felt its mysterious attraction and subtle influence seep into my being in a manner that could not be ignored. With an inner conviction that precedes any great decision and that finds its resolution in feelings of certitude, I became Muslim, formally made the profession of faith, and proceeded to experience my life; but not as the same person and not the same kind of life as I had lived until then.

Soon I commenced the spiritual practices that mark the Muslim life, such as prayer and fasting. I grew to like the Islamic rituals for their liberating quality: the heightened spiritual awareness that results from praying to God five times a day, the awakened consciousness that comes from giving to the poor, the intensely moving spiritual experience that is the pilgrimage to the Kaaba in Makkah, when a life journey becomes a spiritual journey to the inward Kaaba of the self. Even the fast of Ramadan, whose broad avenue of self-denial opens the soul to nearness with God, has provided an intense physical experience rendered spiritual by virtue of its substance and meaning. I have grown accustomed to abstinence from alcohol, preferring the clear awareness and self-control that comes with sobriety, rather than the fleeting pleasure of a light-headed drunkenness with its bitter aftertaste of artificiality and depression. Also, the meat of the pig no longer holds any special attraction over me. If the religion asks me to refrain from pork, I am willing to do so out of respect for the injunction and out of love for the God who imposes it upon me.

In addition, I have prayed in the three places designated as sacred in Islam. I have visited the holy Kaaba in Makkah, the "city of peace," where I made the pilgrimage (*hajj*) to the house of God on earth and kissed the sacred black stone. I have driven through the black hills of western Arabia to Madinah, the "city of light," the second holiest sanctuary in Islam, where the body of the beloved Messenger is buried and where endless streams of pilgrims raise their hands in aspiration and respect to the beloved Prophet who brought them this miraculous way of life. Before his tomb, I wept with sacred emotion before sending my humble greetings and *salaams*, and thereafter I sat down and meditated in an area of the mosque designated in the Holy Traditions (*hadith*) as a part of paradise. I have also been to Jerusalem and worshipped within the sacred precinct of the Dome of the Rock and al-Aqsa Mosque, the third holiest sanctuary in Islam, where the prophet ascended during his night journey through the seven heavens unto the Throne of God. If participation in the rites and rituals offers me the possibility to become the "universal" and "perfected" man of Islam—the aboriginal self according to the American Transcendentalist Ralph Waldo Emerson—then I will gladly abide by the strictures and guidance of the religion.

Since that crossroads and turning point many years ago, my life has been enriched beyond measure or reckoning. I can now speak and read Arabic, and this gives me entry into the sacred experience that comes with Quranic recitation. I feel closer to the inner self that knows God, especially when I sit in the early morning as the dawn light begins to emerge in the eastern sky, and read from the sacred book, the Holy Quran, revered by all Muslims as the absolute Word of the Divinity. Behind every verse lies the knowledge and light of God, whose spiritual energy and blessing course through one's entire physical being with a spiritual emotion that leads to the very threshold of tears. In return for the efforts demanded from the doctrine and the worship, I have been compensated with an overwhelming sense of well-being, with inner reservoirs of tranquility and peace that the word *islam* both means and promises. Altogether, I am a happy man. Can anyone ask for more than this?

The desire to write a book was conceived many years ago in my childhood; but the idea to write this particular book was born out of a suggestion by my brother-in-law to write a book about Islam that could state the framework of beliefs and the practical application of the religion in a simple, clear, and convincing manner. Indeed my brother-in-law, who is an intelligent and inquiring fellow with simple demands of life and easily satisfied, wanted to know in a concise and straight-forward manner what true Islam set forth as the principles of a virtuous life. He had watched the progress of my life as a Muslim since the time when I converted to Islam, in a more benign age long before the threat and hysteria of terrorism had raised its ugly head over the horizon of the world. He had witnessed with a non-judgmental interest my early years as a growing Muslim and recognized the extent of my determination to follow the practices of Islam and to adapt myself to its exotic and unique way of life. He was smart enough to realize that the Islam I pursued with such devotion was not the same

Islam portrayed daily through the mass media, either the stark images of fanatical, hooded, and veiled Arabs expressing their frustration and rage through acts of terrorism and suicide or the alien otherworldly culture of the desert Arabs with their distinctive clothing and their strange ways. He wanted to know about the other Islam, as he called it, meaning the true Islam, groping for the right words to explain his desire to know more that could touch his mind and heart with the inner revelation of the religion, and not just the outer form of fanatical devotees twisted by the misguided mission of *jihad* that calls for the slaughter of the *kafirun*, or disbelievers, and world domination.

Every piece of writing addresses a particular audience and this endeavor is no exception. In writing this book, I wish to address all those people who believe in God as a matter of spiritual instinct and are ready to examine their experience in light of a professed faith in a Divine Being. These reflections are intended for those who find themselves on the threshold of a new spirituality that can take root in the traditional forms, but whose experience conforms to the existential, psychological, and metaphysical needs of today. This book is meant for all those people who are looking for an experience of God as a real and truly felt spirituality within themselves, and for those who understand that these anti-spiritual times offer new spiritual possibilities for lifting the veil and transcending human limitations precisely because we are so close to "the brink," and so near what the traditional writer Martin Lings has fittingly called "the eleventh hour." We are writing for none other than ourselves, a search for knowledge that must eventually lead within, in order to uncover and expose the message of spirituality that lies dormant within every human being and awaits the fullest of expression.

In order to preserve a kind of simplicity of approach to truths that are fundamentally both mysterious and profound, the work has been structured around five key components, including the Awakening, the Foundation, the Descent, the Ascent, and the Journey.

The Awakening of Part I explores the notion of the primordial mystery whose fundamental question lies within us as the impetus and inspiration to turn toward God, especially during the spirit of these times when the very concept of mystery has been neutralized by the imposing certitudes of modern science, when all the while a broader, deeper mystery envelopes all scientific knowledge like the cloud envelopes the mountain and the sea envelopes the land. Beyond the mystery or somewhere deep within its well lies the ineffable secret that, once revealed, opens the door to knowledge of the infinite and the means to experience that knowledge. The English poet William Blake has observed: "If the doors of perception were cleansed, everything would appear to man as it is, infinite."[2] In Islam, the method of cleansing our "perception" lies with the *shahadah* (the witnessing) or testimony of faith, the first duty of the religion and the profound secret that cuts through the heart of the universal mystery with its sword of perception.

Part II lays the Foundation of an Islamic spirituality that begins with faith and comes to fruition through virtue and its corresponding behavior. The hot wax seal of both faith and virtue bears the stamp of the *shahadah*, a divine and revealed knowledge that shatters the mystery of a thousand million galaxies into the Spirit of the One, a revelation that becomes wisdom and blessing when internalized through the impulse of faith and the beauty of the virtues. As such we explore the meaning of these two components, the one a force and the other a quality that propels the aspiring soul on a journey of a lifetime—wisdom's journey through time—that becomes known through the expression of a life well lived within a traditional framework of a revealed religion, in this case the Religion of Islam.

Part III recalls the great Descent of knowledge in the form of a sacred revelation, a formal descent of the Divine to the human that has taken place across the millennia to make known what could not otherwise be known. Islam claims that there have been hundreds of thousands of prophets who have come to multitudes of generations over time with the essential knowledge they need in order to understand the true nature of Reality. Every aspect of the Quran is explored and reflected upon, from its sublime quality of blessing embedded with the rhythms and harmonies of the letters and sounds to the knowledge and worship that guide every Muslim during the course of their life, from the first whisper of the *shahadah* into the infant's ear to the dying breath at the threshold of death.

Part IV describes the meaning and significance of prayer as ritual and intimate means of communication from the human to the Divine,

[2] Chet Raymo, *The Soul of the Night* (Saint Paul, Minn.: Hungry Mind Press, 1992), p. 156.

the metaphoric Ascent through prayer, in response to the metaphoric descent of the Quran as revelation and absolute word of God, in the lives of the Muslims. All these elements—the mystery of the Unseen and the secret revelation, the impulse to have faith and the blessing of a virtuous life, the descent of a knowledge from the Divine to the human, complemented by the ascent from the human to the Divine through prayer as communication and intimacy—culminates in the Journey described in Part V, a sacred pilgrimage to the Kaaba in Makkah and the tomb of the Prophet Muhammad in Madinah, a physical journey that embodies through effort and physical hardship all the spirituality and aspiration of the journey to the inward Kaaba of the self as prelude to the great crossing of the divided self that ultimately comes to fruition in Supreme Union with the Divinity.

No doubt everyone makes their own choice regarding the purpose of their life and the means to fulfill that purpose. We have chosen to pursue the knowledge of Truth that has come to humanity from the Supreme Being as expressed in the Religion of Islam. We have chosen to follow the "straight path" of Islam—alternatively known as "the middle way"—that will lead us back to God through the purification and perfection of the self. Ultimately, truth's vital pursuit rather than truth's utter attainment will portray the human being as he or she is intended to be and is in their essence: A perfect inspiration of God and a human creature unique in kind who aspires to find its meaning and salvation in God alone. I may not be a virtuous man, but I have learned to struggle with myself to become virtuous. I may not be a good man, but I now realize that simple human goodness can only come from the discipline and efforts of an effective spirituality. A life lived in the shadow of the truth demands that we strive to free ourselves from the illusions of this world. It requires us to substitute the relative with the Absolute and to rise above profane existence through an awareness of the sacred quality at the heart of all existence. The Muslim life requires the believer to meet the moment of truth with his own truth. The present moment becomes a moment within eternity, while the eternal moment superimposes itself on the existing moment, thus making the presence of God real and truly experienced.

The idea of God must be conceived in the mind as a Truth, but it must also be felt in the heart as a sacred and divine Presence. Human intelligence conceives of the Absolute Being as a vital and living reality, and the free will of humanity proves its validity in pursuit of a life of spirituality that reflects that Truth. Ultimately, the Divine Mystery of the Unseen must be internalized within the heart and soul as a sacred possibility leading towards the kernel of a truth—the Overwhelming Truth—that needs to be experienced in order to be known. The spiritual path is straight, although it is difficult to follow. Human goodness is simple, yet sometimes impossible to achieve. Truth is accessible to all, but infinitely profound. Through the perennial search for the truth, the seeker can once again become as God created him to be. He can be the most human of beings, the repository of divine knowledge, a narrative of love in bodily form, and a channel of grace in a world in which he lives as a central and vertical being. Thus, the true Muslim can face the reality of this life with the perception of human nature *in divinis* and with a knowledge that allows him to experience the vision of God through the window of the soul.

With these thoughts in mind and asking God's help, let us now proceed with the following reflections.

# PART I

# THE AWAKENING

# 1. The Encounter with Mystery

The mystery of the unseen belongs to Allah.
Then wait; I too will wait with you. (10:20)

The sacred journey inward in pursuit of a traditional spirituality in the modern world must commence with the human confrontation with the Divine Mystery. As point of departure on a voyage that will never end, the idea of mystery commences the ascending journey through the byways of this world in search of an essence that will resolve the questions that, though often not consciously articulated, lie sequestered deep within human consciousness. Our challenge is to lift the veil that separates the manifested world of forms from the unseen world of the spirit and discover thereby a conscious experience of the truth. Embedded within the external world of forms lies a passageway to the internal world of spirituality, which, when experienced, comes alive and breathes spirit and life within human consciousness. To give oneself up to this ancient presence is to begin the process of transcending human limitations; to seek answers to the universal enigma we are confronted with in life is to set the heart on fire with the vision of the Spirit of God as the Origin, Source, Center, and End of all spirituality.

Prior to my conversion to Islam over thirty years ago when I was in my mid-twenties, I felt strangely torn between the forces of two conflicting realities and deeply confused by the experience of modern life that offers people of our time two convincing possibilities. People today can either deny the fundamental mystery of life altogether, or they can confront this mystery by lifting the veil that separates the seeming reality of this world from the true reality of the spiritual world.[1] Because the physicality of this world imposes a superficial

[1] The Prophet has said in a well-known *hadith*: "God has seventy thousand veils of light and darkness; were He to draw their curtain, then would the splendors of His Aspect (or Countenance or Face [*wajh*]) surely consume everyone who apprehended Him with his sight." Also, the Archangel Gabriel (*Jibril*) has said: "Between me and Him are seventy thousand veils of light." The veil of veils in this context suggests the absolute barrier that exists in the modern world between the knowledge of God and the ignorance of man based on a human attitude that precludes any opening to the spiritual world, much less to the Spirit of God itself.

and surface reality onto the human consciousness that is as unsatisfactory as it is overwhelming, many people today have second thoughts about the kind of life they are leading and are searching for a deeper meaning by discovering within themselves a genuine "sense of the sacred." Many people today seek to lift the existential mask of their modernist self to reveal the true soul that lies within the core of their being. In many ways, we are still confronted with a mystery that is both fundamental and sacred: fundamental because the unseen side of reality will always remain mysterious by definition, and sacred because its presence imposes a holy quality that renders the Divine Mystery less obscure and more accessible to the human sensibility. To deny the mystery or neutralize its sublime attraction would be as if to shoot a bird in flight, expressing a willingness to see in its fall to earth the end of the mystery that keeps its afloat, and to destroy the courage it takes to fly over mountains and across oceans in its wanderings.

The story of my conversion to Islam over thirty years ago has already been told in another place,[2] but suffice it to say in this context that by becoming Muslim, I was acknowledging, indeed embracing, the existential challenge to confront and lift the aura of mystery that overlays all of human existence as a transparent veil. One traditional saying (*hadith*) of the Messenger Muhammad, upon whom blessings and peace, expresses it this way: "Human excellence lies in worshipping Allah *as if* you saw Him, for even if you do not see Him, nevertheless He sees you."[3] The modern psyche already has a number of questions that haunt it with the specter of missed opportunity and

[2] *The Seeker and the Way: Reflections of a Muslim Convert* (Kuala Lumpur: Noordeen Publishers, 1998).

[3] Faith requires a leap of mind through the conditional "as if" in order to see with the inner eye and thus to understand that which cannot be seen with the external eyes. The veil separating man from God is both opaque and transparent—opaque because "man is his own veil," and transparent because "man is his own revelation" and as a consequence can lift the veil. If God is a mystery, then we are expected to live the mystery of God through the mystery of faith. "Man must feel that faith is something other than ordinary logic and that it sees things in terms of God and not in terms of the world; and by this fact, the believer is himself not entirely of this world, his faith is not a 'natural' thought, but a 'supernatural' assent . . . and this divine transparency of earthly things . . . confers on faith a sort of concrete and sacramental mystery, in short, an element of the marvelous which makes the believer a being marked by the supernatural" (Frithjof Schuon, *Christianity/Islam* [Bloomington, Ind., World Wisdom Books, 1985], pp. 220-221).

unfulfilled potential. If the sky did not reflect its mysterious message of infinite space, then we might not be able to see the world of the spirit that is the hidden side of reality. If the planets did not stream on course around the sun and if night did not revert into day as a sacred verse (*ayat*) of God, then we might not be able to realize the implicit harmony and order of the universe or the progression of time within eternity. If the world were not so absolute in its creation and so relative in its manifestation, then we might not be challenged to transcend our limitations and escape the world of relativity for the world of permanence and certitude. If the conditions of life had been other than what they are, the modern mentality might have been able to justify the irony of its existence by clinging to a purely secular and externalized understanding of human existence. Perhaps we should be as daring and bold as the traditional saying of the Prophet suggests and worship Allah as if He really exists, rather than worshipping this life as if He does not exist. Perhaps we should live as though in possession of a secret that we struggle every day of our lives to make real through our thoughts, words, and actions.

One question we need to ask is: How do we understand the word "mystery" and how does it define and shape the way we understand ourselves and the world we live in? Many people today may even be surprised by a question that has little relevance to their daily lives. Who today is prepared to assert that there are mysteries surrounding us that will never be resolved, mysteries that actually heighten human consciousness, mysteries that promise alternative worlds and a deeper experience of life than we could ever imagine on our own. The question of mystery and its power to resolve the human dilemma no longer inspires the modern psyche. The modernist mentality of today wants answers not questions, facts that neutralize the mystery pertaining to our origins and final end through scientific speculation, when once there was a time when certain questions were not asked lest a person risk destroying the very forces that keep us asking them.

On the surface, the question of mystery is profoundly simple; we ask it because its subtle inscrutability confronts us at every turn and stimulates the desire to discover what lies at the heart of the human condition. On the other hand, the question of mystery is quite simply profound, so deep that although it will never be resolved within this world, it fuels the desire to transcend human limitations. Elements of the mysterious substantiate for humanity an ancient purpose to life's procession through time; that which is knowable or provable through the evidence of human investigation is superseded by an ancient mystery—a *mysterium tremendum*—that positions us within a framework of time that does not pass us by and that creates an ambiance of wonder and bewilderment that opens onto the grace and beatitude of the supra-natural.

From within the cosmic wilderness there is placed within each person an initial spark—call it a form of energy, a vibration, a sound, or a light[4]—that initiates the line of human inquiry into the cosmic mystery. It is a spark that begins as a mystery, that becomes a hidden secret of the Supreme Being, that flowers into a revelation of the essential knowledge of God, that enters into the human soul as an eternal flame, that expresses itself as worship and praise of the Divinity, and that ultimately reflects through human virtue the qualities and attributes of God. Before a person can adopt a religious tradition, before any active participation in the life of the spirit, and before any true understanding of the role of a personal identity within a universal plan, this spark and the mystery it represents must be acknowledged and confronted.

The Divine Mystery is the Objectivity beyond the horizon of the human mentality, a metacosmic and infinite projection of both Truth and Reality; but this mystery comes down as a sacred presence in order to enter the ground of the human soul as a central and subjective experience. Because of the descent of the knowledge of God through the formal religions, humans know at least superficially that God exists and affects them in some way, but it may take a lifetime for that knowledge to become an inner realization that reflects back out into the world as forms of wise and virtuous behavior. When the human spirit meets the Spirit of God within the ground of the soul, that is the moment and the place when the knowledge of Truth becomes an experience of Presence.

The Divine Mystery in its objective and infinite mode is portrayed at a glance through the canopy of the night sky with the stars shining down their message of eternity and infinitude. The night sky, apart

[4] In the Islamic tradition, the universe is initiated through a vibratory sound with the words "*Kun fa yakoon*" ("Be and it becomes"), while the Biblical rendition of the creation begins with the words: "Let there be light."

from its serene and mysterious beauty, presents a pictorial representation of the cosmic reality. It is as if the heavenly bodies of the night sky have been designed by the Divine Mind to give humanity the experience of the presence of the Infinite. Despite their monumental distance on both physical and mental planes from true human comprehension, the stars offer a compelling experience of the mystery of the Divine. Yet we see this marvel every day of our lives without taking note of its profound implications. Ralph Waldo Emerson has put this thought quite eloquently and even a little mischievously: "One might think the atmosphere was made transparent with this design, to give man, in the heavenly bodies, the perpetual presence of the sublime. Seen in the streets of cities, how great they are! If the stars should appear one night in a thousand years, how would men believe and adore; and preserve for many generations the remembrance of the city of God which men have been shown! But every night come out these envoys of beauty, and light the universe with their admonishing smile."[5]

At the heart of the cosmic universe lies a fundamental mystery that will never be resolved on the human plane of existence. Yet this mystery, like a lingering scent, stirs up desires and emotions that lead us to the edge, not of some forlorn darkness but of an ineffable light that illuminates a vast universe of aspiration and hope, a mystery that will witness the destiny of humankind as cloud-covered mountain peaks witness the valleys to which they are enjoined.

> Nor will Allah disclose to you the secrets of the unseen mystery. (3:179)

Modern science's claim to objectivity in its relentless investigation of physical reality negates the traditional conception of mystery as the point of departure toward an unseen reality and denies what according to the Quran is the interplay between what is seen and what is hidden. The universe has been reduced to a horizontal cross-section of a flat, expanding universe, although the infinite nature of the galaxies and the eternal projection of time through light years recalls the Quranic

[5] *Selected Essays of Ralph Waldo Emerson* (New York: Penguin Books, 1982), p. 207.

phrase, "verily a day in the sight of thy Lord is like a thousand years of your reckoning" (22:47). It has become for us "this narrow world," and remains so even though we are regaled by images of billions of stars populating billions of galaxies, images that settle on the modern mind like so much dust permeating the air with nowhere to go. Nature has become "a dull affair," as Whitehead has observed, "merely the hurrying of material, endlessly, meaninglessly."

For the ancients, the mystery actually protected the integrity of the physical universe since they believed if God were to fully reveal Himself, the very focus of His attention would reduce the universe to ashes. Even Einstein, father of modern physics, did not rule out an appreciation of the fundamental mystery that lies at the heart of the universe, declaring that: "The most beautiful emotion that we can have is the mysterious. It is the fundamental emotion that stands at the cradle of all true art and all true science. Whoever does not have it and can no longer wonder, no longer marvel, is as good as dead, and his eyes are dim."[6] Yet most scientists of today follow more in the footsteps of Newton, who once irritably remarked, "'Tis the temper of the hot and superstitious part of mankind in matters of religion, ever to be fond of mysteries and for that reason to like best what they understand least."[7]

The reality of the Divine Mystery is contained within any number of spiritual traditions, from the Indians of North America who acknowledge the Great Mystery (*Wakan-Tanka*),[8] to the Muslims who acknowledge the mystery of the Unseen (*al-ghaib*). If the Divine

[6] Einstein, quoted in Bruce Vinall, *The Resonance of Quality*, unpublished PhD thesis (Bendigo: La Trobe University, 2002), p. 110.

[7] *The Betrayal of Tradition*, edited by Harry Oldmeadow (Bloomington, Ind: World Wisdom Books, 2005), p. 85.

[8] The name *Wakan-Tanka* means literally "Great Sacred" (*wakan* = sacred) and has been translated alternatively as "Great Spirit" or "Great Mystery" and even "Great Powers." "As regards these Indian expressions, so needlessly the subject of controversy, we see no reason for not translating them as 'spirit,' 'mystery,' or 'sacred,' depending on the case. It is obviously unreasonable to suppose that these expressions have no meaning, that the Indians speak in order to say nothing, or that they adopt modes of expression without knowing why. That there is no complete equivalence between one language and another—or between one thought and another—is an entirely different question" (Frithjof Schuon, *The Feathered Sun* [Bloomington, Ind: World Wisdom Books, 1990], p. 9).

Mystery were not central to the human mentality as a latent secret that demands exploration as well as explanation, then for thousands of years humanity would not have manifested the impulse toward the sacred and the mysterious through devotional worship and sacred art; nor would the yearning of the human consciousness for a higher consciousness have existed for millennia.

The Quran repeatedly calls upon the images of the Seen (*al-shahadah*), or the things of this world, and the Unseen (*al-ghaib*), or the Mystery that is implicit within the concept of the Supreme Being. The Quran elaborates on this mystery of the Unseen by identifying 99 names and qualities of the Divinity that humanize the image of the Divine Mystery of the Unseen so that humanity can understand what is required and what they must focus on in order to be truly spiritual beings. Among His many names, God is known as the Subtle and Mysterious (*al-Latif*), thereby establishing Himself once again as the unknowable as well as the All-Knowing (*al-Alim*). He is also the Near One (*al-Qarib*) and the Friend (*al-Wali*). As such, humanity can identify itself and approach the Divine Being indirectly, through a transparent veil as it were, because of the supra-human qualities and attributes of Allah set forth in the Quran. In Islam, to be human means first and foremost to attempt to model oneself on the divine names and qualities because these are "the best of names" (*al-asma al-husna*).

If Allah is the Divinity, the First and the Last, the Outer and the Inner, mysterious and paradoxical, He is also characterized by the Quranic revelation in terms that humanity sees within its own being and can understand implicitly and "without question." The qualities and attributes are elusive and possibly unattainable on the one hand, but direct, spontaneous and above-all personal on the other hand. As *Homo sapiens* we are none other than a mirror reflection of God, a humanity that can internalize the Objectivity of the Divine within its own subjective being. Because of our intelligence, we have access to the knowledge of God. Because of our human will, we can internalize that knowledge through experience, thus overlaying the purely subjective being with the Divine Objectivity. The human "I" can be subsumed into the Divine "I" and we are gathered together into the unity of the cosmic We.

The Divine Mystery is the cosmic enigma of all time. Its inevitable presence within the human mind marks the absolute horizon to the mind's cosmic inquiry beyond which exist realms that no voyager will ever reach. We do not need to know fully the universal mystery that confronts us. We do, however, need to maintain an attitude of open spiritual inquiry, and this may serve as the key to the unfolding of this macrocosmic mystery within the microcosmic world of humankind. All people must discover, through their own experience, the inner ground of their own mystery—where the wind of the spirit begins to blow—and how this "hidden treasure" relates to the Divine Mystery. Having once crossed the threshold to the inner self, there to have experienced the human mystery, we can begin to develop an appreciation, if not the elusive comprehension, of the Divine Mystery, in keeping with the *hadith* of the Prophet Muhammad, upon him blessings and peace, who said: "Know thyself in order to know God."

I remember myself as a devout child with a burning desire for God. As a matter of spiritual instinct, I felt the holy mystery that was embodied in the idea of God as a Supreme Being and Creator of all things. It seems that my "spiritual instincts" were still finely tuned in the manner of all young children who have newly "fallen from Heaven" and who are still close to the source of all Truth or what I have called elsewhere "truth's Truth." I remember that heightened consciousness of my childhood as an experience of true spirituality that I attempt to recapture even to this day. An example may serve to illustrate my point. When I was ten years old, I inherited a paper route from my two older brothers that, for two reasons, I hated with all my heart. First, it gave me my first taste of hard work, as the dark predawn of winter saw me rise from the warmth of my bed to face the bitter winter cold as I drove my bicycle down to the local newspaper outlet where I collected the newspapers. Second, it interfered with my near fanatic desire to attend daily Mass. Only if I rose at 5:00 a.m. did I have just enough time to deliver the newspapers (avoiding the neighborhood dogs that terrified my childhood sensibility) and get myself to the 7:00 a.m. Mass at the local church which was a 15-minute bicycle ride away from my house in the suburbs of Boston.

One cold winter's morning, I awoke later than was my custom and soon realized that I didn't have enough time to deliver the papers and make my way through the emerging dawn to attend the beloved ceremony of the Mass. I burst into inconsolable tears. This was my initiation into the world of true desire for the mystery of God. Everything up to that point had been the ordinary experience of life; but this represented an experience of profound emotion that was as mysterious as it was raw and unexpected. The tears that fell down my cheeks opened my heart so that I began to yearn to transcend life's limitations and to seek the inner spiritual ground of my outward self. Many years have now passed, but this childhood memory is still vivid and continues to motivate my efforts in pursuit of the way. I remember this experience as the origin of my spiritual quest, the first initiatory "gift of tears."

St. Augustine has bequeathed to us an interesting insight about the nature of mystery and of ourselves. "People travel to wonder at the height of mountains, at the huge waves of the sea, at the long courses of rivers, at the vast compass of the ocean, at the circular motion of the stars; and they pass by themselves without wondering." Mystery can teach us something about ourselves, the world, and the universe that proclaims its marvels and wonders, but the value of mystery itself cannot be taught. No one will take you by the hand and teach you the miracle of the Mystery of the Unseen, for every person must find and face the mystery on the inner ground of the soul. We are confronted with a mystery of what lies outside us, and of what lies within us. To understand the outward mystery, we must understand the inward mystery, or to echo the sentiment of St. Augustine, it is time to start wondering, as we pass ourselves by.

The resolution to the perennial mystery that shapes our lives finds impetus and direction through two symbolic images, namely, the horizontal plane and vertical ascent. The world of the spirit is represented by the vertical perspective,[9] while science and the world of provable facts are presented by the horizontal plane. It is important to understand the subtle differences implicit in these two points of view. The horizontal or scientific perspective proposes facts that seem to have no intrinsic meaning or symbolic value; while each thing is "something"

[9] "The traditional vision of things is above all 'static' and 'vertical.' It is static because it refers to constant and universal qualities, and it is vertical in the sense that it attaches the lower to the higher, the ephemeral to the imperishable. The modern vision, on the contrary, is fundamentally 'dynamic' and 'horizontal'; it is not the symbolism of things that interests it, but their material and historical connections" (Titus Burckhardt, *Mirror of the Intellect* [Albany, New York: SUNY Press, 1987], p. 25).

with respect to its factuality, it is "nothing" with respect to a possible significance or inner meaning. Thus the universe—its origins, its constitution, and its future—is merely a puzzle awaiting to be solved by human ingenuity through the application of the scientific method and the faculty of reason. The purely scientific response to mystery is not deference or respect, let alone reverence, but a relentless pursuit of "the answer." When a scientist accepts the premise that there are some enigmas that will never be solved, he or she is no longer within the bounds of the science framework.

From the vertical or spiritual point of view, the brash, but ultimately meaningless,[10] certitudes of the scientific perspective intrude upon God's space and His mystery. From a properly spiritual perspective, every external fact has its own fundamental mystery and corresponding meaning. Even a grain of sand is "not nothing" and has its own mystery and meaning by virtue of its very existence. No matter how much we may attempt to deny it, mystery comes bubbling up like a mountain spring. We only need to turn our sights upon the stars in the night sky to realize that a science of the finite needs knowledge of the Infinite, just as the body needs a soul in order to be animated, and just as a human intellect needs the Divine Intellect in order to be illuminated.[11]

At the heart of the Divine Mystery lies the notion that God is completely incomprehensible on the one hand, yet completely self-evident on the other. God is perfectly intelligible and uncondition-

[10] Much may be made, for instance, of the scientific theory of black holes or of parallel universes; but without a perspective that leads beyond the physical facts, there is no mystery, revelation, or secret disclosed by this knowledge that transforms the physical fact into a meaning that transcends the abstract theory.

[11] "He (the man of our times) sees the sky above him like any child sees it, with its sun and its stars, but the remembrance of the astronomical theories prevents him from recognizing divine signs in them. The sky for him is no longer the natural expression of the Spirit that enfolds and illuminates the world. Scientific knowledge has substituted itself for this 'naive' and yet profound vision, not as a new consciousness of a vaster cosmic order, an order of which man forms a part, but as an estrangement, as an irremediable disarray before the abysses that no longer have any common measure with him. For nothing now reminds him that in reality this whole universe is contained within himself, not of course in his individual being, but in the spirit or intellect that is within him and that is both greater than himself and the whole phenomenal universe" (Titus Burckhardt, *Mirror of the Intellect*, p. 32).

ally plausible to the intelligence of people who must respond to that Being. Yet He must also remain obscure, unknown, and unknowable, and beyond anything that human beings can really fathom with their present consciousness. There is, however, nothing in our intelligence that prevents a belief in the supernatural, although it is invisible and obscure. On the contrary, our native intelligence draws its substance from a natural inclination to believe in the mystery of some unseen higher Reality. Thus, ultimately, we believe in God, because He is who He is, the Subtle (*al-Latif*) and the Wise (*al-Hakim*), and He and only He makes sense.

The Divine Mystery presupposes a veil, or a tissue of veils, that protects its universal secret and maintains its integrity in the face of the lower order of human inquiry. Creation itself could be said to be that veil, and all of nature is thereby the formal representation of the mystery that pervades the entire manifested universe, from a bubble floating on the river to the black holes of cosmic space. The atom is a veil and so is the distant star. The universal cosmos cast as a dome of darkness in the depths of the night sky is a veil as is the cave within the heart of man.

From a more specific point of view, there are essentially three veils that preserve the integrity of the mystery without compromising the possibility of human inquiry. First, there is a supra-natural veil between man and God, the veil of veils. It provides the isthmus beyond which no one will pass, forever reminding mankind of the mystery of God that lies hidden behind the veil. Then, there are the natural veils that exist between man and the world and between man and his inner self, veils that hide the full disclosure, but often signal a revelatory message of some kind. The signs of nature are an example of such veils. Finally, there are the artificial veils that man creates for himself that are forms of illusion rather than sources of knowledge. These numerous veils of illusion are the ones we most often confront.

The veil between man and God remains absolute given that man will not see God, and for no other reason than that he simply cannot, any more than Moses could see God, and Moses was a prophet. "'Oh Lord,' Moses said to God when he reached the appointed place.

'Show Thyself to me, that I may look upon Thee.' But God replied: 'By no means canst thou see Me'" (7: 143). If not for a prophet, then certainly not for an ordinary human being will the supra-natural veil between man and God be lifted.

The veils between man and the world and between man and his inner self are relative and temporary. If we understand these veils in their aspect of revelatory meaning and not as ends in themselves, we can begin to see through the veil that separates us from the direct perception of the truth. If, however, we understand the manifested world and our own being as "absolute," without the support of the absolute Divinity, then the world and our human nature become permanent and opaque veils that exclude us from the truth. Behind the veil of the world is a mystery that cannot be fathomed in and of itself, but only through a meaning infused into the world through the vision of the Divine that is, as it were, filtered through the veil of His creation.

The majority of modern individuals have created their own artificial veils by adopting attitudes that darken and obscure, rather than reveal and protect, the life of the spirit. For example, the contemporary assumption that the physical world is the bottom line of reality amounts to a man-made veil, whereas in reality the phenomena of nature both protect and reveal the knowledge of God as well as preserve the mysterious sense of a unified reality that exists beyond the abrupt physical horizon of this world. Other artificial veils include an abiding belief in evolution as the explanation of our origins, the belief in progress as constituting our destiny, a materialism that is believed to form the basis of true happiness, and the general worldview of secularism. Taken together these beliefs form a thick and hardened veil that renders contemporary global society a closed and terminal system rather than a symbolic gate that opens toward the other side of reality.

Is it strange to commence this work with reflections on the mystery that strikes at the very heart of the life force and that shapes the way we understand the world? Perhaps, but only because we live in an age that does not see the forest for the trees or that in listening to the sound does not hear the sweet melody of the music. The Divine Mystery may go beyond the ability of words to contain it, but the presence and force of that mystery is undeniable for those who have eyes to see and ears to hear. And as compensation for the mysterious secret of the Divine Unfolding, every human being has his or her own secret that only God can truly fathom. "He knows every thought and hears the secret whisperings of what the soul itself may be less than fully aware, for He is the sole Owner of our souls, our minds, and our senses. Above all, He knows the *sirr*, the innermost nucleus of each human being, and no man can know another's secret."[12]

The meaning of the Great Mystery hovers in the background of our mind as the absolute interrogative of the human condition.[13] No one can deny its compelling presence, no matter how much he would like to be free of its implications. Like a watermark, mystery is embedded within the very parchment of our lives. But by acknowledging this mystery we create a bridge between the relative and the absolute, between doubt and certainty, between ignorance and knowledge. The unfathomable Mystery of the Unseen then becomes truth's associate, and its holy secret stirs the human heart with an inspiration that will one day lend the soul wings.

[12] S. H. Nasr (ed.), *Islamic Spirituality: Foundations* (New York: Crossroad, 1987), p. 374. Cf. footnote: "The *sirr* may also be said to contain the seeds of the future, which is concealed from mankind but known to God, and none can foresee what a man may become in the course of time."

[13] People today may consider themselves knowledgeable, but this does not mean that they have tasted necessarily the fruits of that knowledge, nor that they have internalized it as an operative wisdom. In fact, the knowledge they possess may have no genuine fruit in terms of experience. Secular knowledge may fascinate and intrigue the modern mind, but ultimately it "leads nowhere" and as experienced is actually as "dry as ashes."

## 2. The Secret Revealed

God! There is no god but He. (2:255)

The greatest of all mysteries lies in the intimate encounter between the heart of man and the Spirit of God. Within the mind, heart, and soul of humanity lies an inner ground in which the bud of a universal mystery can blossom into the fulfillment of the human spirit.

In the Islamic perspective, this unexpected awakening becomes a life-long endeavor to unfold within the human heart the spark of a divine mystery that finds its origin in a sacred, revealed formula in four simple Arabic words *la ilaha illa-Llah*, a negation of this world in affirmation of the one true reality, "no god but (the one) God." This simple message comes down into the human domain as a sword from heaven to strike open with a single blow the proto-mystery that hovers over conscious existence to reveal within its heart the message of oneness and unity that surrounds us as the secret revealed, that penetrates our lives as an existential reality, and that gives us a sacred identity and makes us who we are. At the utterance of the single, revealed "sacred formula," the creature meets the Creator; the human soul encounters the Spirit of the Divinity; the human being expresses readiness to become one with the Divine Being. The mystery of Oneness sews up the fragility of the universe with its permanence and certitude. It showers its certitude upon the mystery of the universe and casts transcendence into the soul of humanity. Its simplicity says a firm "no" to the permanence of this world and all that it contains as a prelude to the resounding "yes" in surrendering to the supreme principle of the one God, the Friend (*al-Wali*) and Guide (*al-Huda*).

In today's highly charged world of media hype with its exaggerated sense of importance, excess money, and uneven bias on issues; in today's dark world of Islamic fundamentalism and the terrorism that is its by-product; in today's world of alien concepts of a crazed and fanatic *jihad*, the issue of why a person becomes a Muslim has again come to the fore for Muslims and non-Muslims alike. Of course, over thirty years ago in 1974 when I first became Muslim, the manifestations of the collective psychic aberrations of the global mentality steeped in the maelstrom of the modern world was less manifest than it is today. People were worried less about random acts of wanton terrorism and more about the rising cost of oil which in 1973 had quadrupled in price almost overnight to serve a wake-up call on the world that the Sheikhdoms of the Middle East had control of a commodity that forms the underpinning of the Western economies. Not surprisingly, the question why I became Muslim was an important one then and continues to be so now in today's radically altered world, following me through time like a shadow across the more than thirty years of my Muslim life.

In any event, without delving into the politics of today's cultural environment and in spite of the profound climate of misconception and confusion surrounding the Islamic tradition and the opportunities of living Islam as the religion was intended to be experienced, I have now passed beyond the point of no return, and have lived more years as a Muslim than as a carefree, Western professional in search of success and personal happiness. The reasons behind conversion have been a religious, social, and cultural question from which I could not easily escape. In the eyes of the Muslims you are always a convert, forever new to the religion and eternally young in the expression of your spiritual life, and not born into the religion as they are. To them you are freshly fallen down from heaven having been newly born through an active choice and not cast from a mold that has robbed them of the privilege of a freely-willed choosing. For the non-Muslims, you are always under suspicion for having abandoned a way of life and a point of view that the majority of Westerners hold dear, including such hallowed values as independence, freedom, self-reliance, progress, and success. Living outside the envelope of two complete and integral worlds, one needs to find ways to come to terms with the reality of one's place in the world in addition to one's own destiny within the adopted religion.

There are many things that I have thought about only to myself, thoughts that I never had the presence of mind to divulge to anyone else. When asked about my conversion and why I became a Muslim, from whomever these questions may have come, I could never find the right words; or rather my inmost thoughts were buried so deep within the inner sanctum of my mind and heart that they could never find their truest expression in the light of day. How does the eagle in flight convey the magnitude of the blue sky that fills its soul with truth or give thanks to the wind under its wings allowing it to soar on high. But perhaps the moment has come for me to attempt to express the reasons for the loving reverence I feel toward the Religion of Islam and the beloved Prophet who delivered the divine message to humanity.

Every conversion, indeed every sincere turning toward the Divinity, is a blessing that comes from God. God chooses and man is chosen. Nevertheless, one can discern a pattern of spiritual evolution within a person's life that is worth mentioning as part of the process of becoming a Muslim or as some people prefer to say of reverting back to the acknowledgment of and surrender to the Supreme Being that lies within the heart of an infant child as well as within the heart of Islam. When I reflect upon my own childhood, I can remember some of the instinctive fear akin to spiritual awe that I felt in my heart for the idea of God. I remember an innocent and natural attachment to the Divine Presence that today I can only recreate with studied concentration and the discipline of spiritual devotions. An amazing characteristic of childhood is indeed its sweet and uncomplicated naiveté that reaches out and instinctively remembers the divine source. This is before children can learn to consciously separate from God and attach themselves to the world. The innocent young soul has yet to abandon its newly lost connections with eternity and the ambiance of paradise, and the desire to partake of its plenitude and benevolence is still instinctive and fresh. Indeed, this is what we see when we can upon the countenance of the infant baby.

Infant children seem to belong there no matter where they are and have no need to be anywhere else. They look out unconcernedly at the world around them as if they have claimed ownership and already taken possession of it. Of course they fuss when they are uncomfortable or cry when they are hungry since the world they are beginning to experience is not the paradise they remember, but by and large they behave in that primitive infant condition with nobility and contentment, as if they have brought from their mother's womb a knowledge of their own unity, as if the sea itself flowed in their veins and a crown of stars rested fittingly on each of their heads. In the detached gaze of an infant child, the wisdom of the world is wiped clean. A child at rest and free of care can teach us that it is not what we see, but the way we see a thing, that marks the difference between a pure, virgin mentality and the corrupted, over-worldly veneer that envelopes the adult mind, trapped within a labyrinth of its own human weaknesses and foibles and weighted down by the experience of the world. In fact, what does the child see but the same world as we do; but in a manner infinitely different, in which everything is at first new and strange, rare and delightful, and inexpressibly beautiful.

Infants are strangers unto themselves, but their entrance into the world is compensated by the world itself saluting them and surrounding them with innumerable joys. They know nothing of sin and protest, insecurity or fear. They neither know nor dream of poverty, vice, sickness, or death. Everything seems at rest, free of sorrow, and having an immortal quality. Everything is manifest in the light of day and behind ever created thing something infinite and eternal lies in waiting. Time for them is still a part of eternity, the universe itself is an Eden, and the world that infants experience make them heir to the mysteries which the books of the learned never fully unfold.

When I observe these holy sentiments in the young children of my extended family, and when I therefore glance back upon my childhood, I am struck by the boldness of my spiritual feelings and the purity of my loving attachment to God. These genuine spiritual emotions lasted well through my adolescence until the time I entered the mainstream of life during my twenties. When I entered the university, I was already beginning to suffer some inner confusion and self-doubt. My traditional attitudes had begun to weaken considerably as I was confronted more and more with the secular and contemporary attitudes of my friends and the anti-spiritual environment I lived in. The traditional dogma of Christianity didn't make sense to me anymore, and the demands of the secular world were simply too imposing, too tempting, and too convincing to refuse them outright. I eventually abandoned my spiritual inclinations in what amounted to a worldly naiveté and I fully embraced what the Muslims call the *dunia* in the life of this world.

I don't mean to exaggerate. My experience was common enough when I was coming of age during the turbulent era of the early 60s and is reflective of the experience many people today have, perhaps unconsciously on the inner level, as they shed their spiritual attachments and cling to the illusion of an earthly freedom and a human fulfillment that is clearly impossible without the aid of Heaven. As I mentioned earlier, a profound religious choice almost demands a rite of passage that amounts to a kind of "dark night of the soul." It is an inner passage of self-doubt and inner despair that is fully in keeping with the Quranic verse that states Allah has created man "in the best of forms, and then cast him down to the lowest of the low" (95:4-5). I was slowly becoming an empty glass, drained of all value and substance, without meaning or vision, an ego without a soul, or a fragment in search of the Whole. I tried to cultivate a kind of personal religion, if for no other reason than to keep feelings of confusion and despair at bay. I never denied the idea of God outright as many people willingly do nowadays. The secular attitude, for all of its attractions and subtle temptations, never really convinced me. But my personalized religion ran out its natural course. I finally realized that it was merely the delusions of my own ego, as if the mind had successfully outwitted the soul and closed off all doors to the latent spirituality within me.

Eventually the dark night of the soul reaches its ultimate conclusion, its lowest, most intense point, when a person is either lost to its shadowy depths or begins to see the light and turn towards God. For one brief moment, there is a realization, if one is so blessed, of how insignificant we truly are without the Supreme Being who sends blessing down to us and guides us through the mystery of life in spite of our pretensions to live on our own and insincerity in coming to terms with the truth. There is a brief second that amounts to the spark before the flame or the flash that precedes light. A person realizes that the choice is there for the making. It is either God or nothing, and one summons the presence of mind and the will-power to choose God. Perhaps this happens on some unconscious level. A person is made to feel once and for all the absolute need for God, and he feels this in his innermost heart and soul where the Absolute resides as a latent and unexplored truth. According to the well-known traditional *hadith qudsi*, in which Allah speaks directly through the Prophet in words: "The heavens and the earth cannot contain Me, but the heart of My believing servant does contain Me." At the threshold of spiritual discovery, a man of doubt and insecurity such as I was at that time becomes finally a man of faith, ready for the absolute experience of full surrender to the divinity as never experienced before in life. From that moment on, there is no doubting the Divinity, and faith begins to take root once again in the ground of the soul as the foundation of true spirituality. "Say: I worship Allah, completely sincere in my religion, for Him alone" (39:14).

I did pass through such an existential crisis just prior to my conversion to Islam and if this be a necessary prelude to the opening of the spiritual eye, then so be it. There is no doubt that this dark experience represents for me the winter solstice of my life. It was the absolute low point of a divine test, a pause before the turning and an inner hesitation before a new spiritual initiative that could replace the doubt and confusion about the purpose and meaning of my life. Beyond the inner spark and flash of light lay an inner burning to pursue a life of spirituality and follow a path that would lead towards perfection and enlightenment, an inner burning to identify oneself through a witnessing and surrender to a reality that is in fact the Higher Intelligence, the Creator, and the Absolute Being of the Godhead.

This inner burning was nothing short of a desire to perfect oneself through a process of knowing oneself, or to try to become what one is in the true light of human nature, namely a reflection of the Highest Spirit and the imprint of Ultimate Reality. The alternative is to run the risk of loosing one's identity, one's dignity, one's intelligence, and one's sense of self to forces that have no meaning or direction. God sets man free with His infinite possibility in a way that the world never can, and provides the keys to an understanding of the grand mystery of the cosmos that can be found within the human heart as the simple impulse to believe and have faith in God.

Many years have now passed since I first traveled to the Middle East to teach English at one of the local universities. At the time, I was seeking experience beyond the known world, impelled perhaps by the same spirit that stirred Christopher Columbus to cross the seas on his epic voyage to the very edge of the horizon in search of an earthly paradise. Little did I know then that I was setting off on an epic voyage of my own to places I had never dreamed of going, but that lay hidden as latent possibilities of the soul rather than anything so prosaic as a literal journey in search of famous landmarks or raw adventure. The details of the setting and the locale are not important to these reflections; what is important is the encounter that took place between me and Haneef, an Indian professor of Cybernetics whom I had the good fortune to meet when I first arrived in the Middle East. I fully appreciated his crisp intelligence, his electric presence, his unrelenting mirth, and the freedom that he allowed me to be intellectually curious without overpowering me with the force of his own will and the knowledge that powered it. He never imposed himself or his ideas on me, in keeping with the Quranic injunction that there is no compulsion in religion. On the contrary, he had a subtle, gentle way of not insisting upon anything in our discussions about religion. He had answers, but he withheld them until I asked the appropriate questions. A person can accept the truth, he told me at one point, precisely because he has the freedom to deny the truth. Eventually, the seeds he planted began to grow, so that the spiritual knowledge he wanted to impart could eventually become a wisdom rooted in the ground of my own evolving soul. Wisdom's journey through the course of my life began with the laughter and good will of a Kashmiri Muslim who planted seeds and tilled soil of the ready and willing.

Every religion has its own particular form that contains its own spiritual message, Haneef told me, but the final end is always the same.

"And what is that," I asked him, perplexed but intrigued by the force of his gentle persuasion.

"The transcending of human individuality through a grace called down by worship and sincere devotion," he said with assurance. "Throughout history, but especially now, people need to regain the lost contact with the Spirit of God. We are living in difficult times," he told me frankly. "Life has always been conditional and precarious, but never with such intensity as during these times that have all but witnessed the disappearance of the traditional world. Life may have always been conditional, but until now traditional people have always enjoyed an inner consciousness that made them a gate of departure and the only true exit from the confines of the individual ego. Through the effort of sincere devotion and spiritual discipline, a person could escape from the entrapment of this world, in Arabic and Quranic terminology the *dunia*." Haneef repeated a beautiful expression of the Prophet Muhammad, peace be upon him. "The *dunia* is the prison of the believers and the paradise of the disbelievers."

My laughing Sufi was dead serious. Haneef never tired of discussing these issues, and I for my part never tired of listening to him. He seemed to be bringing me to the threshold of spiritual experience within the context of the Religion of Islam through a process of psychology, by imprinting on my mind an understanding of the psychology of man and the necessity of the life of the soul. Perhaps he already sensed what I was beginning to realize and was guiding me like a lighthouse on some dark coastal headland, but I was in fact standing on the rocky outcrop of a new awakening, hovering on the knife's edge of spiritual realization, a hair's breadth away from being turned inside out. I was beginning to understand that the Religion of Islam is as simple as it is profound, and that the divine message is fully accessible to the extent that the human heart is open and ready to receive this knowledge. I was beginning to see that the truth of Islam can be reduced to an infinitely simple and clear sacred formula, and still retain its profundity, its depth, and its mystery.

One day, Haneef laid aside all discussion and summoned me to meet the moment of truth. "Now, I would like to ask you a question," he said, as I sat with him awaiting further words of wisdom to nourish my dry and expectant soul.

"By all means," I replied. It was the least I could reply after the multitude of questions I had asked him over those past few weeks many years ago.

"Do you believe in God," he asked me point-blankly.

I was taken in surprise by the directness of his question. My first impulse was to say no as if my modern sensibility had been affronted; my second impulse was to say yes as if the ancient certitude that lived within me could not be denied. The denial in me reflected years of conditioning and the latent desire to retain pleasures and liberties I had grown accustomed to. But I realized later that it was a necessary first step. One has to take a stand somewhere, sometime, and for me the moment of choice had come. Is it no or yes to the implicit truth of my life?

"I have always believed in God," I frankly admitted to him. "I have always taken comfort in the idea of the existence of God, even if I had no idea how to realize His presence and had no inclination to pursue the matter."

"Do you believe in a superior Intelligence that has no equal?"

Once again, I said "yes," thinking that God would not be God if He fell short of this noble description.

"Shall we call this intelligence Allah?"

"I don't know," I hesitated. "If you say so."

"It is not I who say so; He has identified himself with the name of Allah in the Quranic revelation. He is Allah, meaning the one to be worshipped, and the revelation is God's communication to humanity."

I closed my eyes for a moment, thinking: Yes, everything has a name, and so too God has spoken to man in this way and given Himself an identity so that a willing mind such as my own could communicate with Him and experience His presence. I opened my eyes and looked into Haneef's own. "Allah," I said, but more than merely saying a name, I was asserting a desire to believe and he knew it.

"If Allah speaks sacred words to mankind, He needs a man big enough, strong enough, deep enough, complete enough, and human enough to be able to receive these words and this knowledge with openness and humility," Haneef went on. "He needs a go-between, a messenger, a perfect man, to absorb and then to convey this simple yet profound message to future generations of humanity."

"Muhammad," I replied, thinking once again in the affirmation, yes, this must be so. "Is God going to speak to every man or any man, to me or to you, or is He going to send down His knowledge to His own messenger (*ar-rasul*) and friend (*al-habib*)?"

"You have said it, not I," Haneef intoned.

"What have I said?" I asked perplexed.

"The *shahadah*."

"And what is the *shahadah*?"

"It is the testimony of faith and the great witnessing in Islam," Haneef said. "God and messenger, knowledge and action, doctrine and practice, the two essential elements of a single all-encompassing truth. A sacred formula simple enough to say with the tongue; yet powerful enough to shatter false worlds, and profound enough to penetrate into both the human heart and the heart of the universe itself. A phrase that tumbles off the lips of the faithful with the sweetness of myrrh and gives expression to what lies beyond the mind and heart."

"What are the words of the sacred formula?" I asked.

"There is no god but God and Muhammad is His messenger," Haneef replied. "It is the formal summary and complete synthesis of the entire message of Islam. For the believer, it is the source of the ultimate knowledge and sets the seal on the one Reality. There is no reality, but the one Reality; there is no truth but the one Truth."

"How does it sound in the original Arabic," I asked Haneef, wondering about the cosmic sounds of the divine speech, a sound that must be the meeting point between distant thunder and the beating of angel wings.

*La ilaha illa-Llah, Muhammadan rasulu-Llah*, my friend Haneef intoned slowly and sonorously.

Outwardly, with my voice, I repeated the Arabic words, taking immediate note of their harmonious, other-worldly quality; but inwardly, I was not my usual normal self, a piece of driftwood floating on the open sea of this world. I was beginning to come to the realization that faith and practice bring real experience—an inner spiritual experience that is both real and undeniable and which amounts to a parting of the waters, revealing a straight path through the contingencies of this world.

Haneef shook with laughter.

"What's so funny," I asked him.

"You're a Muslim and you don't even know it."

"How so," I asked.

"You already have in your heart, what your mind is reluctant to place on your lips. With a gentle shove from me," he added.

I frowned outwardly; but smiled inwardly and said: "Perhaps you're right, yes, perhaps you're right." On some deeper, unconscious level, I knew that my Muslim life had already begun; indeed that instinctive surrender to a Higher Being had always existed within me as an inner reality that needed only the catalyst of a human experience to make it known once again. This unique encounter with Haneef had finally brought this truth to the surface of my mind so that I could see its light. The great journey had begun, wisdom's journey through the life of the soul as the soul journeys through the frontier landscape of a new life.

The moment passed quickly, but its memory lingers on and its enduring significance has never failed to keep me on the "straight path" of Islam. The moment of truth, however, never passes us by. It exists in time as an eternal reality, just as humanity exists in time as a temporal reality, spiritually human in order that they may become humanly spiritual. We have only to meet life's moment with our own moment of truth in order to incorporate the wisdom of the *shahadah* into the life of the soul. This meeting prefigures the divine meeting, when God and man are reunited once again through the doctrine of Unity, the one at one with the only One (*al-Ahad*), not just as an abstract reality prefigured in heaven, but as an existential experience lived on earth.

Witnessing and surrender are the categorical imperatives of the Islamic spiritual life. They represent the two sides of a double-edged sword—both creative and destructive—that cuts through human illusions about reality on the one hand and rips away the veils of the aspiring soul on the other, in order to expose the complete wisdom of the unity and oneness (*at-tawhid*) of God. Although the sword has erroneously been associated with the rapid spread of Islam across what is now called the Islamic crescent,[1] its inner, true meaning lies in its symbolic image as an instrument of discernment in which the mind uses the "flaming sword" of the *shahadah* to eradicate all falsehood and ignorance and strike open "as with lightning" the unity that lies at the heart of existence. Humanity witnesses through an intelligence that is both conscious and contemplative; humanity surrenders through a human will that is powerful, decisive, and free. Without the commitment of an active surrender, human witnessing of the truth is an abstract intellection or an empty word. Without the knowledge of a firm witnessing, human surrender to the Divinity becomes an empty gesture and a hollow sound, a form without substance, or worse, "the letter of the law that killeth."

Every religion approaches the sacred mysteries of life from a particular perspective. Islam's unique vision lays emphasis upon the dual role played by knowledge and action, combining the knowledge from above with the activity from below, for which witnessing and surrender are the human modes of spiritual expression. The Quran relates the sacred narrative in which the primordial soul of man proclaimed its cosmic affirmation of God as Lord with the words: "Yes! We witness You." The eternal norm was established once and for all eternity, as the prototype human soul recognized its place as God's servant in the great hierarchy of being, in exchange for the knowledge of God and the consciousness of self.

In response to the divine inquiry, the human soul bore witness; but this was only a prelude to a cycle of human witnessing, as the soul hovered on the horizon of an unfolding cosmic process. The witnessing

[1] The sword is not an image that is exclusive to Islam. Christ himself said in the New Testament: "I come not to bring peace, but a sword" (Matt. 10:34).

began as an instinctive and spontaneous overflow of knowledge and love between the Creator and His human creation—it was a direct communication between soul and Spirit. There followed the compulsory test of wills and the fall from beatitude. The prelude of this courageous witnessing gave way to an interlude in which humanity needed to seek out the essence of a lost truth. The harmony of interacting wills gave way to the need for the human will to surrender to the supreme will of the Divinity.

Once human beings fell from the beatitude of the paradise and the veils had been drawn before the inner eye, they needed the knowledge of God once again, and they needed the means to absorb and assimilate that knowledge into their beings. The witnessing testifies to the veracity of that knowledge, while the surrender of soul provides the means to assimilate and absorb it. Thus, the very concept of religion itself was born out of a knowledge that descended to the earth followed by surrender to the source of that knowledge in God. With this knowledge, humans could make the ascent once again back into the beatitude of the divine milieu. The Religion of Islam is the religion of surrender, the primordial *islam* reawakened and the primordial religion reconfirmed.

Witnessing commences a life of the spirit that acknowledges the all-powerful God as the Creator and Source of all existence. In fact, witnessing is both acknowledgment and verification of the truth. The Muslims witness through their intelligence, their mind, and ultimately their tongues, which repeat the great witnessing in Islam, the *shahadah* or the sacred formula that is on the lips and in the heart of every true Muslim. In addition to the words of the *shahadah*, however, the Muslims attempt to bear witness to the knowledge of God in every detail of their lives, by following the words of the Quran and imitating the behavior of the Prophet. Every word, every action, every attitude become meaningful statements that give back to God, through this formal surrender and witnessing, the essential knowledge He has sent down to humanity through the various forms of revelation.

The act of surrender provides the balance and the equilibrium for the knowledge contained in the witnessing. The believer's witnessing remains insufficient in and of itself, just as knowledge in the abstract, without its corresponding action, becomes merely an unexpressed inner process. A child learns the true meaning of fire once he has felt its painful power. The Muslims witness Allah because they have a genuine sense of who they are and who God is. They surrender, not so much because of who they are, but because of who they are not; they surrender because God is who He is and because they have not yet become what they are intended to be. Through their surrender to the All-Powerful and Supreme Being, the Muslims can express their humanity and spirituality as they were intended to be expressed. Otherwise, they run the risk of becoming less than human as they drift away from the divine norm established for humanity to follow. The active mind surrenders its own will out of deference to the Will of God, freely and willingly. Through such surrender, the Muslims place themselves within the code of the universal norm that must apply to all created things, including the human being. To actively desire to be outside that norm can further result in an imbalance and a disequilibrium that is most characteristic of the periphery and is actually to court damnation.

As with the primordial religion, the Religion of Islam identifies itself as the religion of surrender as well as the religion of faith. The Muslims identify themselves formally as *muslimun* (those who surrender) rather than as *mu'min* (those who believe), since one proclaims the privilege of surrender, while the other aspires to a deepening faith in God. However, both faith and surrender are fully integrated elements in the overall process of spirituality. The essence of the religion, without its legal, formal, and ritual aspects, can be summarized by a single divine command directed exclusively toward God's thinking creation: Surrender! This is verbalized in the sacred Quranic language through three letters: s (*sin*), l (*lam*), and m (*mim*). These three letters are the basic root that forms three key terms of the religion: These terms are *islam* or the concept of surrender itself, *muslim* or the person who surrenders, and finally the Arabic word *salaam* which means none other than peace. In addition, the meaning behind this Arabic root also suggests an inner soundness that leads to well-being, just as peace leads to peacefulness, and just as surrender leads to the security within the Divine Beatitude.

Surrender and peace, uniting as they do in a single root, are the spiritual antipodes of earthly existence. They represent effort for the sake of contentment, conformity for the sake of freedom, denial for the sake of affirmation, and contraction for the sake of expansion. Through surrender to God, the Muslim comes to feel a peace within his or her soul that can only grow out of conformity to the divine norm. It is the peace implied in the awesome serenity of the night sky or the calm tranquility of a placid, moon-lit sea. All of nature underscores a mood of sober other-worldliness with the signature of peace. This feeling culminates in a peacefulness of heart that serves as a motivation for humanity and promises the soul the quiet stillness that it knows instinctively to be the rightful inheritance of the good life. Heaven, which is the realm of perfection in Islam, is referred to as the *dar-as-salaam*, the mansion of peace, since the paradisal environment is a reflection of the inner condition of those near to God. In the gardens of eternity, "the believers will not hear any vanity, but only expressions of peace" (19:62).

Similarly, through physical attitudes and movements, the Muslims adopt postures that suggest human surrender at its most elemental, physical level. Certainly when the Muslims bow during the prayer ritual, they immediately assume a physical attitude of humility before the King (*al-Malik*). Similarly, the full prostration during the ceremony of prayer, forehead to the ground, must certainly be the most eloquent statement of total surrender that a person can express with the human body. Moreover, the Muslims express their instinctive surrender through a number of other bodily attitudes. The folded hands, the hands cupped in prayer, the arms raised on high, the head bowed in silent and solemn repose all capture within the body itself the sincere sentiment of humble surrender before God.

The religion of surrender that commences with Adam terminates with Muhammad, who is the seal of all the prophets (*khatim al-anbiya*). The cycle of revelation that began with the descent of Adam when God gave him *some verses*, concludes with the verse from the Quran: "Today have I perfected your religion for you, completed My favor upon you, and have chosen surrender (Islam) for you as your religion" (5:4). This was one of the final verses to descend to the Prophet before he died, thus terminating his ministry on earth. With the completion of the Quran came the completion of the religion itself, since the primary source for the knowledge of the religion comes from the revelation. Through the revelation, the religion of Islam began and through the revelation, it continues to live.

Faith and surrender form a subtle latticework of inner spirituality that distinguishes one man from another and advances the Muslim along the stations of the Islamic way. Faith precedes surrender from the point of view of time. One cannot surrender to a superior will without first having some consciousness of the efficacy of faith, just as intelligence normally precedes willing—at least in principle—even if a person can will a thing without necessarily being intelligent. Surrender rises over faith's horizon and takes root in the ground of a person's faith. Knowledge comes down from heaven because the human mind has the capacity to receive it through intelligence, but human aspiration reaches up to heaven and makes its ascent through surrender because humanity has free will and can act upon their desires.

Faith expresses itself most completely in the *shahadah* or witnessing, *la ilaha illa-Llah*, there is no god but the one God. The sacred words proclaim the divine prerogative and oblige the Muslims to witness the substance of its necessary truth. Through faith and surrender, the Muslim is able to superimpose an absolute reality on his or her own relative reality, thereby conferring on their immediate reality an absolute quality that represents the absoluteness of the Divinity. Faith expresses the knowledge of God; surrender expresses the desire for human goodness precisely because the freedom implied by willful surrender to the divine norm is an essential prerequisite of the Good. Without free will, humanity would not be able to experience the subtle and intricate harmony of their witnessing and surrender, and human goodness as such would have no real meaning for him. "As a trial, We shall test you with good and with evil" (21:36). Because we are free to conform to God's will by choosing between good and evil, our goodness, having been earned, arises out of the soul's free surrender to the moral ideal and is not the result of some kind of compulsory predetermination from above.

Total surrender of the human will amounts to a knowledge that has truly been carried out by the body and assimilated by the heart. God commands and humanity surrenders in an interaction of divine and human wills that are joined together in the unity of God. Abraham proclaims in the Quran: "Indeed, I am the first to surrender," having passed the divine scrutiny and earned his right to be the "first" among those who surrender. Every Muslim, however, wishes to claim that he is the first among those who surrender. Of course, this bold statement is not meant to be understood in its literal and quantitative sense, but rather in its qualitative one. Every act of surrender is a reconfirmation of one's way of religion (*din*) and a proof of the sincerity of one's inner life. *I am the first to surrender* must mean that I am ready to be first by way of anticipation and sheer will power, if not always in actual fact.

Man is the servant; Allah is his Lord. Through a willful surrender, humanity earns its freedom rather than becoming an eternal slave through a will devoted to the pursuit of a personal freedom that follows every earthly passion and whim. Humanity is free, but only insofar as God grants His human creation that freedom and only insofar as they earn freedom's divine rights and privileges. God's will is the divine model and the eternal prototype of all free willing: His Will takes precedence and His Command prevails. The human being is but a copy of the original and a mere functionary of the Divinity. Through surrender to the Divine Being, human intelligence and faith unite to form a virtue that provides the very atmosphere in the soul wherein the presence of the Divinity becomes not only possible, but fully manifest.

The Religion of Islam is an invitation, a call, a summons, and a promise. It is an invitation to a journey of return to the origin and source of all existence, a call to action and striving (*jihad*), a summons to perfection, and a promise of salvation. As such, Islam addresses itself to all that is vital in humanity, namely knowledge, action, and purpose. The existential human condition is one of exile just as it is a journey of return. By following the whispering of Satan and choosing the Tree of the Knowledge of Good and Evil, Adam had deliberately chosen a path of self-discovery and human fulfillment that required him to fall down from the paradise. "Go down from here," God has said definitively in numerous Quranic verses. Ultimately, the human soul responds to the divine call to salvation precisely because it contains within itself the very real possibility of damnation.

Conversion is an opening, an initiation, a challenge, and an act of pure surrender. A person opens the "eye" of the heart to the message of truth and embraces not only what is essential but what is inevitable. The challenge implicit in conversion involves none other than free will, for it is not enough to "become" Muslim, one must also "be" Muslim. The one is a single, decisive choice, the other a lifetime of choices. To the non-Muslim it may seem paradoxical, but to the Muslim surrender means freedom, the freedom to be most truly oneself through a submission to the truth, a truth that is known to be just, beautiful, and above all merciful (*rahmah*).

The distance between arrogant human defiance and surrender to the truth is actually infinitesimally small. Still, for a person to cross that small distance can be as difficult as touching the fire. In my own case, once I had crossed this invisible line, once the subtle distinction between faith and disbelief had been erased from my active consciousness, surrender to God could express itself within the context of a truly Islamic spirituality whose focal point is the Quranic revelation itself as the ultimate source of all knowledge and action. The *shahadah* is the ultimate remembrance of God and amounts to a fusion of the soul with the spirit of God through remembrance. Armed with the knowledge contained in the sacred formula, the soul takes part in a conscious inner life that allows man to superimpose the awesome reality of God onto the surface of the human consciousness in order to expose the fragile, dream-like quality at the heart of material existence. Of course, as a new Muslim, I was like an infant and a child again on the psychic and spiritual level. I knew nothing of the history or philosophy of the religion, nor had I read a single word of the Quran at first. All I had to hold onto was the *shahadah* itself, the great witnessing in Islam, but it was virtually a sword of lightning that had the power to pierce the heart with vital energy.

Eventually, I came to know that the sacred formula was actually the key to a sacred psychology of man and not just a formal doctrine of the religion. It is not just a theory and an abstraction, but a practice and a way of life. It provides the handle and the key, the means and the method to order and integrate the entire life of men and women, their waking and sleeping moments, their work and their rest, and their interaction with one another. Increasingly, I felt as if I had fallen out of a dense cloud only to arrive at the door of my true inner self. I could finally say: Now I am myself as I was intended to be, under the protection of Allah. What I do is in His name. I could finally affirm after years of self-doubt and uncertainty: I have located my true self through a revelation from God, without fear and without falsehood. Previously I had existed, but everything happened to me and I was confronted by people and the world with an insistence that could be frightening. Now, I happened to myself and I happened to the world. I finally know that I exist as an absolute reference point to the divine Authority. Now I know who I am and who Allah is. There is authority in me because I take part in the Divine Imperative. I enjoy a "relatively absolute" quality because I have surrendered myself to the Absolute. I affirm, witness, and worship my Creator and Lord. In return, a heightened spiritual consciousness is sufficient proof of all that I aspire to.

The pursuit of an Islamic spirituality involves devotion and worship to the straight path mentioned in the *Fatihah*, the opening chapter of the Quran. It requires much of the Muslim, including self-discipline, conscientious attempts toward piety, inner restraint, and the exercise of the spiritual instincts of charity, love, submission, fear, and hope. Gradually, the Muslim feels the momentum of this inner process having a profound effect as he begins to lay aside the externalized world of alternatives for the spiritual world of clear choice and vision; I can confirm this now after many years within the traditional, Islamic fold. As a Muslim, I know the secret of my heart's desire and can begin the ascent and return heavenward to the paradise lost. I am the human mosque, providing the setting for a sacred drama that takes place within my very being. My physical shape and vertical stance make me the human minaret. My head and shoulders form the towering porch where the call to prayer is made. My heart is the mosque enclosure itself. My soul becomes the inner sanctuary of my body and the *mihrab* or prayer niche of my being.

The Religion of Islam remains a vital and living spiritual tradition in the world today. The modes of worship such as prayer, fasting, and the pilgrimage to Makkah are still performed as they were fourteen centuries ago, and they still have the power to heal, purify, and sanctify. The call of the minaret still beckons the faithful to prayer, and the grace called down by sincere worship still has the power to transform the human soul into a perfected being. Modern man can still connect himself with God's sacred Presence in the world through his own spirituality and he can still escape the limitations of his own earth-bound ego.

Eventually, the Muslim convert must abandon his status as convert and become a Muslim, which is none other than one who surrenders his or her "self" to the will of God. Beyond conversion lies a vast realm of spiritual identity and experience that through effort, striving, and worship continually connects man with God. The Muslim life is not one choice, but many choices; it is not a solitary act of faith, but a mode of existence and a way of being wherein faith continues to narrow the gap that exists between the known world and the unknown frontier that the Quran identifies as the mysteries of the unseen. The servant approaches the Master and the vice-regent gives account to the King, and in so doing can lift the veil that separates the purely human from the spiritual world that finds its center in the Divine Being. Allah is infinitely transcendent, while at the same time infinitely close to man. "We are nearer to him than his jugular vein" (50:16), a well-known Quranic verse says in order to emphasize Allah's proximity to man, and reinforces this major idea in another verse: "God comes in between man and his own heart" (8:24).

The central purpose of the religion of Islam and its accompanying traditions is to keep alive in the mind and heart of the Muslims the truth of the one God. Through the duties and other spiritual disciplines, the knowledge of God must be made manifest in the lives of the people and not just as a token gesture to truth. Muslims face the idea of God and the eternal preservation of the soul as a matter of conscious reckoning as they make their way through life. They know that the exterior personality is merely a temporary form and façade, a house, as it were, or preferably a human mosque. They realize that they have obligations to Truth, and they fulfill these obligations with a willingness to act upon that truth.

I must confess that my capacity to intellectualize the human dilemma has its natural limits. At the time of my conversion, I had finally come to realize how difficult it really is to be a human being. It is not easy to be ourselves, and it is not easy to transcend our own limitations, especially in today's complex and fragmented world. The purely secular and materialist attitudes of modern-day society with all of their hype and pretence do little to satisfy the inner urgings of the heart and soul. We see plainly that we come into being, the world is the way it is, and ultimately we must take our leave. Somehow, we must arrive at an explanation in a world that does not explain itself.

This perspective is based on a revelation from God and has a formal structure in a way of life that is uniquely Islamic. However, it has also evolved from both an intellectual and an emotional process: intellectual so that those who think can grasp the message from Heaven with their minds, and emotional so that a person of spiritual sensitivity such as myself or anyone in today's world can come to love God with all his mind, heart, and soul.

I, a man approaching old age, abandoned my other self over thirty years ago for the promise of a spiritual reality that I understood already existed within me. The Religion of Islam introduced me to a mysterious world held aloft by the sacred formula of the one God and the revelation of a unified Reality. With a clear mind and a hopeful heart, I will endeavor to derive meaning from the subtle intuitions of the divine mystery and to experience the world through the force of the *shahadah*, whose vision identifies the Absolute as the supreme principle of Unity and portrays the human being as the human representative of that singular Reality.

# PART II

# THE FOUNDATION

# 3. The Certitude of Faith

Consider life for a moment as a river whose source and destination are not fully known. The river of life flows through a landscape that does not fully explain itself and it contains for humanity a topography of secret thoughts and conflicting emotions that are never fully satisfied or resolved. We must become one with this river and fully integrate ourselves with the environment that the river serves, but we do not know how precisely to do this. We must become like the river that flows inevitably within us; a river that irrigates the near and distant lands of our being, but as a living thread never loses its connection and never forgets its source. The question that haunts us as humans is this: What is the means to set free the inner current of our being and become one with the symbolic river that runs through us? The true existence of faith is no mystery; it lies in waiting as the backcloth to all our perceptions and as the pivot of the inner faculties. The mystery of faith lies in the certitude that springs from it, a certitude that shines like a farmhouse lamp beckoning weary travelers on some great prairie in the darkness of the night.

Remember childhood—that kingdom of native innocence and time of virgin faith. The infant soul still clings to the memory of its origin and source, as though it had unexpectedly fallen down from heaven without any surety of its whereabouts, yet providentially without a care in the world. The mysteries of life suggest not only a promise, but also a reality for this carefree and noble "infant being" who still enjoys an intimacy with the life of our primordial beginnings and has yet to forget the spirit of the remote golden age from whence it is born. The limitless sky with its vivid color of blue reminds the child of Heaven with its magical vistas of clouds and rainbows and stars. The field of tulips blowing in the wind brings joy to the infant soul as do the flight of the butterfly and the color of the rose. The whisper of the wind through the trees and the sound of the wave in a seashell create a reality of ghosts and distant shores as clear and well-defined as any scientific theory. There was no mystery, no dilemma, and no question that the child's mind could not resolve with satisfaction through instinctive faith and pure imagination, as if all the soft edges of their mind had not yet had time to sharpen and the tight ball of their infant beings had not yet had time to unravel. Life was like a house with a wide-open door: It held the peace, security, and contentment of pure spirit at bay against this mysterious and miraculous universe. The whole world lies at the feet of the infant and there isn't a sight or sound that enters the *tabula rasa* of its mind without passing through the sieve of its primordial innocence.

Perhaps we should somehow prepare ourselves during the innocence of our childhood and youth, when the river of life is still fresh and still remembers its source, for the uncertainty and discontent that manifest with the coming of maturity and adulthood. Perhaps we should keep telling ourselves as we grow older that we can never break through the illusions of this world and we will never be able to transcend the limitations of the human mentality unless we can maintain and preserve the virgin faith of infancy and childhood as an instinctive faith during the time of maturity and adulthood. Perhaps we will never know the meaning behind the face of the world and perhaps we will never achieve the certitude of mind and the serenity of heart that seems to be an instinctive desire of all men and women the world over. Perhaps if we could remember the poignancy and immediacy of childhood's imagination and faith, we would never let these vital instruments of perception go in maturity and adulthood as the scarred tissue of our lost dreams and deepest imaginings.

Prior to my conversion to the religion of Islam so many years ago, I was experiencing the confusion, isolation, and uncertainty of what I thought to be the ruins of my young life, far removed from the privilege of infant innocence and proximity to the source of our fundamental instincts and intuitions. What saved me then, and what continues to save me now, was a fundamental faith embedded within the spiritual instincts of my being that reaches out from some deep well to temper and tone my thoughts and desires with the sweet glow of its sacred sentiment. My childhood faith was still with me and still had the power to lift me out of the confusion and turmoil within myself by virtue of a consciousness that still yearned for an experience and a reality beyond the purely physical reality of this world. By the time I came of age in my early twenties and entered university, this lingering faith of childhood had weakened considerably. The spontaneity and instinctive imagination of my childhood and youth had vanished without a trace and I had no direction, no path, and no destination in life beyond an impulsive and primitive desire to be comfortable, secure, and happy.

Just before my conversion, my faith was a raw and primitive longing for an ill-defined spiritual path, a faith without coloration or substance, and a faith without the support of a traditional and God-revealed religion with its knowledge of the Reality and the blessing (*barakah*) that always accompanies a valid traditional religion. It was faith nonetheless, though only a kind of smoldering ember rather than an enlivening spark, a faith that still had the power and potential to lead me in a direction I could not have conceived of solely within myself and "on my own." This lingering faith was enough to set me apart from the multitude of my colleagues and friends who were drifting souls in pursuit of a purely secular existence, willing to live life without any other-worldly perspective and without the possibility of an inner spiritual life that could lead not only to fulfillment here on earth, but also to an evolution of soul rather than merely an evolution of body. They lived within a time frame and society whose culture supported a belief in a theory of evolution rather than a faith in the mystery of God, and trusted in a modern-day science that finds an answer for everything except the "one thing needful."

My faith at that time was naive and innocent, yet shallow and unstructured. I had no religion and consequently no clear path, because I had abandoned the Christianity of my youth during my university years like some worn out coat and embraced what the Muslims call "the life of this world." It was not enough for me just pretending to believe, without the support of a traditional path and without a genuine religion with its descent of knowledge through revelation, such as is found in the Religion of Islam and many of the other great spiritual traditions. I eventually came to the realization that my pretense to faith needed to give way to a true faith built upon desire, direction, and action. I deeply felt the sense of isolation and restlessness that seems to overlay our 21st century existence, not to mention the discontent of soul that is felt everywhere today. I felt separated from all that should have been meaningful in existence and I felt that an invisible barrier existed somehow and somewhere that inevitably cut me off from real possibilities, leaving me with a sense of despair and doom. The river of my life had flowed into a stagnant pool and I was no longer moving forward inwardly within the active stream of life.

Plato had an amazingly accurate perception reflective of a universal truth when he wrote several millennia ago: "It is not the eye that sees, it is the I that sees." In order to open my mind to the "I" consciousness mentioned by Plato, I needed to first close my physical eyes and turn them inward to the inner "I" which represents a consciousness of self, a consciousness most notably that sets humankind apart from the rest of the creation. I had to look far down into the depths of the inward self in order to ask: How could I make the connection and bridge the eye of the contemporary "ego" with the "I" of the eternal self? How could I cross the chasm that exists between the "passionate and egoistic" soul (*al-nafs al-ammarah*) and the "soul which blames" (*al nafs al-lawwamah*), or the discriminating soul that the Quran so clearly identifies? How could I change from being a believer in myself only and a believer in the power of this world as a satisfactory reality? How could I become whole again and not just an insignificant fragment disconnected from the totality of the life experience? How could I transform myself into a conscious being in search not of myself and my own personal truth, but rather a conscious "self" in search of truth's truth? How could I become one again with the river of life that flowed within me? There was one final question that I did not directly ask, but later learned that the Quran asks for us: "Is it not to Allah that sincere devotion is due?" (39:3).

These questions forced me to search for a knowledge that could effectively replace the ignorance at the heart of my understanding of myself and the world. These questions ultimately provoked a profound desire to search for a more meaningful approach to life. I was searching for something that could bridge the chasm that existed between my superficial understanding of the self-serving ego and the inward consciousness of the discriminating soul. I wanted to find a way to bridge the chasm that existed between the known world I saw before me with my eyes and the unknown world that I could sometimes feel with the inner "I" of consciousness. By the grace of God, I ultimately found myself at the crossroads of a new mindscape and on the threshold of a new heartland, through which flowed a river that circumvented both myself and the world. In what direction this new premonition would lead me I had no idea; it was enough to realize that that crossroads and threshold were in front of me, beckoning me with their symbolic meaning to reach beyond myself and my immediate world.

I have always been intrigued with the significance and implications of faith, partly because a fundamental faith made my initial interest in Islam possible, and partly because faith has played such a vital role in my life after my conversion to Islam, to the extent that I can honestly state that I am no longer the same individual that I was before becoming Muslim. The dynamic range of faith is in fact limitless and embraces countless possibilities. Men and women everywhere must find their own meaning and their own inner identity if they want to come to terms with the mystery that confronts them in life. This is true for those with faith and those without faith, true for Muslims and non-Muslims alike. To simply profess a faith in God with words is never enough. It is not enough to have faith, the believer must also live faith's meaning and implications.

Initially, the meaning of this new faith was a profound mystery to me; its practical application had yet to unfold and make itself felt in my life. The more I pursued faith's mysterious and elusive quality, however, the more I wanted to explore its inner meaning for my own spiritual development and its place in shaping the life experience. Why is it that one person is ready to believe in God and act upon that belief with all his mind and heart and another person refuses to believe and have faith in a Divine Being, but rather chooses to have faith in the progress of a purely material form of existence that begins with the evolution of the body but leads ultimately to the cul-de-sac of human mortality. It is perhaps the greatest irony of the modern-day world that the culture through which contemporary society expresses itself seems to deny the feasibility of a faith in a Divine Being. The purely secular point of view has become a worldwide cultural phenomenon, a worldview that encourages the pursuit of a purely materialistic life experience, a worldview that assumes a hereditary affinity with the apes through the now sacrosanct theory of evolution while aspiring paradoxically to a progressive development of the human race that never seems to emerge. It is a purely horizontal point of view and a linear mode of thinking that refuses to engage the possibility of alternative worlds and other modes of thinking about the self.

We can, in fact, safely assert that there is no such thing as a faithless person or a person without some form of faith. There are those who exercise their spiritual instincts and believe in the power of a Divine Being who has created the human being through an expression of infinite mercy and love: "I was a hidden treasure that wanted to be known. Therefore I created creatures and made Myself known to them" (*hadith*). Similarly, there are those who choose to believe in the concept of an evolutionary progression of *Homo sapiens* from the kingdom of the apes that affirms the natural progression of man from the animal kingdom and thus implicitly denies the possibility that a Supreme Intelligence has created the human being as an expression and reflection of the Divine Being, creating this human being "as is" and "from nothing" (*ex nihilo*). The belief that humanity has advanced over the course of time from the insensate nothingness of inorganic matter, and will somehow progress both mysteriously and miraculously into a superior form of being has become as sacred and definitive as the faith found within the family of religions. Its exclusivity does not permit or tolerate any counter-argument. Yet what is the significance of such a faith and what are its implications?

Once I had gained a feeling of conviction and adopted the path and the practice of the religion, faith was no longer a passive belief or an attitude of mind looking for a confirmation. It became the operative filter through which I was able to see through the inner "I" of the self and experience the world through a heightened consciousness that lent substance and meaning to everything I encountered. In adopting a spiritual identity through faith in a Divine Being, the world had become spiritualized and I had become a spiritual being once again as in the innocence of my childhood. When I began to experience the world through the prism of faith, it was as if nature everywhere and the universe itself came to witness all that was real and true. "Everywhere you turn, there is the Face of God." When I looked at the sun, I was able to see the Light of God, for "Allah is the Light of the heavens and the earth," and God is "Light upon Light" (24:35). When I looked at the night sky, I no longer saw merely the accumulation of stars and galaxies, but rather I beheld the symbolic image of the city of God and in return my life began to steer itself by the cyclic movement of the sun, moon, and stars, whose harmony and synchronicity was a reflection of the Divinity. Everything in the world of nature became a "sign" (*ayah*) and symbol of God. Through faith in God, I was whole again and took part in the totality and the unity of the universe which is its supreme truth. I became once again a part of the river that draws upon and remembers the source, a river that moves through a landscape of miracle and wonder and leads once again to a destination with meaning and promise.

This sacred saying of Christ has as much relevance today as when he spoke two thousand years ago: "Blessed are they that have not seen, and yet have believed." Perhaps we will find that the role of faith in the modern world is similar to the role of faith in the traditional world, at least from the spiritual point of view, as a means of activating the spiritual emotions and bridging the gap that would otherwise exist between the mind and the will, between what we know to be true as a matter of conviction, and what we are willing to act upon. At its best, faith initiates a process of inner inquiry that provides a vision into the true nature of reality and opens the possibility for people to appreciate and develop a sense of the sacred in all aspects of life.

Faith flows like a river through the being of faithful people everywhere and transcends both time and space by placing human beings within their own center and situating them within the eternal moment. Faith has the capacity to lift the veil of the Divine Mystery, to enliven the sacred traditions, and to overlay the symbolic image of the human being with a projection of the perfected being that we are destined to become.

As the point of departure for all spirituality, faith is both knowledge and belief. As knowledge, faith represents a modality of mind—an intuition if you will—that can awaken human spirituality by acknowledging the existence of an Absolute Being as the originating force of the human being. Faith as a basic intuition represents knowledge of a doctrine whose implicit blessing is the certitude that what one believes is the absolute truth. As belief, faith represents a modality of will that activates the human "free" will to believe in God, a Divinity who has created and who sustains the human soul, and who will ultimately save the soul that is worthy of perfection and fulfillment in Paradise. As such, faith contains a power that transcends form, and a power that can formalize the abstract into a clear image of the Divine, a power that can link outer and inner worlds like a bridge, and a power that can be a veil to protect as well as the key to unlock the dam of spiritual forces that lies at the center of our beings.

Because faith implies intuition based on knowledge of the Divine and a desire to turn toward God, it has the potential to become a force that can "move mountains." Faith permits those who have it to manifest inner realities through external actions, and to reduce the great impasse that exists between matter and spirit to a modern myth. By shattering the mirror of all earthly illusions, faith actually begins the process referred to earlier as "lifting the veil" of all cosmic mysteries.[1] Ultimately, faith has the power to lift the human soul onto the plane of realization of immanent and eternal realities.

Faith has the possibility of becoming a force too powerful to be denied by the men and women of our time and its significance and implications are too subtle to be summarily rejected or ignored by modernist sophisticates. Faith within the context of the modern world must no longer be labeled as merely psychological or blind, a thing to be dismissed as sufficient only for children, sentimentalists, antiquated spiritualists, and possibly fools, as though faith can only be explained as a human need to believe in fairy tales. Faithless men and women of today have been content to pass off faith's dynamic range as being mere childishness or sentimentalism that is sufficient to satisfy people who do not want to think, but which "thinking" people have no need of. When faith isn't passed off as a thoughtless sentimentality, then it is labeled as "blind," a pejorative word intended to imply that it is nothing more than a sightless vision founded on the basis of a human psychology that needs faith to explain the unknown nature of reality. Simple human psychology suggests, however, that people do need faith, not as a sign of weakness and inadequacy of mind or as a childish way of explaining the unknown to a frightened psyche, but rather as a measure of courage and strength, in which individuals overlay their thoughts, emotions, sentiments, actions, goals, and purpose with the power of the knowledge of God that accompanies faith.

Herein lies the secret of faith. Men and women of all times and places are faced with a number of unknown factors that demand of the thinking mind a faith either in the existence of a Supreme Intelligence who creates, guides, and sustains or a faith in some alternative, what in modern times would amount to a belief in the verity of an evolutionary process that originates somewhere and proceeds along a path of natural selection and survival of the fittest that promises a human

[1] "The veil is a notion which evokes the idea of mystery, because it hides from view something that is either too sacred or too intimate; but it also enfolds a mystery within its own nature when it becomes the symbol of universal veiling" (Frithjof Schuon, *Esoterism as Principle and as Way* [Pates Manor, Bedfont: Perennial Books, 1981], p. 47).

progress that will eventually bring modern man to a superhuman, rather than enlightened, state of being.

The modern-day alternative to faith is nothing short of a faith in religion's counterpart: modern science. Modern man cannot escape the parameters of a faith in something, as unknown factors continue to haunt us and force us to retain either a faith in God or a faith in evolution, for neither are provable according to the demands of scientific scrutiny and both require faith with its implicit leap of mind and imagination. In that regard, evolution is no different from religion, as much as modern scientists hate to admit it.

Modern man's commitment to faith can, in fact, be reduced to the level of lowest incredibility. Is it more incredible to believe in God as Divine Being, Supreme Intelligence, and the Absolute than to believe in the process of a human evolution in which the human body was arrived at after a complex progression of chance and accidental factors commencing with disparate atoms that combined somehow, somewhere, to form a complex grouping of molecules that ultimately formed a living cell that built itself into a thinking creature with a consciousness of self? Is it more incredible to believe that *Homo sapiens* is made in the image of God in terms of human consciousness, a consciousness that is self-aware and a consciousness that can be raised to a height of purity of mind and a pristine clarity? Isn't it more incredible that human consciousness has somehow derived from matter and that it is a sophisticated, refined, or somehow highly evolved form of matter? The modern-day approach to the mystery of faith should be from such levels of incredibility. Only then can we as modern civilized beings arrive at a satisfactory answer to the contemporary challenge to faith consisting of the less believable and utterly phantasmagorical suggestion that the higher has evolved from the lower, that consciousness has emerged out of the elements, that life and spirit have burst forth from matter as "spontaneous effulgence."

At the heart of this exacting dialectic concerning faith and its implications lies the seemingly absolute barrier that exists between matter and spirit,[2] a barrier needless to say that eventually must be

[2] ". . . The Origin of the Universe is, not inert and unconscious matter, but a spiritual Substance which . . . finally produces matter by causing it to emerge from a more subtle substance, but one which is already remote from principial Substance. It will be

faced—if not fully transcended—by all who want to articulate what is both meaningful and real within the range of their own existence. The relationship between matter and spirit,[3] between the world without and the world within, has a transcendental quality that defies clear explanation and cannot be explained fully with words, much less with terms that are purely scientific and thus non-transcendental and non-supra-rational. The relationship between matter and spirit lies at the core of the human difficulty in understanding and accepting "reality" as such, not as one understands it within a limited range of perception, but reality as it is manifested in the cosmic realm, namely as the Absolute Truth.

Matter and spirit are the two imperatives of life that shape human understanding and affect the experience of reality. These two great modalities of earthly existence play on us like the bow on a violin to produce an *andante* or the *largo* movement of a great soulful sonata, a melody that cannot be predicted or described within the context of a particular life, except as that melody is manifested through the formulations of the mind and the movement of the heart to emerge as a song among songs. Both matter and spirit contain their own mystery, and neither one is ever fully revealed to us as the basis for our lives or as an explanation of reality until they are played out on the strings of our being to become real experiences and truly felt realities. We are con-

objected that there is no proof of this, to which we reply . . . that there are infinitely fewer proofs for this inconceivable absurdity, evolutionism, which has the miracle of consciousness springing from a heap of earth or pebbles, metaphorically speaking" (Frithjof Schuon, *From the Divine to the Human* [Bloomington, IN: World Wisdom Books, 1982], p. 6).

[3] From the scientific point of view, matter and spirit antagonize each other with irreconcilable differences, denying each other their legitimate rights. "From the spiritual point of view, matter and spirit represent an enlightening paradox that exists in reality and must be what it is, just as facts and truth interrelate and ultimately harmonize" (Herlihy, *In Search of the Truth*, p. 35). Schuon, our ever-faithful mentor and guide, also sheds light on the matter: "Matter . . . is nothing else but the extreme limit or precipitation-point in the process of manifestation, at least for our world; consequently, it is the 'lowest thing' to be found within that reality that concerns us" (S.H. Nasr (ed.), *The Essential Frithjof Schuon* [Bloomington, IN: World Wisdom, 2005], p. 359). Because modern science relies so heavily on the validity of matter and on the human senses to substantiate that matter, Schuon elsewhere points out: "Modern science, by its own showing, remains strictly horizontal and linear; at no point does it reach above and beyond the plane of sensible manifestation" (*Ibid.*, p. 360).

demned to know them in part and only through their consequences on us, even though we are composed and fully enveloped by both matter and spirit. As we cross the threshold of a new millennium, the absolute division between these outer and inner worlds has become more difficult to identify, especially in light of recent findings in quantum physics. Today even the most rational scientist doesn't exclude the possibility of a complete theory of knowledge that would transcend the purely physical world of matter with the macrocosmic application of its law. The shift back to the spirit has already begun to the extent that it is naive now to think solely in physical terms and foolhardy not to leave a crack in the door of perception that leads back toward the unknown mystery of the Spirit.

Faith is the formal bridge between two realities: between matter and spirit, body and soul, outer and inner modalities, earthly and celestial realities. As such, faith brings about the sacred encounter and makes possible the meeting of man and God.

Firstly, faith strikes down the apparently absolute barrier that exists between matter and spirit with its wand of inspiration and insight. Through an accepted knowledge incorporated into the mind and through a kind of imaginative yearning of the heart that becomes an experience that is very real, faith bridges the vast distance that separates humanity from the Sublime. The sacred intuition of faith permits an understanding of unity to be possible between the world of form and the world of spirit to the extent that it could be said that the physical world is spirit seen from without, while the spiritual world is the external world seen from within, an interactive and harmonious blending of earthly and celestial realities. Because of faith, the physicality of the world of matter does not become a stumbling block in man's perception of reality. Faith allows the believer to understand, if not actually see, the forces of spirit at work within matter. Nature itself is the prime example of form virtually glowing with spirit. In this way, a barrier that seems absolute to the human mind takes on a more transcendental quality through the interaction of faith with the human mind and heart.

Secondly, faith bridges the great divide that exists between man and his own self on the one hand, and between man and God on the other. This gap of self exists on existential levels wherein people understand themselves to be living beings without explanation, a fragment of a whole that is both mysterious and questioning. It is as if we project two personalities out of ourselves, an outer self personified in the ego that responds to the demands of the world and our immediate environment. The second personality lies further within us and runs as a deep undercurrent that emerges at moments in our lives when we are able to discard all our worldly presumptions and preconceived attitudes for a spiritual intuition that projects the inner self out into the outer world of people and forms.

Faith as a bridge to inner worlds sets in motion a movement of the spirit that needs to be activated, lest the spirit should lie dormant deep within the individual. Faith becomes a coloration of the soul in which the believer prepares himself, stands firm, opens his being, and puts himself on the line as it were for the discovery of that which cannot be explained in words, but which can create a music of the spirit, a bow on strings, and which can articulate for the individual the greatest truth of which he is capable. Faith permits, indeed begins, a dialogue between oneself and the Divine Being, whether He be identified as the Hindu Brahma, the Christian God, the Jewish Jehovah, the Islamic name of Allah, or the Great Spirit of the North American Indians, permitting once and for all a softening of the heart and an opening of the soul toward the Spirit through the music of one's own being.

Finally and above all, faith as an essential knowledge based on intuition is a humble acknowledgment of our place with regard to ourselves and our own abilities, with regard to other members of society, with regard to the world generally, and finally with regard to the Divine Savior. Perhaps the time has come, as we terminate the second millennium after the coming of Christ and approach the new demands on mankind that will be inevitable in this 21st century, to abandon once and for all time our earthly pretensions and adopt once again the humble attitude of faith as the necessary prelude to unknown realms of experience and as an initiation that could activate a new life of spirituality. Only then can we begin to approach one another as human beings, not with the superficial mask of a false persona whose investiture into a faith in evolution underscores the fundamental illusion at the heart of our beings, but with a deeper expression of self that is based on the eternal truths and modeled by the great prophets, saints, and mystics of recorded history. Perhaps then we can meet each other based not on a superficial knowledge of matter and form as the true nature of our reality, but on a knowledge that transcends the physical plane to reveal mysteries humanity would not otherwise have thought possible. We can meet each other out of a knowledge that we have truly experienced, a knowledge that brings with it a human commitment to transcend our limitations in ways that only a faith in God permits.

Faith based on such knowledge can become the vehicle of a legitimate interaction among people because it communicates not only facts and statistics, but also something of the person who passes it on, and because it conveys a truth beyond the purely physical entity. Such a faith would represent a knowledge that contains the fragrance of primordial meaning that existed at the heart of the world as an original faith and still lies dormant somewhere near the horizon of our time.

The face of faith contains many profiles. Initially, it manifests itself as a purely abstract idea that seizes the cognitive mind with its inscrutable and mysterious possibility. There arises in the human mind the possibility of moving across the isthmus between known and unknown worlds to experience a reality that would not otherwise be known. A choice is then made and the believer says *yes* to the possibility of higher levels of reality. The affirmation of faith is timely and permanent on the one hand and reaffirmed every minute of the day through conscious application on the other, since our thoughts and actions must reflect our faith. Throughout life, the believer pursues a process in which thoughts, actions, and accomplishments take on the "coloration of a faith" that illuminates the soul.

In its abstract and sphinx-like configuration, faith is free of the constraints of the dogma and form contained in religion and lives as a purely personal and intimate presentiment of mind and heart that often manifests as feelings of promise and hope. Faith is first and foremost an attitude of mind that serves as the foundation and backdrop of a person's active life, lending meaning and purpose to all that the life experience contains. Humanity can face the existential reality of the world with the armor of a faith, the penultimate spiritual attitude as a prelude to enlightenment, that predisposes them to a belief in the knowledge of God and in the power of His guidance and mercy. Faith reveals its knowledge in relation to the predisposition of the believers to incorporate this faith into their work and life as an existential reality. As such, faith becomes a sign of the sacred within life that gives definition to the mystery that lies at the heart of earthly existence.

The bold visage of faith also manifests as an argument[4] that can become a predisposition of will to proclaim the existence of God, not just in words but more importantly through actions. "Verily I am God, there is no god but I; so worship me!" (20:14). It is our responsibility to understand and accept the clarity of the argument whose light touches our very core and affects our human nature to the extent that we are predisposed to the argument and have a sentimental inclination for the knowledge that faith contains. Faith, however, is an argument without words. It begins as an alternative and ends as an action done in the name of God. One person can argue on behalf of the necessity of a faith in the one God and the spiritual realities implicit in that faith, while another can argue against such a faith. Neither argument can create the spark of a faith that can "move mountains," since faith begins within and is both personal and intimate. The distance between faith and disbelief is the thinnest of threads; the impasse that separates outer and inner worlds is but a hair's breadth across according to one tradition that inspires the feeling of being "infinitely near yet infinitely far." On the other hand, another tradition suggests that faith is actually like touching the fire: some people simply refuse to believe in the possibility of a supreme Divine Being that creates and sustains the universe and everything in it.

Because faith exists as a natural predisposition within humanity to explain the unexplainable and to bridge the chasm that exists between the sheer physicality of the human form and the world on the one hand, and the invisibility of God and the spiritual world on the other, the human being is never without some kernel of faith that eventually reveals the secret disposition of his inner self. In my own experience as a faithless man, I realize now that I was never completely without faith and would have been reluctant to deny faith outright since I saw no advantage to an active disbelief. In retrospect, I now realize that crossing the invisible barrier that exists between faith and disbelief

[4] The human argument may be interesting, articulate, and close to us, but God's argument must prevail: "Say: With Allah is the argument that reaches home. If it had been His will, He could indeed have guided you all" (6:149).

was as simple a snapping one's fingers, as easy as a simple affirmation that is based on the fundamental human desire to believe. Once having crossed the bridge between worlds and having experienced briefly the "other side" of reality, I developed a taste for faith and a readiness to act upon the knowledge contained within faith, and I began to realize the blessings that accompany such faith.

I began to realize that faith was actually an alchemy of spiritual forces under my control. Since faith is based on a revealed knowledge, it is not the acquired knowledge of a profane learning, but rather an immediate recognition and grasp of things as they are in reality, have always been, and eternally will be, a knowledge that is inborn in humanity but later becomes covered over and obscured by the spiritual ignorance that arises from a life of superficial and surface experience on the purely physical plane. This essential knowledge is potentially available to all humanity, and when internalized and realized within ourselves, this knowledge becomes virtue. The alchemy of the forces of interaction between knowledge and action fuse together to produce a faith in the believer with the power to translate a simple experience into an internalized knowledge that becomes a certitude. Ultimately, this certitude is the only proof that the believer needs because it creates a circle of faith that moves from knowledge through action and experience to a certitude that leads back once again to the initial impulse of faith. It is a circle of experience that is both sacred and total.

I realized that one of the most important things that had been lacking in my life was the impetus of a spiritual force that was not based on a purely philosophical argument, but rather was based on a simple knowledge, an essential knowledge, indeed a revealed knowledge, that could be verified by direct experience and then internalized through effective action. I soon discovered that nothing short of experience could be translated into a certitude that proves that our spiritual aspirations are not merely abstract ideas, mere shadows of a thought, but an attainable state of mind, the only "tangible" reality of which we can speak. Of course, the initial impulse to faith does not necessarily make a faithful man or woman, but the effort to incorporate a sincere faith into one's life does make both faith and the reality behind that faith both immanent and real.

If faith is to survive as a spiritual force in the modern world, several things are necessary. Firstly, people living during these times must abandon their preconceived notions about faith, notions that have perhaps accumulated over the centuries and have now solidified into an attitude toward faith that is both negative and counterproductive, not to mention misleading. With regard to the dynamic spiritual force that faith contains, we must become once again a *tabula rasa*, in which all our mental projections, preconceived notions, and transitory prejudices can be abandoned for a working hypothesis of faith whose key can unlock inner doors and create vistas of experience that the modern person has never dreamed possible, much less experienced. Life has become more provisional and transitory than it ever was during more traditional times and people today have become but a passing phase, an insignificant projectile on the trajectory of time, turning through the modern scientific understanding of humanity into a virtual pygmy of their true selves by virtue of their faithlessness and singular lack of readiness to open themselves to realities that are greater and more profound than they could ever hope to find in and of themselves.

Contemporary people still have the power to spiritualize themselves—they still have the capacity for a faith in God—because faith is a basic predisposition within human nature. Because faith is ultimately based on an essential knowledge with the power to affect action, it contains the key to the doors of perception and experience. The existing religions and their accompanying traditions still exist for humanity as religious forms, though forms are not intended to be ends in themselves, but rather means to an end. These religions and their traditions do not exist for themselves, but rather they exist for people who are willing to adhere to the religious forms in order to achieve a higher perception of reality. With the support of the orthodoxy of one of the revealed religions and a well-grounded faith that is the sincere reflection of true spiritual affirmation, the faithful can escape from their own limitations and pursue the salvation of soul that ultimately leads to unity with the Divine Being.

Needless to say, there can be no spirituality without faith, modern or traditional. Faith can be "modern," insofar as it exists during these times and takes into account the dynamic range of the 21st century mentality, while continuing to be "traditional," insofar as it is based on a revealed knowledge which alone has the orthodoxy and the divine power to enlighten and save. Our duty during these times is to align the knowledge of the religions with the spiritual forces that exist within humanity: namely, a clear intuition of God and faith in the power to transcend the limitations implicit in the human being. A formal religion can become once again a living religion, just as we have the power and the resources available to become a source of consciousness, will power, and light.

Human beings can activate the spiritual forces contained within the religion in order to humanize the face of the religion with their own spiritual experience; while the religion can activate the spiritual forces contained within humans in order to spiritualize the face of *Homo sapiens* with the knowledge of God and the promise of the eternal life of the soul.

It is not easy to think about or to explain through words the meaning of faith in such a way as to clarify rather than obscure faith's essential mystery and its promise of certitude. It is an issue at once subtle, sensitive, and profoundly personal. There is nothing more precious or intimate than a human faith in a Divine Being, and perhaps nothing more fragile. It is the *mihrab*[5] or inner precinct of the mind and heart and holy sanctuary of the spirit. Through faith, true Muslims put themselves on the line and identify with a spiritual identity that trusts in God. It is a sacred trust whose blessing permits the individual to transcend human limitations and escape the narrow and self-serving drive of the individual ego. Through faith, the believer can transcend his own humanity and lift the veil of the inward self—an act of self-revelation that is outwardly human and inwardly spiritual. "On the earth are signs for those of assured faith, as also in your own selves: will you not then see?" (51:20).

Central within the universe are the men and women with hearts of faith, Allah's thinking creation within the hierarchy of being, whose perspective of belief serves as a bridge between the reality of this world and the world of the universal reality. Central within humanity, therefore, must be a faith that proclaims that God exists as the supreme and absolute Being, a faith that expands with the passing of the days into a coloration of mind and a firmament of soul, a faith that

[5] The prayer niche within a mosque where the *imam* stands to lead the prayer and that indicates the direction of Makkah.

represents a knowledge of God within one's being and a willingness to act upon that knowledge throughout the course of one's life.

Knowledge of the Divine Reality lies at the heart of the cosmic universe. The desire to realize this knowledge within oneself remains the central aspiration of our inner universe. The fact is, however, that we are veiled from direct knowledge of God and cannot cross this inseparable barrier on our own terms and by ourselves. The Prophet Muhammad, upon him blessings and peace, has said in a well-known *hadith*: "God has seventy thousand veils of light and darkness; were He to draw their curtain, then would the splendors of His Aspect (Countenance or Face [*wajh*]) surely consume everyone who apprehended Him with his sight." Also, the Archangel Gabriel (*Jibril*) has said: "Between me and Him are seventy thousand veils of light." The veil of veils in this context is reminiscent of the absolute barrier that exists in the modern world between the knowledge of God and the limited scientific knowledge that scientists are able to unveil. This natural barrier that separates humanity by a veil from direct knowledge of the Reality has become during these times more like a steel shutter that effectively closes the human being off from the experience of the Reality through a human attitude that precludes any opening onto the spiritual world, much less to an understanding of the Spirit of God as the one true Reality.

Faith unites the knowledge of the Divinity with human aspiration in order to realize that knowledge through action and through the power and force of human behavior. Faith is meaningless without the dual elements of knowledge and action, for knowledge and action are brothers, the Muslims say, in a sacred alliance. Through action, through behavior, and through the very personality of the faithful person, an active faith grows and nourishes the being like a tree with deep roots, expanding, enlivening, and enriching the life experience of the individual with a view to the divine reality that lies at the heart of all experience. It grows solid and strong, rich and deep, and this is why the Quran refers to "levels" of faith within the human entity and emphasizes the importance of a faith that grows. "But Allah has endeared the Faith to you, and has made it beautiful in your hearts" (49:7).

Paradoxically, faith begins as a mystery within the human mind and ends as a certitude within the human soul. In the earthly sphere, humans are confronted with a fundamental mystery at the heart of themselves, their world, their universe. In addition to the perennial questions that confront humans within the scope of this world—questions as to origin, meaning, purpose, and ultimate end—there also exists within the conscious, human experience a fundamental mystery that is incomprehensible to the human mind on the one hand, and yet curiously accessible to the human heart on the other hand. We, as the most human of "beings" in God's creation, know that the mystery exists and virtually underlies our conscious existence. No one questions this without questioning the basic nature of human experience. As such, it is instinctive within every individual to yearn for and pursue the meaning of this mystery within his or her life and to place it within both a reasonable and understandable context here on earth. After all, the longing for the Divinity is deeply engraved within human nature. Therefore, faith becomes the instinctive and primary response to all that is incomprehensible and unknowable within the world. Faith becomes the operative factor within humanity and the human resolution to life's mysterious and most valued secrets.

Faith addresses the mystery in life, but it carries with it no inaccessible secret. On the contrary, faith becomes a personal affirmation once the human mind has realized that it is "veiled" from the true nature of reality. Faith as a spiritual expression of the self is both individual as well as universal, individual as a personal response to a cosmic mystery and universal in so far as faith reaches across barriers that inhibit full realization of the mysteries and lifts the veil that separates humanity from the true nature of reality. Every man and woman, from the simplest peasant farmer to the most erudite of scholars, can enjoy the blessing and certitude of a simple faith in God precisely because faith is a personal and intimate aspiration as well as a universal manifestation of knowledge and desire. The human aspiration of faith draws upon the knowledge of God, while the universal forces available to humanity reach down from the sublime to the terrestrial, from the Divine to the human, and touch both the simple peasant and erudite man and woman with wonder and awe. Faith lives within the individual as a field of vision whose horizon gives way to the certainty of the truth. If there is a secret associated with faith, it is a revelation rather than a mystery.

Faith is the plain and simple affirmation of the Divine Mystery within the human heart and within the universe itself, a mystery that finds its resolution in the knowledge of the Divine Being, because

"Allah embraces all things in His knowledge" (7:89) and "Such is He, the knower of all things hidden and open, the Exalted (in power), the Merciful" (32:6). As we mentioned earlier, this affirmation is made powerfully explicit in the sacred formula of the *shahadah* (*la ilaha illa-Llah*), usually translated as "There is no god but the one God," or alternatively expressed as "There is no reality but the one Reality." The mystery embedded within this sacred formula provides faith with its own sufficient reason. In other words, faith exists as a fundamental human impulse, a spiritual instinct if you will, because a fundamental mystery exists within creation that a person needs a lifetime to explore and come to terms with. In return, faith resolves this mystery for humanity when the believer simply accepts in principle all that the mystery implies and all that the mystery has to offer. Faith permits the believer to absorb as it were the unknowable essence of the mystery without necessarily comprehending it in any measurable way. The mystery becomes for the believer an "intuition" of all that is possible or probable within the human being and the world, while faith makes possible the practical experience of life lived within the reflection and shadow of the Divine Mystery.

Humanity seeks God by responding to the impulse of faith in the Divine Being precisely because there is this fundamental mystery at the heart of human existence. We have faith and through faith unknown worlds emerge and become accessible to us. Perhaps this is why one often refers to faith as having the capacity to "move mountains." The believer is able to communicate with the Divinity precisely because God is the Divine Mystery of which all other temporal mysteries are the manifested earthly prototype. All things in the universe, including both the natural and human order, manifest the mystery of their origin in what the Islamic perspective calls the secret (*as-sirr*) and in what the Quran repeatedly refers to as the unseen (*al-ghaib*).

We are a mystery unto ourselves and therefore need God to substantiate for us the knowledge of our individual reality as well as the Ultimate Reality. Without faith in the Divine Being, the human being would be adrift amid a conflicting multitude of uncertainties concerning himself and the world. We have faith, we pray, we fast, we perform good works, in short, through our faith in Allah as the Supreme One we attempt to spiritualize our existence and lift ourselves out of our mundane manner of living in order that we may cope with the inevitable mystery that pervades every aspect of life. It is as if the mysterious and the secret realms of the universe are fundamental to the faith that permits us to explore the true nature of our own being and the true nature of the world in which we find ourselves as a human mystery facing a cosmic mystery. Faith makes possible the lifting of the supreme veil that exists between the world of humanity and the world of the Spirit.

The mystery is the divine challenge; the pure impulse of faith is the human response. If it were otherwise, we could not identify ourselves as being human, nor would our humanity have a true identifying quality to distinguish us from the animal kingdom. The Divine Mystery is actually the Cosmic Secret of the universe. This is no more fittingly prefigured than in the night sky with its canopy of stars, a miraculous panorama that has been called by St. Augustine the "city of God." Its infinity of space and eternity of time reaches down nightly to remind humanity of our other self that is a reflection of the Supreme Self. Human beings, both men and women, have the potential for faith just as the blue sky has the potential to become the landscape of God and a symbolic image of other worlds. This faith then becomes the human secret that makes the meeting between the human and the Divine possible, a secret that is embedded within the Divine Mystery as knowledge and actualized within the human being as aspiration to meet that Mystery through a pure faith in the Supreme Being.

We began these reflections by associating faith's original inspiration and *raison d'être* with the fundamental mystery that confronts humanity in this life. We will conclude these reflections on the mystery of faith in a Supreme Being with a comment concerning faith's certitude. We have suggested that faith is required of the human mind because of its confrontation with the fundamental mystery at the heart of the self and the known world. Thereafter, faith begins to grow within the mind and heart of the believer who takes part in a life of spirituality and follows the path of an orthodox and God-revealed religion such as the religion of Islam. The full range of faith's influence eventually invades the inner world of the believer like a starburst from heaven and enters the ground of the human soul as a certitude and a certainty. The mystery that inspired faith into an action becomes a certitude within the soul of the knowledge that is already there in faith's initial assent.

Faith, at first, is grounded in the completely mysterious as a single ray of light amid the total darkness of the unknown. It is based, of course, on the knowledge of God, but it would go nowhere without the human desire to believe. It becomes a kind of illumination through a great and generous leap of mind in which vast chasms are crossed and monumental heights are scaled and the believer arrives upon a field of vision whose plane expands the inner horizon of the mind and heart beyond all human reckoning.

Faith is based upon an essential knowledge and a fundamental desire. Its knowledge is based on the knowledge of God, that He exists, is One, that He creates, shapes, defines and sustains the Reality, that He encompasses all Truth, that He is the Beloved One and Sustainer of all life. Faith's desire is based on a free will that is purely human, but, like all true human desires, it is founded on a knowledge that is divine. Faith, as such, is of the earthly realm; temporal and pristine, purely personal and humanly intimate, it represents the meeting of the human with the Divine. Faith's desire is of this world in the sense that it actualizes, here and now in this present moment, the eternal moment of God. It represents the human desire to turn toward God and believe in Him in thought, word, and deed. Like the roar of the lion and the cry of the peacock, faith's voice emerges from the human depths to reach beyond the solitude and isolation of the human entity; it is the voice of a single soul, alone in an unexplained world and on its own with this simple yet sacred spiritual response.

The divine mystery belongs to God, but faith belongs to those who believe. As such, it becomes the summative statement of what they think is true and what they are willing to act upon. It serves as the font of inspiration and the headwaters of their impulse to act upon their desires in order to understand and experience the world. Genuine faith is expressed through the totality of the human entity, through thought, action, sentiment, and spiritual aspiration. It provides the inner structure and framework for the pursuit of a life of spirituality. Without an abiding belief in God, there can be no real knowledge, no holiness, no salvation, and above all no certitude. Faith opens the inward "I" of the human consciousness and this inner eye becomes a panoramic window into the true nature of the one Reality. Through faith, the believer can resolve the enigmas, uncertainties, and mysteries woven into the fabric of this world. We live in a world of shifting sands and our lives rarely exhibit any consistency or continuity. Without an abiding faith in a unitive reality, our outer and inner worlds quickly become a bundle of conflicting feelings and emotions that ultimately manifest themselves through an intolerable isolation, loneliness, and doubt. We are nothing if we believe in nothing. We are everything if we follow our true nature and place our trust in God.

Through faith, the enigmas, mysteries, and uncertainties of this world can be transformed into feelings of certitude that always accompany any genuine faith in the Divine Being. Knowledge of God brings with it a desire for faith. With a desire for faith comes the experience of faith. With the experience of faith comes realization through faith. With realization through faith comes certitude. Finally, certitude brings with it its own compensation and its own ambience. Faith's certitude becomes a kind of compensation for the mind and heart because it increases faith's desire. Faith's certitude thereafter manifests itself in an ambience of tranquility of soul and serenity of spirit, this element of serenity, or peace, being the very essence of what the word *islam* has come to mean and promise: "It is He Who sent down Tranquility into the hearts of the believers, that they may add faith to their faith" (48:4). It amounts to a circle of spirituality that moves from knowledge, to desire, to faith, to experience, to realization, to certitude, and back again to an enriched faith fortified by experience.

Within the hierarchy of creation, only the human being has faith and expresses this faith as a sacred sentiment and as an active participation in the Divinity throughout the course of life. This faith sets a person apart from the angels, the *jinn*, the animals, and plants in the kingdom of God, all of whom enjoy a knowledge of God and act upon their spiritual instincts on fundamental, supra-natural levels of expression. The angels execute the Divine Command, the *jinn* surrender to the Divine Being, the animals pray and praise, as the Quran tells us, even plants turn their faces to the light of the sun in praise of the Divine One. Only humans actively choose the Divinity with their mind and heart through the profession of a faith in God. Only humans choose God, and because of that, their faith is the spiritual expression par excellence of all living beings.

Faith commences as mystery and comes to fruition as certitude. It begins as a subjective inspiration of the human mind in order to deal with the fundamental mystery, uncertainty, and doubt that confront the human entity in this world. With time, faith grows into an outward expression of spiritual virtue that actually shapes the ambience of the mind and provides the coloration of a person's inner being. Through the excellence (*al-ihsan*) of spiritual virtue, ordinary faith finally develops into an inward certitude that takes part in the objective Reality of God. Through the power of faith, the human subject is able to experience, if not actually see, the mysterious presence of God, and this experience objectifies for humanity the Reality of the Divine Being and encourages people to worship and "fear the Most Gracious Who is unseen" (50:33).

The meaning of faith is embedded within the mystery of the knowledge of God and this mystery is symbolized through the image of the veil. The certitude of faith and its very object is the doctrine of the unity and omnipotence of God. It promises eternal life for the aspiring soul, who sees and experiences with the spiritual "I" what can not be seen with the human "eye."

# 4. Wisdom's Journey

> Now have We removed thy veil, and sharp is thy sight this Day! (50:22)

Late one afternoon just after sunset, I drove out into the virgin desert that lay wondrously close to the small university town in the Middle East where I worked, ostensibly to escape from the turmoil of a busy city and all that it represents. The flaming orange orb of the sun sat on the rim of the horizon for several seconds as if in a final salute to the tribulations of the day before sinking like melted butter beyond the hem of the world. As I approached the rolling dunes that swept across my vision as some predatory ocean of undulating sand, I abandoned the car as the final vestige of all that I hold dear to the routine of my day, namely the ability to move about efficiently and in comfort. On foot within this primordial sea of shadowy dusk, with nothing but the sand under my feet and the thin line of the horizon to define my vision, I felt suddenly alone and afraid within the sheer physicality of raw nature in all its purity and uncompromising truth, in counterpoint to the solitary twinkling of the North Star that interrupted the emerging night with its inviting message of light beyond the ages of mankind.

What is it about the great deserts, forests, and oceans of the globe that render us insignificant when we confront them alone in all their sublime grandeur? When you come to think of it, Mother Nature has no real outside or inside—no skin and no heart—but is instead some vast combination of outer and inner worlds whose unity creates a reality that cannot be denied, a meta-cosmic symbol that transcends itself by being much more than the sum of its materiality. In the presence of pure nature we stand alone, while the mind is enveloped by the innocence of Nature's beginning and enduring magnificence.

By the time I had left the road and walked beyond the crest of a nearby dune amid that eerily silent stillness, darkness had conquered the land. I found that the immensity of the desert had suddenly become the venue of some vast infinity. I had fallen through a crack in the universe and in doing so something within me had also broken open to allow the in-pouring of a knowledge that transcended the mere input of the senses. Overhead the night sky was rippling with stars, like diamond stones set against black velvet, highlighting in their infinitesimality the blackness of the heavens and sending their infinite specks of light across millions of light years to reach my curious eye and enter my mind to create a profound sense of wonder and awe that complemented the halo of descending dusk that cast shadows across the land. The faint light of multiple star clusters seemed to pulsate and beckon one another through those vast distances as though they were in some kind of conspiracy to confound the insignificant mortals that gazed up in wonder upon them from the vast distances below. From the vantage point of that desert plain spread clear to the horizon, the canopy of stars overhead created great rivers of light across the celestial dome. The Milky Way streamed across the sky with its several tributaries. And the great river of light whirled through the darkness to create a grand promenade through the city of God. There seemed to be no ground under my feet but only the abyss of a star-studded space falling away forever, while those falling stars fell into my open soul as strange thoughts of the magnificence of God Almighty amid the infinite whispers of the human spirit that cascade across the deserts of the night.

And let us not forget the awesome silence that bears witness to the reality of sound by virtue of its peculiar emptiness. "Nature's silence is its one remark," Anne Dillard has written, as if in making this one remark, silence has uttered the iconic essence of what needs to be known. I was no longer in the desert and beneath the night sky; I felt above and beyond it, as though I had passed through these symbolic images of nature and arrived on the other side of some invisible door to witness a revelation whose significance and import would last me a lifetime. It is interesting to take note of a corresponding silence that lies within us as a premonition of something great that lies just beyond the reach of our own inner horizon. The expanse of the desert epitomizes the reality of a foreboding silence that lies within us as some primal secret awaiting the arrival of a divine whisper. In traversing the vast stretches of sand amid such silence under the depths of the night sky, one quickly comes to realize the voice of a silence that lies within us once we are able to shed the turmoil, fear, confusion, and all the other psychological idiosyncrasies that make up the limitations of our mentality and inner psyche. "What makes the desert beautiful," said Antoine de Saint-Exupéry's little prince to his pilot, "is that somewhere it hides a well." The hidden presence of the Spirit that lies within me is my hidden well and I am willing to cross the landscape of a desert that lies within me to give expression to what lies beyond the mind and heart amid the turmoil of my days.

I was in the Middle East when I was first introduced to the aesthetic charm of the desert with its austere panorama and the night sky whose stars shine overhead as divine envoys in the absolute darkness and shimmer like plate-glass the wisdom of eternity down upon us through its symbolic metaphors. It was in this grand arena of the desert that I was able to experience the subtle influence that the metacosmic symbols of nature such as the horizon at sunset and the empyrean of the night have on the human mind. One of the first and most enduring lessons I learned early on from the Religion of Islam is that there is not one revelation, but three distinct sources of knowledge that descend from on high to give shape and definition to the essential knowledge of God. The Quran is of course the divine Word par excellence that has come down to the Muslims in the form of verses that comprise a book; but in addition to this noble book, Islam identifies both virgin Nature and humans themselves[1] as unique sources of knowledge that reveal in their own manner the secrets of the true nature of Reality. The primordial forces and images of Nature are none other than verses and signs (*ayat Allah*) of God; while human beings have a range of abilities including the human faculties of intuition, reason and intelligence, the higher emotions including spiritual instinct, imagination and the spiritual sentiments, the impulse of faith that bridges knowledge and action, and finally the unique capacity of self-consciousness and free will that drive humanity forward into the realms of higher awareness and human fulfillment. The Quran manifests the Divinity through sound; the natural order manifests the Divinity primarily through the symbolic images of Nature; the human being essentially manifests the Divinity to the extent that every individual activates the essential knowledge of God—His Truth and His Reality—through every thought, word, and action they undertake during the course of their lives. Ultimately, the human revelation makes itself known through virtue.

In Part One, we commenced this work with some reflections on the perennial mystery that lies in wait as some preternatural source of

[1] Identified as *insan* in Quranic Arabic.

inspiration that aids us in coming to terms with our human identity and our place in the universal scheme of things. It is as if the mystery of the Unseen (*al-ghaib*) becomes visible to the human eye through the expression of an individual destiny whose every thought, word, and action become the threads of some rich and miraculous tapestry of life. Set against a dark and velvety backcloth of mystery whose warp is the Unknown and whose woof is the Unseen, we live our lives in search of a meaning that will substantiate who we are and what we need to accomplish within the context of a world that does not fully explain itself; but whose mystery beckons us to intelligent thinking and rightful action with every breath we take and with every beat of the heart. Its austere charm gives little of itself away and yet still holds us in thrall as the fundamental challenge of our existence. All of the great scientific minds of the modern centuries have erected a grand architecture of scientific knowledge as the means to identify the true nature of reality based on a premise that physical matter and the human capacity to reason can determine what that truth may be. Yet, this attitude toward truth has not been able to neutralize the sublime force of the mystery or render it as insignificant to the human experience.

Embedded within the perennial mystery lies a secret that only a divine revelation can reveal and which will ultimately clarify the relationship between the seen and the Unseen, the human and the Divine, the known world and the universal specter of the Unknown, all of which preserve the aura of the *mysterium tremendum* that we live with every day of our lives. As bud to the divine flower and kernel to the human husk, the sacred intimacy that unfolds through the human interaction with the Universal Spirit begins with the acknowledgment that the great proto-mystery at the heart of the universe is nothing more than the absolute truth of the one Reality in disguise, an enigma awaiting resolution and a secret waiting to be told. The Quranic revelation contains this profound secret in the form of the *shahadah*, the great testimony that reduces the entire doctrine of the religion to a double-edged sword of knowledge and action, truth and way, the divine singularity as sublime overlay to the human multiplicity. We live with the force of a mystery and we live with the promise of a secret, two complementary realities or the single blade of a two-edged sword.

Between the reality of the divine mystery and the knowledge of the sacred *shahadah* lies the human impulse to have faith and believe in a Divine Being. Through every "act" of faith—indeed the impulse to believe carries no weight without a complementary action that gives testament to one's belief—the Muslim takes the first step that leads beyond the confines of some earth-bound vision by establishing a spiritual identity through an instinctive faith in a Supreme Intelligence. It is the hand that leads the believer beyond the horizon of the cognitive mind and opens a "straight path" to the Infinite. The face of faith shines as an initial spark of light that can illuminate human consciousness with the knowledge of God. This knowledge of the Divinity helps to resolve the mystery that surrounds the origin and true nature of both man and the universe, and acts as an antidote to the darkness and uncertainty that the life of "this world" embodies when it is understood to be an independent reality of its own. What begins as a presentiment and grows into a ray of light, ultimately becomes a burning conviction in which we commit ourselves to the principles of a sacred and essential knowledge that defines for us the true nature of Reality. Our imagination alone cannot reconcile the invisible and the visible, the metaphysical and the physical, the Creator and the creation. It is only through the light of the *shahadah* and the certitude of faith that the mind, heart, and soul can come to understand the divine qualities of the visible, the physical, and the creation by acknowledging the inner reality of things that are veiled and embedded within the invisible, the metaphysical, and the Creator.

Is faith enough to lead us beyond the morass of our own inner turmoil when we are left on our own? Does the knowledge that faith implies provide the keys to the kingdom that lies within?[2] Indeed where would we humans be without the dome of Heaven reaching down as in a dream to touch our souls with its wondrous mystery and encircling the earth with its enduring message of transcendence and infinity? Because faith amounts to a human intuition based on knowledge of God combined with the desire to turn toward Him, the impulse of faith has the potential to become a force that can "move mountains," that permits the faithful to manifest inner realities through visible actions, that reduces the great impasse that exists

[2] "We are nearer to him than his jugular vein" (50:16).

between matter and spirit to a modern myth, and that shatters the mirror of all earthly illusions and actually begins the process of "lifting the veil" to reveal the cosmic mysteries at the heart of the creation. Ultimately, faith has the power to transform every thought, word, and action into a human revelation that will raise the human soul onto the plane of realization of immanent and eternal realities.

At the heart of faith lies the beginning and source material of what is referred to in Islam as *ihsan*,[3] or human excellence as represented by the principle of virtue and its corresponding virtues. In response to the question what is the true nature of *ihsan* or human excellence, the Prophet of Islam responded by saying: "*Ihsan* is worshipping Allah as if you actually saw Him, and even if you do not see Him, nevertheless, He sees you." It is an intriguing paradox that we disbelieve the very Being that bears us witness on the ground that we cannot see such a Being with the human eye.

This was one of the first Islamic sayings (*hadith*) of the Prophet that I became aware of when I first became Muslim. Conceptually, I found it an interesting challenge and the counterpoint to the tendency of the modern mentality to live in this world as if we will live here forever. This modern-day adage has great meaning for people, a practical phrase that virtually drives them forward and provides the fundamental motivation to their every thought, word, and action. The desire for pre-eminence, the love of wealth, the impulse to control our destiny, the illusion of free will, the myth of an earthly progress or a purely human happiness, all contribute to the fantasy that the world is enduring and that we will endure with it, when in fact we pass the world by and the world takes no notice of us except to take us back within its embrace in the awesome finality of death. What, then, of the incisive concept of living "as if" a Supreme Being truly existed, amounting to a grand universal conditional with the power to transform the earthly experience into a life of profound experience of an eternal reality?

In today's world, we use words like faith and virtue as if we knew what they truly mean, when in fact they are alien concepts that when

[3] Interestingly, the humanity of *insan* in the Arabic root comes from "intimacy" (*ins*) with Allah; while the *ihsan* of virtue comes from the implicit blessing (*hasanat*) of good works.

fully experienced as genuine sacred emotions would rise up from our souls like hesitant butterflies taking flight from a leaf in the summer wind. The truth is we do not know what they truly mean or what their full implications may harbor for our perceptions and destiny here on earth unless we embrace their promise and make efforts to explore and experience their potential efficacy in fulfilling our heart's desire. Virtue as worship of the Divinity jars us out of our complacency and forces us to consider the implementation of actions that will have a bearing on how we live our lives. To worship Allah as if we actually saw Him obliges us to dedicate ourselves to the task of imagining what is not there and then living in its presence; while in compensation, everything in the manifested universe promises to bear witness to the suggestion that something invisible is making its presence felt within us as the only enduring reality worth striving for.

The key to human spirituality and the means to inculcate the spirit of virtue within the soul in order to achieve true human excellence lies with the simple conditional "as if." The believer should worship God "as if" he or she could actually see God, and this conditional, the greatest of all "ifs," is actually an invitation to open the inner eye of the heart to witness the deepest aspect of ourselves. The more people realize that God can and does see them, the more intensely and the more sincerely they can feel—if not actually see—God with the inward eye of the heart, which is the eye of perception and understanding. In this way, the conditional gives shape to the external reality that we experience every day and raises our consciousness to the inner reality that cannot be seen with the human eye. A Zen master once remarked that if you sip the sea only once, you will know the taste of all the oceans of the world. Indeed, during the brief walk in the desert that evening in years now passed, I witnessed ten thousand stars. In walking into the soul of the night and taking note of its mysterious presence, I have witnessed the universe. If only I could retain the miracle of this experience in my daily life and live in the consciousness of the universal Presence.

Although we have called upon, perhaps, far too many words to conjure up a meaning to the concepts of mystery, knowledge, and faith, we hope we have left an impression on the reader that exceeds the superficial—if not downright misleading—sense these words are commonly understood during these times: What does mystery mean in today's world but an enigma awaiting human resolution by the scientistic[4] and secular mentality of today, knowledge being the mass of speculation and theories that pass themselves off as facts in the age of information, and faith being a naïve sentimentality that serves as a crutch for people in facing the unknown quality of life. In Chapter 1, we explored the true meaning of a perennial mystery that every human must confront and cannot escape because it lies at the heart of the physical universe in terms of first origins and final ends. In Chapter 2, we highlighted the secret revealed in the Religion of Islam as the great testimony of the *shahadah* that proclaims the knowledge of the one God and the straight path through the example of the Messenger Muhammad—peace be upon him—that leads the Muslims back to their source in the Divinity. In Chapter 3, we commented upon aspects of faith in God that could possibly lead us through the vicissitudes of the modern world with the dignity and courage befitting a firm belief in the Supreme Being.

Faith requires the essential knowledge of God and surrender requires proactive affirmation of that knowledge, but virtue requires both human intelligence and free will functioning at the height of their efficacy. To understand the true nature of things—which is what human intelligence is supposed to do best—and to assign to all things their just proportion is a wisdom reflective of the essential knowledge of God. To live according to the nature of things is to take part in the true nature of Reality. To fuse one's thoughts and actions with the knowledge of God and the sacred feeling that is its natural by-product amounts to a devotional love that transcends mere thinking and doing. In other words, wisdom's journey through time takes the believer down the road of virtue which has no limit and is truly miraculous.

[4] The term "scientistic" conjures up the attitude and approach of the scientific way of thinking that precludes any other possibility in the pursuit of the knowledge of reality other than that which conforms to the assumptions of the scientific method based on human reasoning and the laws of observation and experimentation that objectify the veracity of a given truth. Authentic scientific knowledge refers to things that are observable and verifiable; scientistic beliefs on the contrary represent ideas that are taken as a dogma without the accompanying verifiable proofs.

That is why we are encouraged in Islam to live within the force of a conditional—living Islam as if you actually saw Allah—that sets all true Muslims on a voyage into the unknown with only the knowledge of God and His loving remembrance as the guiding compass.

I lived as a Muslim for over twenty-five years before I actually developed a true understanding of what it means to internalize the knowledge of God within one's being as a personal statement of wisdom and virtue. By witnessing a fellow Muslim live his life as if Allah actually saw him, I was able to come to terms with what it means to live a life of true Muslim spirituality, where the knowledge of God is so penetrating and so deep it actually shines back out into the world as living virtue and true spirituality. Of course, I had taken part in the prayer rituals in the mosque, fasted with the Muslim community during the holy month of Ramadan, and had otherwise witnessed and incorporated into my own life the various social and cultural components that make the Religion of Islam a way of life. It is one thing to bow in prostration five times a day and wear a flowing robe and turban, and another thing to reflect through one's attitude, way of thinking, and behavior the very forces of spirituality that reflect the knowledge of God and His abiding presence. One feels in the presence of a genuine Lama or Sheikh the true eminence of the person's presence, in the same way that you feel the sublime presence of Nature when standing in the midst of a grand patriarchal forest. Occasionally, if you are very lucky indeed, you will also experience as I did a seemingly ordinary soul exercising an extraordinary faith and worship in the manner in which he conducted his life.

His name was Farman Allah, the son of Saleh, native-born in the upper regions of Pakistan known as the North West Frontier Province, the traditional home of a stoic and warlike tribe of mountain men called the Pushtu or Pathan people. I have already briefly recounted the blessing I received in having been taken by the hand and brought through the door of Islam by my "laughing" Sufi, whose compassion and understanding showed me the way into the true spirit of Islam. Once inside this rarefied environment of traditional history and spiritual culture, it took another person, my friend Farman, to show me the true Islamic way of life, amounting to a way of thinking in his approach to life that formed the basis of his every thought, word, and action. He didn't wear his virtue as a cloak to be thrown at people's feet as a dramatic gesture of his own goodness; on the contrary, he took a noble pride in a strict adherence to the practical dictates of the religion in what amounted to his ability to "worship Allah as if he actually saw Him."

The very sight of him inspired wonder and awe. I remember the day he implored me to come and visit him and his extended family back home. "Come Yahya," he proclaimed grandly for such was his way of speaking, his loud, sonorous voice emanating from deep within the incredible hulk of this mountain man. "The people in village is waiting for you. If you not come, whole village is very sad and I will kill you."

I thought for a minute, then looked at my Pathan friend and beyond to the inner being of the man. At a glance, he could have passed as a tender giant of childhood fairy tales. His frame was larger than life, well-proportioned, solid, and suggesting a feeling of strength and nobility that went beyond the normal course of a man. There was a bigness in him that transcended his body. Dark-skinned and toughened by hours of hard work out in the grueling elements of the Emirate desert where he worked as a foreman for an irrigation company, he wore his thick dark hair closely cropped and had a well-trimmed jet-black beard covering his face, offsetting the brightness of his eyes and the light of his facial expression. I knew he was kidding, not because of the broad smile and the gleaming row of white teeth, but rather because within that incredible body was a simple, innocent, uncorrupted, noble soul incapable of committing any true outrage. Indeed, he was a formidable being by any account and a rare and unique friend that I truly valued and trusted, even with my life. When he invited me to visit his village, I accepted, knowing the import and implications of such a rare invitation. He was drawing a line in the sand by inviting me to cross over into a very private and conservative world that few have ever seen, much less experienced.

What epitomized his ability to live his life as if he were actually being watched by God was his attitude toward money, a sure barometer that more clearly than anything else in the world measures the pulse of a person's desire for the amenities of "this world." When he spoke of the importance of honesty and his attitude towards money, his words sounded into the atmosphere with all the quality of a solemn vow: his voice spoke to me directly from another, more traditional world as the voice of a conscience that I fear we no longer possess.

Perhaps no other commodity highlights more succinctly the modern tendency to make excuses for our inner sense of morality and ethics than does our attitude toward money and the extent to which we will go to accommodate its pressing demand to have more and more of it no matter what our need. It happened that he was required to carry and handle huge amounts of money in his capacity as foreman for a small irrigation company. The farm projects that he was responsible for organizing and bringing to completion—including everything from wining the tender to the installation of the tubing and water pump with his team of Pathan tribesmen hand picked from his own village—required him to collect and bank huge sums of money that often amounted to hundreds of thousands of dollars. In a world in which bribery is the norm, where corruption and pay-offs are rampant, and where people are able to justify cheating the boss in the name of retribution and just cause, Farman was the rare exception. He could have easily doctored the books as it were; a few thousand dollars could have easily disappeared without his boss being any the wiser or any more the fool. But he prided himself on his honesty. "I not take a single cent, Yahya, this is not my way."

"Why not," I asked him pointedly.

"This is not the Pathan style," he replied proudly, but quickly added, "and Allah knows even if no one other knows."

"How do you know," I said, prodding him on to explain his meaning.

"He sees us, Yahya, what you thinking."

"But you don't see Him," I reasoned.

"I doesn't need to see Him, Yahya, not with these two eyes; but I know He is there."

"But the owner of the company cheats you of your holidays and your vacation. He doesn't pay you on time and doesn't pay you what you deserve for the work you do and the responsibility you accept." I argued without much success, trying to play the devil's advocate and wondering just how far he would take his argument. "He has cheated you," I said finally raising my voice. "You can take back what is rightfully yours without his even knowing about it."

"That's his account, but not mine. I doesn't cheat the people, Yahya, even if they cheat me. We all have our destiny and in my destiny I doesn't take money that isn't my work. Allah knows and I know. Anyway, whatever I have comes from Allah. If I need more money, then I will have it; but not because I cheated the people. This is enough."

I stopped in my tracks. It was enough that I could see the wisdom of his virtue. The great conditional of life that he lived by was his reality to experience and enjoy. Upon it he had built an empire of wisdom and virtue that no one could take away from him and nothing could conquer. Here is an honorable man, I thought, and a happy one. If we applied this attitude to everything that we did, then we would indeed know the true meaning of a living spirituality and what it means to be virtuous. It is not the number of times we say the prayer and bow in prostration. It is not the amount of money that we give away to the poor as a means of showing ourselves to be generous. It is not the extent to which we announce to people that we are true Muslims or that we follow the virtuous way. No, it is like my friend Farman said: "He see us, Yahya, what you thinking," even if no one else recognizes the lies that we speak or the promises that we break. The knowledge that even if we do not see God, "nevertheless, He sees us" had been internalized within his mind and heart as wisdom that, when executed through his daily decisions and actions, reflected back into the world as virtue.

Wisdom's journey through the life of a soul is nothing less than a journey beyond this world, traveling toward a supreme certainty as voyagers embarking on a maiden voyage beyond the realm of facts and figures, a journey to the very limits of the way we imagine our world. It commences with the acceptance of the *shahadah* or testimony of faith in Islam when the Muslim acknowledges his or her place in the Divine Plan with a mental, psychic, and ultimately spiritual surrender to the Will of the Supreme Being, a surrender that ultimately becomes physical through the full prostration during the prayer ritual when the Muslims arrive in close proximity with the Presence when their forehead meets the ground. The wisdom implicit in this surrender takes the road of virtue in order to make itself known within the life of an individual through thoughts, words, and actions that form the basis of people's lives. It is a road of virtue that has no true limit because its final destination is truly unattainable at least within this world.

Wisdom's journey is as perpetual as the river of life until this incredible journey merges once again into the sea of universality that Islam identifies as the Spirit of the One (*al-Ahad*).

Within the Islamic perspective, when God created man, He endowed him with an intelligence that is both integral and intuitive, a will that is both powerful and free, and a soul that is both radiant and translucent. These three divine gifts allow the Muslims the possibility of a faith (*iman*) that is enlightening as well as total, a submission (*islam*) that is both courageous and liberating, and a virtue (*ihsan*) that is both innocent and perfecting. Virtue brings about the full realization of the knowledge of the *shahadah* and the certainty of faith, thereby bringing to near perfection human intelligence, faith, and willful surrender to God. Intelligence reflects a mode of thought and perception; free will reflects a mode of choice and of action; virtue reflects a mode of living and thus a mode of being. The soul participates in the perfect equilibrium of knowledge and love through the human excellence of virtue, which generously lends its sweet aura of innocence to the formal modes of knowledge. In other words, knowledge finds its purpose in action and action finds its purpose in virtue.

Faith is a secret alliance between humanity and God. Surrender is a proclamation of the faithful who identify themselves as Muslims, as a formal religious posture. Virtue, however, is the definitive statement of the soul as it sheds its colors and hues and spreads across both the inner and outer life of the seeker. Through virtue, the human aura glows.[5] As such, it requires a heightened presence of mind and a devotional piety that goes well beyond the standard norms of the faith and surrender required of every believer. To see the Unseen (*al-ghaib*) with the "eye of the heart" is not one of God's gifts, but rather one of His challenges. As we have already suggested, faith may be a mode of thinking and surrender may be a mode of living, but virtue is a mode of being. Like happiness, the sustained effort to achieve a life-long spirituality is very difficult to achieve and maintain. Most people are fickle, inflexible, and weak and need the rituals and spiritual disci-

[5] The visualization of spiritually harmonized forces are common to the religious traditions. The halo is a common feature of the Christian tradition, whereas Buddhism assigns a similar manifestation to the entire body in the form of a spiritual aura called the "rainbow body."

plines of the religion to liberate them from their inherent limitations. Still, if happiness is the motivation, then virtue is the means through which the aspiring soul expresses itself and makes itself known to the world.

Virtuous actions are direct references back to the Divinity, when a person becomes their own proof of the existence of God by virtue of their reflection of the divine light. More than anything else, virtue expresses the best of a person as he or she is summarized within the soul. It remembers most directly the primordial condition of the paradisal man and woman, who enjoyed a natural state of virtuous innocence. The object of knowledge is Truth or the Reality that projects that Truth. The object of the will is to choose the Good and reject the evil alternative. The object of virtue is to love God in such a way that the full range of the virtues becomes apparent. Essentially we make shadows in this world; something else beyond the horizon of the known universe shines down its light upon us.

The individual virtues are the endlessly varied modalities of the principle of virtue, just as the colors of the spectrum are the subtle variations of the one light. Each of the virtues is an individual key that unlocks the latent perfections of the soul. They are attitudes and modalities of the mind that become imprinted on the soul as qualities and beauties once they have passed through the heart of the believer as intelligence and through his behavior as virtuous actions. The individual virtues enter the soul and find their place gradually. As in the movement from darkness to light mentioned in the Quran, they slowly uproot and supplant the imperfection and darkness that are polar opposites to the perfection and light of the virtues.

Humility represents a quality of soul when the believer fully recognizes his true position as one of utter dependence on the beneficence and mercy of God. Humility elevates one's nothingness to the level of sincere awareness and can be called the greatest of the virtues because it ultimately implies a denial of the ego and the assertion of the soul in the Spirit of God.

Charity recreates the denial and affirmation that rests within the heart of the Islamic witnessing (*shahadah*). Charity effectively denies the individual through the giving of the self, for the sake of a greater whole represented through the society at large. Charity leads to greatness of soul because it allows a person to take leave of the self in a practical way and put himself in the place of others, thus enlarging his perspective and softening his heart to the needs of those around him.

Truthfulness gives voice to the truth on the practical level through the power of the word. Human beings can only fully represent themselves through speech, so that the truthfulness of their word represents the truth that exists within themselves. Watchfulness holds its breath in conscious introspection and waiting. The watchful man is an aware man, who restrains himself through the sheer joy of inner self control. Watchfulness partakes of attention to detail, together with a vigilance against negligence, or worse, extravagance. Watchfulness represents a presence of mind that calls the believers back to the remembrance of the Divinity. As such, it makes of the present moment a moment of true remembrance.

We need also mention patience which the Quran says "is beautiful." Patience is the sweetest of the virtues that overlays the soul with its implicit blessing. It is the virtue most difficult to achieve, the virtue most in demand in the course of one's everyday life. Life demands patience and often draws on the reserves of patience to see a person through. Indeed, patience requires an inner self-control and an outer physical discipline that can border on the superhuman. For all of its rigor, however, patience is beautiful (*sabr jameel*), as the Quran remind us. It focuses toward the inner self, so that a person has the strength to bear with equanimity the reality of one's unfolding destiny. Similarly, patience focuses outwardly toward mankind and the world with a calm understanding of the eccentricities of one's fellow man.

Virtue cannot lie and still be what it is. Genuine virtue draws its substance and its meaning from knowledge and presentiment of the Divine Reality that underlies everything in life. Whatever knowledge a man possesses about the ultimate reality will shine through his thoughts, his words, and his virtuous actions. The more the believer yearns to become virtuous, the more he will develop the means to attain the divine names and qualities that differentiate the virtues. By way of compensation, the believer can experience as a confirmed reality the benefits of the divine names and qualities once they are firmly fixed within his soul through the virtues.

Thus, the human expression of an Islamic spirituality finds its most comprehensive statement in the combination of the Muslim's faith, his surrender, and his virtuous soul. Faith becomes the human expression of the mind whose intelligence identifies itself with the intelligence of the Supreme Being. His free surrender through conformity to God's law becomes the true expression of his heart's desire and proclaims the witnessing in thought, word, and action. Finally, virtue, with its ethereal fragrance and its aura of luminosity, becomes the outward expression of the soul's essence. The knowledge of God and man's free will unite to form a beauty and a nobility of soul that share in the rays of the divine light. "Some faces that day will beam with beauty and light, as they gaze on their Lord" (75:22).

Virtue lends a brilliance and a depth to the human face that is a reflection of the inner radiance of the soul that only the human being can achieve. The radiance of the human face comes about through a presence of mind that embodies faith and an effort of will that projects complete submission to the truth. This radiance of soul is none other than the soul's fulfillment of an obligation it has borne throughout earthly time: To project into the face of the world the blinding radiance of the Face of God.

Before drawing these reflections to a close, we would like to ask: Are there twinkling flickers of light across the dark plane of the human soul as there are in the dome of the night sky overhead? Are there occasions for small flashes of light, like fallen stars, to slip through the circuits of our brains to reveal the light of universes beyond the ken of our minds, flashes that can light up and fascinate the intellects of those open to the new and unexpected? This is precisely the role of the human intellect, namely to open the mind and transform with a momentary illumination the entire human countryside to the full image of the world with a vision far greater than itself, "from seeing things as men describe them," Thoreau has written, "to seeing them as men cannot describe them."[6] These intuitions become threads of gold that streak through the mind with their perception of the Divinity that lead us toward the serenity and quietism that the inner life of the heart and soul promise.

[6] Quoted in Loren Eisley, *The Night Country* (Lincoln: University of Nebraska Press, 1997), p. 137.

These intuitions most clearly manifest through an inner triad whose mode of expression in the mind can be identified as separation-attachment-detachment. What better way to "see things as men cannot describe them" than by separating ourselves and becoming detached from the things of this world. Separation refers to a basic disentanglement from the world and from the false promises that the world projects towards the vanity and desires of people the world over. Attachment refers to the affection and intimacy Muslims endeavor to develop for their Lord as the Supreme Being, Protector and Friend. Detachment refers to an attitude of heightened other-worldliness to the outcome of the affairs of this world (*al-dunia*) and a supreme indifference to the demands of the ego. Detachment displays a profound respect for the cosmic universe that reveals a sacred and intelligent design that keeps everything in its proper place, a detachment that allows every individual to know the true value of things at least in principle if not in fact.

We admit that we are taking a step and venturing beyond the normal limits of a formal inquiry into the spiritual life of man. Yet, this work would remain unfinished on fundamental levels if its inquiry were abandoned at the threshold of expanding horizons for the sake of a technicality that insists on staying within fixed and established parameters. Every literal form has an inner value and meaning. Beyond every dogma lies an essential truth. Behind every good work lies the enlightened knowledge of a virtue. Within every thread of gold lies a golden light that casts a radiance that remembers the golden age when every man lived according to the inward revelation and who radiated his own inner light.

Even in its simplest and most unpretentious dimension, the inner triad separation-attachment-detachment seems to take on the flavor of a paradox, if only to stimulate the human inquiry into the mystery of the unseen. For example, from the earthly point of view, humans appears to be separated from God by an invisible shield; but strictly speaking, from the spiritual point of view, God cannot be separated from us without disconnecting the sacred thread of the lifeline that leads back to the Spirit. Similarly, we are attached to the world; but, in fact, the world could care less about humanity and lies spread out in silent detachment, lending an air of indifference to its perennial questions.

The angle of vision alters the poignancy of a paradox considerably. From the Islamic point of view, a separation and a distance, both existential and psychic, exist between *insan* (humanity, or man "as such") and God. *Al-insan* is not what God is; on the contrary, the *insan* is what God is not. An imbalance exists between the earthly and heavenly spheres that has to be compensated for in some way. God is formless and all-powerful; we are formal in body and mind and limited in everything we are and do. Moreover, our consciousness, both of self and God, betrays our separation from Him. Yet, the revelation itself fuels the essential paradox concerning man's fundamental relationship with the Divinity in the well-known Quranic verse: "He is nearer to you than your jugular vein," and if that isn't striking enough, an additional verse reveals the potential for intimacy in which God "comes between man and his own heart."

On inner levels, the pattern of this triad follows a spiritual progress that leads from separation, through attachment, to a pure and free detachment of mind and heart from the turmoil and pressures of life. Separation from the world automatically attaches man to God. This leads not to a denial of the world as such, but to a refined detachment of soul from the external forces and pressures that are inevitable on the dissonant plane of earth, a detachment that is shaped by the serenity and calm repose offered by the certitudes of spiritual knowledge and wisdom. Within the mode of separation, everything matters less and less with regard to the world. Within the mode of attachment, everything matters more and more with regard to God. Within the mode of detachment, nothing at all truly matters, except God.

Separation means an elemental departure from the demands of the ego and the attractions of the world. The seeking soul attempts to live *in* the world without being *of* it. After all, a turning toward the inner life of the spirit does require a separation from the cares of the world, nor even less their outright denial. The world is useful and functional in its own right and we have to cope with its demands. G. K. Chesterton wisely suggested that we must find a way to love the world without trusting in its ephemeral promises. "Somehow, one must love the world without being worldly." The seeker lives in the world, respects it, even loves it in a manner of speaking, but he also keeps his distance from the world through an inner separation from all that tends to draw him away from the reality of his spirit and the remembrance of God.

Separation anticipates attachment: It is its motive and goal. Man's separation from himself and from the world must lead to an attachment to God as the sole and saving Reality. The satisfactions of his demanding ego shall then become less and less insisting; his hold over the world less and less tenacious; his presentiment for the things of the spirit more and more meaningful; and his desire to re-orient himself inward and upward more and more intense. Attachment allows the soul to follow the way of return to God that is characterized by a spiritual identity which directly connects man with Heaven.

The surrender of worldly attachments works in harmony with a spiritual identification of the subject with the Object, in which the seeker senses the proximity of God within himself, and he understands himself to be in the presence of God. As such, he takes part in the divine milieu in which it is impossible for him to be separated from God. "He is with you wherever you are" (57:4). His spiritual identity protects him from the negative impressions and the temptations of the world. The religion offers him the methods and the spiritual disciplines with which to intensify and deepen his sense of identification with the Divine: Through prayer, through the earthly duties, through the recitation of the Quran, and through the quintessential prayer that is the repetition (*dhikr*) of the sacred name of God. Even the prayer carpet and prayer beads are spiritual supports that aid in the remembrance of God and the development of a spiritual identity. All the modes of worship work together in harmony toward the central and unifying theme of the knowledge of God and His eternal remembrance.

Pure and loving attachment to God must be the natural harvest of man's surrender and spiritual identification. The Muslim attaches himself as a matter of spiritual instinct to all that will lead him along the path of salvation toward the otherworldly condition of paradise. Through surrender and spiritual identification, God becomes the sole Object of the believer's innermost desires. He is the Beginning and the End, the First (*al-Awwal*) and the Last (*al-Akhir*) and all that is between and beyond. Surrender separates the real from the illusory in this world. Spiritual identification imprints the knowledge of God and His supreme vision on the mind and heart of the believer.

Separation and attachment share the two ends of the same polarity. If man is separated from heaven by the world, then he must actively separate himself from the world within a loving attachment to God and to all that will lead him toward his salvation in heaven. If he enjoys a natural and sentient attachment to this life on earth, then he must separate himself from this attachment with a presentiment for the life of the spirit and for all that remembers Heaven

The virtue of detachment, however, brings to fulfillment what separation and attachment can only commence and approximate. Detachment is nothing short of the realization that any true separation from God is futile and in fact impossible. In addition, all earthly attachments are nullified by genuine spiritual detachment, which dismisses the demands of the world with an indifferent shrug. All human anxiety, fear, and worry are nullified when the soul detaches itself from the contingencies of the world and comes thereby to rest in the shadow of the divine mercy.

Detachment could, indeed, be called the virtue of virtues, as it renders the world's offerings as valueless illusions, of interest only to an insecure and naive ego. What detachment accomplishes for the soul already proves its precious value, even supposing it were an indifference to the world; but detachment also addresses itself to life's turmoil and uncertainties. It represents an inner calm as a response to all that rudely confronts man during the course of his life. It proposes an attitude of mind that makes our aspirations to God as meaningful and our addiction to the world as meaningless. The virtue of detachment means not to fall in love with anything outside of God in and of itself, but only to love all things insofar as they remember and reflect something of God. Detachment is the opposite of the passionate desire and avidity of the human ego. It represents a greatness of soul that is inspired by a consciousness of the absolute value contained within everything that reflects the truth. Detachment allows the soul to keep its inward freedom and its distance with regard to the ego and the unfulfilled self. The ego makes incessant demands, while the self perhaps does not demand enough, but detachment soothes them both with its perception of the true value of everything.

Enlightenment is the ultimate achievement of all human spirituality. From the plane of enlightenment, humanity can recognize the world for what it really is: A setting and backcloth in which the believer can express his unique identity as a truly conscious and spiritual being. Therefore, the seeker endeavors to unload himself of the burden of himself and the world. He separates himself from the world through the surrender of his will to God's divine plan. He attaches himself to God through attention to worship and devotion to the way, as a means to personal holiness and inner sanctity. As a prelude to perfect security and lasting peace, he detaches himself from the web of the ego and the individual self through his awareness of God.

Through the course of a human life made spiritual by the pursuit of the way of return, the seeker awaits the blessings of peace, perfection, and salvation. Through separation, he anticipates the promises of a peaceful bliss in all its miraculous wonder and heavenly beatitude. Through attachment, he anticipates the perfection of the human being in all its glorious possibilities. Finally, through detachment, he anticipates the salvation of the human soul that finds its fulfillment in the fold of the enveloping Spirit.

The virtue of detachment brings to the human consciousness a surprisingly subtle insight. If a person is truly saved by the compassion, mercy, and love of God, what need is there for the world, for the ego, or for the individual self. These lesser gods are all rendered superfluous in the face of the divine alternative, and "Allah is sufficient." That is why faithful Muslims follow the advice of their Prophet and "worship Allah as if [they] actually saw Him." Striving to worship God with the inner eye will reveal the inner spiritual dimension that we witness and observe every day as a self-evident truth, thus building within wisdom's journey through time its own implicit destination as the true journey unto God that is the destiny of the human race.

# PART III

# THE DESCENT

# 5. Seed Words of the Divinity

> And We sent down the Book to thee for the expressed purpose that thou should make clear to them those things in which they differ, that it should be a guide and a mercy for those who believe. (16:64)

Every spiritual tradition and the corresponding religion that forms the cornerstone of that tradition, contains an initial spark—a miracle if you will—that becomes the smoldering ember at its heart whose perennial glow keeps the tradition alive as it finds its way into the hearts of its followers. Because this "singularity" emerges within this world from an otherworldly dimension that is "unseen," it is referred to as revelation and can take a variety of forms.

In principle and as the ultimate mode of communication from the Divine Being to the human being, revelation—in whatever form it reveals itself—dispels the fundamental predicament facing a humanity that lives under the spell of a "holy mystery" (*mysterium sacrum*), a spell that it cannot avoid and that has been laid on it since the beginning of time. It reveals the secret nature of both humanity and the universe and creates pathways through the perennial mystery that overlays the true nature of the universal experience. Revelation touches upon primordial memories within us that exist as the birthright of our true inner nature. Between the covers of revelation, time becomes eternity; space becomes infinite; light becomes a symbol that reminds us of the primal light that illuminates our source and origin.

While every spiritual tradition has its own unique character, the miracle of the Islamic tradition comes in the form of a book. Its initial descent as verses into the mind of the prophet Muhammad, upon whom blessings and peace, marks the beginning of the Religion of Islam, while the final verse marks the completion and perfection of the religion as the ultimate and final message to mankind[1] and seals

[1] The descent of the Quranic revelation began in the cave of Hira outside Makkah with the word *iqra'* which means "recite" or "read": "Recite in the name of thy Lord and Cherisher, who created, created man from the clot of blood" (96:102). Thus, God immediately identified Himself to the messenger Muhammad as the Lord and Creator of all mankind. His earthly ministry came to its final conclusion with the words of the last revealed verse: "This day have I perfected your religion for you, completed

prophethood for all time.[2] Through the words of revelation, the worshipper can send forth beyond earth's shadow and into infinite space words of a divine discourse that have a Divine Listener awaiting this echo from the human domain.

The Religion of Islam is founded on the principles of a revealed knowledge that originates with a Supreme Being Who is the First Cause (*al-Awwal*), the Final End (*al-Akhir*), the Truth (*al-Haqq*), and the One (*al-Ahad*).[3] This revelatory knowledge forms the baseline of a "science of knowing and perception" that fully integrates the outer appearances of all natural phenomena, as well as their qualitative and numinous value, into a single unified reality. In Islam, there cannot be a knowledge of the outward appearance of things—or what we call natural phenomena—without a knowledge of their inner reality; just as there cannot be a knowledge of this inner reality without a corresponding knowledge of the outer appearance. It is the same with the Holy Book, the integrality of the revelation cannot be understood simply from its letter, from its outward literal sense; it can be understood only when interpreted by the spiritual science[4] of its inner meaning. There is an absolute union that exists between the inner reality of a thing and its external appearance, and it requires both spiritual and natural science to define the true vision of the one Reality.

According to the Islamic worldview, a divine revelation is the vision of the Absolute from the perspective of the Absolute; a Self-

My favor upon you, and have chosen for you Islam as your religion" (5:3). It was not long after the revelation of this final verse that the messenger died, may blessings and peace be upon him.

[2] "Muhammad is not the father of any of your men, but (he is) the Messenger of Allah, and the Seal of the Prophets: and Allah has full knowledge of all things" (33:40).

[3] The Quran officially identifies 99 qualifying Names of God in addition to the reference of other attributes that are implicit in the Quranic text. Needless to say, these "Names" aid considerably the human mentality in coming to terms with the great unknown and unknowable quality—the factor of mystery—that hovers perennially around the idea of God.

[4] We use this term, deliberately running the risk of accusations of misappropriation. The term "science" itself was once understood within a sacred, revelatory, and philosophical context as a true knowledge, a first knowledge of the reality. Its meaning as the source and baseline knowledge of an earth-bound, secular, and strictly rational as opposed to metaphysical worldview is a relatively recent phenomenon.

Disclosure from God to man that recalls the primordial revelation[5] and sends forth knowledge into the world of humanity from the original and ultimate source. Revelation portrays the physical world as the consequence of actions initiated by the Creator and it offers the study of nature as a science of signs and symbols whose intricacy and deeper levels of meaning reflect the design and intelligence of the Supreme Being. The traditional worldview understands human beings to be thinking beings made as the human reflection of the Divine Being, with a consciousness that mirrors the Supreme Consciousness and with a variety of higher faculties that can connect with this higher order of Reality. Thus, the Truth has been made manifest to the human mentality in an absolute and unequivocal manner. Because of free will, human beings are at liberty to accept, turn to, and surrender their minds and hearts to this Supreme Intelligence and this Omniscient Being. Human intelligence, supported by both intellect at its upper range and reason at its lower range, can form its own judgments and the way people live their lives becomes sufficient evidence of the validity of their choice of purpose and direction.

The traditional view in Islam is that there are two Qurans, the one metacosmic and uncreated and the other an earthly document, created in an auditory and ultimately written form suited to the demands of this world and the human mentalities that rely on its knowledge and power to enlighten the mind and awaken the higher spiritual emotions. The celestial Quran is referred to in the Islamic traditions as *al-Qur'an al-takwini* and the terrestrial Quran is called *al-Qur'an al-tadwini* whose mode of expression is determined by certain human contingencies so that the Muslims can actually hold the Book in their hands[6] and partake of its knowledge and blessing. For a Muslim, the written book that we see within this world partakes of a different

[5] The typical point of origin of any well-developed traditional culture was an external revelation whether it be in the form of a man or a book, such as Moses for Judaism, Lao-Tzu for Taoism, the Buddha for Buddhism, Jesus for Christianity. Each of these revelations, which contained multivalent meanings *ab initio*, both remembered the Primordial Tradition in its essential form and resulted in creating an established "religion" that could relate to the aspirations and needs of a humanity that would otherwise be "groping in the dark."

[6] After the ritual purification, while non-Muslims read translations that have no liturgical value and require no special precaution.

dimension than any ordinary book we have ever known or will know, partly because its substance is not of this world and partly because its inner reality is inimical to this world.

The question could be asked why Muslims treasure and love what they sometimes refer to as the Noble Quran. The answer must lie in many different factors. For one thing, the Quran addresses itself directly to the human soul rather than to the human mind, possessing an inner dimension that no literal, philological, or literary analysis can set forth and explain away as a purely human document. As such, it has powers and properties that reflect its celestial origin and when read or recited its influence moves into the innermost core of the human entity to give shape and coloration to the fundamental instincts that emanate out of the soul in search of their fullest expression and fulfillment. Through vibration, through sound, through letters, words and phrases that constitute the holy Book, the divine discourse enters the mind, heart and soul of the believing Muslim as a profound remembrance (*dhikr*) of the Divine Being and knowledge of the reality .

Moreover, it is said that the Book addresses the soul directly because it overwhelms the profane and the earthly with a sense of the sacred and the otherworldly, because it casts the absolute and objective quality of the Real upon the relative and subjective aspects of the temporal world, because it responds to the human yearning for the Beyond with the plenitude of the Divine Self-disclosure, and because it brings the presence of the Source and Center into the world of contingency and periphery. This yearning of the mind and heart for an absolute and definitive knowledge of God is fundamental to the human soul and lies at the very heart of our ambition to transcend the broad range of human limitations through the aid and benevolence of a Supreme Intelligence Who ultimately provides the means for the transcendence of the human condition.

In return for the beatitude of the Divine Disclosure, the soul responds naturally to the Object of its innermost desire. What is it that the soul desires most and reflects within the mind and heart as the fundamental human aspiration? The answer must lie somewhere within the intricate weave of human nature and the aspiration of the human soul to transcend its fragmented and lonely state of being here on earth, cut off as it is both from the knowledge and the experience of the unity that lies at the heart of creation. The great themes of the Quran address the broad expanse of all human endeavors and enlighten humanity on the mysteries of the human condition. The profound doctrinal themes, the great ethical questions, and the sacred sentiments all reflect the fundamental elements that constitute the framework of a spirituality that takes into account the human capabilities of thinking, doing, and feeling.

The trials and insecurity of life are counterbalanced by the serenity and peace that is the promise of a person's *islam* (surrender). The uncertainty reflected in the perennial mystery of life is counterbalanced by the absolute quality and the certainty that is the cornerstone of the Word of God. The imbalance and disequilibrium of the human soul is counterbalanced by the balance and equilibrium implicit in the knowledge of the one Reality. The chronic forgetfulness of our true self-identity is counterbalanced by the consciousness of the Supreme Identity associated with the Name of God. The density of the earthly and the mundane is offset by the ethereal quality of the mystic and the spiritual. The linear quality of the strictly horizontal perception is seared through and revitalized by the incisive quality of the vertical disclosure. Finally, the endless diversity and multiplicity of "this world" is counterbalanced—indeed resolved—by the unity and oneness of the Transcendent Center that exists at the heart of the metacosmic vortex. All these grand themes lead toward the development within the soul of that unity implicit in the human world, the Quranic world and the cosmic world.

The Holy Quran is a written as well as a celestial book, capable of being contained in the heart as well as held in the hand of the Muslims. Its exclusive quality lies in the manner in which it has become audible and visible, and therefore those who come in contact with it without prejudice, and with a traditional sensibility for the majestic and the sacred, are ready to be the human instrument that is played upon by the divine sound and the visual Arabic letters. The Quran is a sonorous and visual universe that enters the mind and heart as forms of audible and visual art that have the power to transform the human form into a living reed, a human calamus and flute. Psalmody is the first art of Islam, while the second major art is calligraphy,[7] constituting the let-

[7] "Calligraphy is the basic art of creation of points and lines in an endless variety of forms and rhythms which never cease to bring about recollection (*tidhkar* or *dhikr*) of the Primordial Act of the Divine Pen for those who are capable of contemplating

ters and words of the Book and reflecting on the earthly plane the writing on the Guarded Tablet (*al-lawh al-mahfouz*) that is preserved in Heaven. Psalmody moderates the sound and modulation of the verses, while calligraphy is a sacred art that man carries within himself from the inception of the revelation since "He taught man with the Pen, taught man what he knew not" (96:4-5).

Another rarefied aspect of the Quran for the Muslim community lies in the "presence"—for want of a better term—that accompanies the physical appearance of the book in a mosque or home. The true presence of the Quran lies not in the pages and binding as with other books, but rather in its resonant splendor and its calligraphic majesty. Muslims read the Quran for the knowledge, guidance, and truth implicit in the words and verses; but they also read the verses because they contain a "spiritual presence" through the recitation and intonation of the divine speech that remembers the beloved personality of the Prophet of Islam, upon him blessings and peace, before literally bringing them into the Presence of God.

As sacred sound, the letters, syllables, words, and verses of the revelation call forth the inner voice of the self, the voice of the prophet, the voice of the archangel, and the Voice of the Supreme Being[8] who has chosen to reveal a knowledge of Himself and speak in words of the knowledge of Creation and Origins, thus recalling the primordial man within each of us through the power of sound. When a Muslim recites the verses, he hears his own voice reciting the words first of all in the here and now. Then as a kind of echo beyond the voice of the individual lies the voice of the Prophet Muhammad, upon him blessings and peace. Through the voice of the Prophet passed the divine revelation of God to humanity, whereby he became the instrument and intermediary through whom the world of the Spirit was

in forms the trace of the Formless" (S. H. Nasr, *Islamic Art and Spirituality* [Albany, NY: SUNY Press, 1987], p. 19).

[8] According to a *hadith qudsi*, which is a saying of the Prophet that quotes the direct speech of the Divine Being, a regular reciter of the Quran is he "who reads the Quran is as if he were talking to Me and I were talking to Him."

able to enter and influence the spirit of the world. Beyond the voice of the individual self and the voice of the Prophet lies the voice of the Archangel Gabriel who as intermediary of the Divinity delivered the verses to the Prophet. Finally, all these voices are earthly echoes of the Voice of God Who communicates through these revelatory words to the soul of every human being a profound sense of wonderment for the numinous and the other-worldly. Through words, the Divine Being is able to pluck the violin strings of a person's inner being to sound a cord of the timeless Reality whose echo reverberates throughout the human entity in all its physical, mental, psychic, and spiritual aspects.

The sounds of these primordial, revelatory words of God emanate a feeling of proximity to the Divine Presence, and once spoken aloud or whispered inwardly they reverberate deeply within the cave of the heart and take root in the ground of the soul. Muslims who read the sacred verses over and over on a daily basis can experience within their minds and hearts a pulsating ripple of energy caused by the sacred auditory rhythms embedded within the letters and words of the text itself. The words of the Quran create an inner harmony that in the eloquent words of Seyyed Hossein Nasr produce "an echo in the minds and world of the men who read it, and returns them to a state in which they participate in its paradisal joy and beauty. Herein lies its alchemical effect."[9]

The Quran cannot be translated without seriously diminishing the spiritual presence that emanates from its sacred letters and sounds. There is a majestic projection of sound that is primordial, central, and eternal; primordial in that the sound and meaning evoke within the heart of the reciter feelings for the mythic dimension of primal origins; central because it brings the Muslim immediately back from the periphery of his earthly existence to the very center of his being; eternal because it lifts the reciter out of the march of a lateral, advancing time to the eternal now, the sacred present, that transcends and extinguishes time with its window into eternity.

There is also the perennial question of the language of a text that fundamentally cannot be translated because of its otherworldly texture and its inherent sublimity. Non-Muslims justifiably wonder

[9] *Ibid.*, p. 77.

what it is about the text that renders it untranslatable any more than another text. The answer is first and foremost that the text is the word of God; to alter the text in any way, especially through the expression and form of another language is to withdraw the Presence by taking away the very words that make the text sacred, noble, and holy. In both its meaning and form, the text is sacred in character: the written word as calligraphy, the sounds of the recited text as chanted psalmody, the physical presence of the book, and the message itself are sacred and liturgically important as a vehicle of blessing and grace. The very form of the book is treated with reverence by all Muslims in their homes. It cannot be touched unless a person is in a state of ritual cleanliness. When Muslims sit down to read and recite the Quran, they go through the ritual washing just as they do in preparation for the ritual prayer. Also, the book itself holds a special place within the household, set aside in an elevated place and never below the level of other books within a room.

Revelation brings a doctrine that conveys a meaning, a morality that establishes a purpose, and spiritual sensibilities that lead to a virtuous life. The depth and profundity of this doctrine containing the Truth of the One Reality, given its supreme luminescence and spiritual consequences for humanity, cannot be fully understood and internalized without the descent of a supernatural communication whose divinely inspired text neutralizes all mystery and whose theurgic radiation suffuses the mind, heart, and soul with its radiance (*al-nur*) and blessing (*al-baraka*).

The Quran has variously been described as a recitation (*al-qur'an*), a discernment (*al-furqan*), the mother of all books (*umm al-kitab*), the essential guidance (*al-huda*), the perennial wisdom (*hikmah*), and the ultimate remembrance (*dhikr*). Its very name "recitation" (*qur'an*) recalls the manner in which it was delivered, the way it was received and remembered, and the means with which it is treasured and preserved, for the Quran is a reading and a recitation first and foremost, a compilation of verses and the word of God on the tongues of the faithful. As a criterion and discernment, it establishes once and for all time the true nature of the Real as opposed to the unreal, the light of truth as opposed to the darkness of falsehood and ignorance. The Quranic guidance shapes all personal and ethical conduct and gives definition to the actions of the believers who would not always know otherwise how to behave given the sometimes conflicting nature of their hidden desires; while its wisdom becomes an internalized knowledge within the heart and ultimately manifests in the world community as virtuous behavior.

As Divine Remembrance, however, the Quran contains the ultimate sacred psychology, leading the human soul[10] back from the periphery to the Center and establishing the doctrinal knowledge and the sacred sentiments necessary for the soul's journey of return to the Divine Fold. The Quran is identified as the *dhikr Allah* which is also one of the names of the Prophet and recalls the Quranic verse: "Nothing is greater than the remembrance of God" (29:45). Its vital presence, with all the crystalline quality of a sparkling diamond within the mind, focuses the human consciousness on "the one thing needful" and recreates the ambiance of primordial beatitude that constituted the consciousness of Adam before the fall from Paradise.

The interaction of human consciousness and Divine Remembrance is subtle and intricate. The very *raison d'être* of human consciousness is to realize within the individual self the knowledge of the Universal Self. Remembrance, then, whether it be through the Profession of Faith (the *shahadah*), through the repetition of the Name of God, through the ceremony of prayer, or through the recitation of the holy Quran, activates the human consciousness with the living presence of the Divinity. To enjoy a consciousness of the individual self without a connection to the Supreme Self constitutes a desire to roam on the periphery rather than to be at the center, to live in an evanescent rather than in a transcending world, and to recognize a fundamental mystery at the heart of existence, while refusing to explore its true origin and source.

[10] "The more traditional mentality believed in the concept of the soul as the ultimate locus of man's individuality; the soul was the ground upon which people invest in a principle that is not rooted exclusively within themselves but that transcends their physical limitations. Behind the intuition of higher truth, behind all the emotive experience that colors and shapes man's inner world, behind all the sacred sentiments and virtues that can result from the rich texture of a human life, behind the free will and the wisdom that adds to the qualitative uniqueness of the human being, behind all the seeing and hearing of our senses and deeper than the deepest thought lies the human soul as the source of the individual being" (John Herlihy, *Borderlands of the Spirit: Reflections on a Sacred Science of Mind* [Bloomington, IN: World Wisdom, 2005], p. 118).

The Quran, as Divine Discourse and Revelatory Word, remains the ultimate source of all essential knowledge, the well-spring of all morality and ethics, and the means of spiritual worship that permits the faithful to transcend their limitations and approach the true knowledge of the Reality as Truth and as Presence. Like the earth with its arctics and tropics, its seacoasts and mountain ranges, its plains and valleys, its deserts and woodlands, the Quran has a broad range of topical representation, including poetic heights and legalistic depths, dogmatic theology as well as mystic aphorisms, lists and litanies, prayers of supplication and praise. Every letter, word, and verse is packed with layers of symbolic meaning that reach the human mind according to the receptiveness of the recipient.

The Book can be summarized in three distinct ways. Firstly, it represents a doctrine containing the metaphysical knowledge of God and science of reality concerning the ultimate nature of things. Secondly, it presents an ethical code of conduct as the basis of an Islamic law (*shari'ah*). After all, one of the purposes of revelation is to ground the morality of humanity within the precinct of a sacred knowledge that has the power to deliver a truth that is absolute and that finds its source and efficacy beyond the whims of the human mentality. As such, it provides an objective, moral foundation that transcends the subjectivity of humanity and finds its root in the authority and judgment of a Supreme Being. Thirdly, the Word of God narrates a history that transcends linear time by appealing to the sensitivities of the human soul, a sacred history of the soul that casts in cameo the great personages of Biblical and Quranic history, from messengers and prophets to pharaohs, conquerors, and kings. In recounting the strengths and limitations of the great figures of sacred history, the Quran teaches mankind a wide range of moral and spiritual principles. These sacred narratives appeal directly to the human soul wherein the battle ultimately is fought between the forces of good and evil. To become aware of the currents of a sacred history is to become aware of the history of one's own soul, for humankind was made from "one soul" and enjoys a unique human nature that is as changeless as it is enduring.

The descent of the knowledge of God in the form of a metaphysical doctrine, a moral law, and a sacred chronicle of the soul remains the one true source we still have available for an absolute expression of an Absolute Truth. The ascent of humanity through spiritual aspiration and experience based on the knowledge of God remains the one true means we still have available to transcend our limitations and perfect ourselves. Knowledge descends as sacred speech because Allah is the Living, the Knowing, and the Omniscient. Consequently, humans can make their journey of ascent and return to God because these divine attributes are reflected within their theomorphic nature as Life, Knowledge, and the power implicit in Free Will. We live as beings who may have access to the essential knowledge, who choose what we wish to believe, and who must put our beliefs into practice through the force of an inner power that actualizes this knowledge. Finally, through the worship implicit in the Quranic recitation, the Muslim has the means to actualize the encounter of the human with the Divine and thereby to counterbalance the sacred encounter of the Divine with the human made possible through the descent of the revelation.

For several reasons, the true value of the Quran as it is understood in the mind of the Muslim escapes the understanding and appreciation of non-Muslims, especially the Euro-American Christian community. This applies firstly to the Quran as a means of worship, and secondly to the language of the Quran as the absolute speech of God and how the worshipper relates to the literal and inner content of the words and phrases. In the Islamic tradition, Quranic recitation is a form of worship on a par with prayer and the other spiritual disciplines, such as meditation and fasting. In Islam, every person performs a sacerdotal role as the celebrant of the sacred rites of worship. The human and the Divine come together in an encounter that is direct and ultra-personal. Reading the Quran provides the perfect means for such a direct and intimate encounter with the Divinity, who according to a well known verse "is nearer to him than his jugular vein." Islamic practice encourages Quranic recitation in the morning after the dawn prayer (*salat al-fajr*), when keeping vigil at night, and upon the completion of the ritual prayer. "Establish regular prayers, at the sun's decline till the darkness of the night, and the morning prayer and reading: for the prayer and reading in the morning carry their own testimony" (17:78).

The true value of the Quranic recitation as a form of worship is borne out by the fact that millions of non-Arabic speaking Muslims read and recite the Quran without necessarily understanding the literal meaning of the words. Yet, they approach the Book with a conscious reverence and a fundamental desire to worship God that transcends the literal meaning of the verses. In addition, it is possible that God may bless the sincere heart and intention of a devout Muslim with a realized knowledge of the doctrine without having to necessarily pass through the gate of a literal knowledge.

There is even a potential danger that could arise from either complacency from habitual reading or an over-familiarity with the text. Native speakers of Arabic who may know the linguistic nuances of the text may fall short of a realized knowledge for one reason or another, such as lack of intent or sincerity of purpose. In other words, a literal knowledge of the language carries with it no guarantee of an assimilated knowledge of the text or of the many and varied levels of knowledge and meaning that are contained therein. On the other hand, non Arabic-speaking readers who struggle through a careful recitation of the text may well approximate a better and more accurate reading then a native-speaking Arab who through habit and routine may rush through a well-known portion of the text and lace the reading with multiple errors.[11] Only intention, effort, and an underlying sincerity can define the parameters of Muslim worship and not a specific race or language type.

The Quran is a miraculous blend of meaning and sound. Obviously the Quran conveys a meaning upon those who understand the literal words, while intuitive meaning can be conveyed directly to the non-Arabic speaker, depending on the intentions of the person reciting the verses together with the mercy and blessing of God. However, there is no doubting the miraculous effect that the sacred sounds and word combinations have on the faithful generally, Arab and non-Arab Muslims alike. In addition to the words, phrases, meanings, aphorisms,

[11] There is a well-defined science of Quran recitation, known as *tajwid* in Arabic, with detailed rules for reading the Quran correctly. These rules must not only be learned, but practiced systematically to be mastered properly, even by native speakers. It is not just a matter of knowing Arabic pronunciation and reading correctly. Arabic-speaking Muslims themselves require training and practice in the skill of *tajwid* which raises the level of Quran recitation to a science as well as a sonorous art.

stories, and symbolic images, the sacred text is replete with rhythms, cadences, intonations, elisions, ellipses, and sacred sound vibrations that, together, add up to a glorious psalmody having a powerful, cumulative effect on the reader, who makes every effort to chant sonorously, clearly, slowly, and above all correctly the holy phrases.[12] "It exercises its effect not only upon the mind but on the very substance of the believer, although it can do this only in its integral character, that is to say as the Arabic Quran."[13] No doubt, the words and their associations have echoes and reverberations in the ear and mind of the faithful with a power that can melt hearts and stir souls. The Prophet once told his companions that "hearts become rusty just as iron does when water gets at it." When asked how this rust could be removed, he replied: "By frequent remembrance of death and frequent recitation of the Quran."

It is not uncommon during Quranic recitation for a Muslim to weep for no apparent reason other than the subliminal and cumulative effect that the recitation has on the mind and heart of the reciter. This phenomenon is commonly called the "gift of tears." These tears are symbolic of the profound emotion present within the person at that time, while the emotion itself serves as a purification and release of repressed feelings and attitudes that often reside unconsciously within us. Muslims often feel spiritually refreshed after a session of Quranic recitation, uplifted and ready to meet the forces and challenges that they may be confronted with during the course of their day. The mind, heart, and soul have been washed clean and a sense of mental and spiritual refreshment hovers like the scent of fresh soap from an early morning bath.

The Quran exudes a mysterious and in a sense miraculous power. In his *Risalat al-Quds*, Ibn 'Arabi quotes the case of Sufis who spend their whole life in reading or in ceaselessly reciting the Quran. This would be inconceivable if not impossible to sustain were there not, behind the words of the literal text, a concrete and active spiritual presence that goes beyond the words and the actively conscious mind

[12] In quantum terms, everything vibrates, even the human body as the physical manifestation of the soul of ourselves.

[13] Charles Le Gai Eaton, *Islam and the Destiny of Man* (Cambridge, UK: The Islamic Texts Society, 1985), p. 78.

of the reciter. Moreover, it is by virtue of the miraculous power of the Quran that certain verses can expel evils and heal illnesses in many circumstances. Christians familiar with the exorcism of devils from the body will not be surprised that Muslims also use the Quran to cast demons and evil *jinn* from the body of human beings that they have taken possession of. Similarly, Quranic phrases are used in traditional massage and other healing techniques, such as energy projection through breathing in which physical methods work together with spiritual aspiration to cure the person of his or her disease. One sees that the Quran is truly "a cure and a mercy" (17:82) for the faithful.

A Muslim's relationship with the Quran involves something more than establishing the facts or acquiring the knowledge it contains. It goes far beyond an acquiring of the Arabic language or appreciating the aesthetic quality and visual impact that Islamic calligraphy has on the mind. There is a harmony and a rhythmic flow to the words and verses that virtually defy close analysis. Non-Muslims who are unfamiliar with the Arabic language liken its mysterious rhythm to poetry, but it is not poetry in the normal sense of the word since its rhythms follow no poetic rules and contain a power that goes far beyond the realm of any earthly poetry. "The eloquence does not reside so much in the ordering of the words into powerful poetic utterance as in the degree of the inspiration as a result of which every sentence, every word, and every letter scintillate with a spiritual presence and are like light congealed in tangible form."[14] The rhythms themselves are subtle and mysterious and cannot be compared with what is found within the great works of literature that have been written down through the ages.

In addition, rhythmic patterns flow out of the Quranic images and symbols into the very soul and have the power to create feelings of primordial bliss. These images and symbols are not classical or literary, rather they are archetypal in their character and universal in their message. They are of two kinds, the macrocosmic and microcosmic. The macrocosmic symbols recall the great and harmonious rhythms of the natural order that include the passage of night and day, the movement of sun, moon, and stars, the magnitude of the zodiacal heavens, the phases of the moon, and the spiral movement of galaxies all ponder-

[14] *Ibid*, p. 5.

ously swirling around a central metacosmic core.[15] These are symbolic images expressive of a rhythm and movement that touch the very soul of those reciting the verses as they sit with the book and intone the sacred words and phrases. "The Quran . . . engenders, in whoever hears its words and experiences its sonorous magic, both plenitude and poverty. It gives and it takes, it enlarges the soul by lending it wings, then lays it low and strips it bare; it is comforting and purifying at one and the same time, like a storm; human art can scarcely be said to have this virtue."[16] We touch the Book, take it to hand, read it, aspire to absorb its meaning and internalize its holy essence; in return we are touched by the very words of God.

Similarly, there are the microcosmic images and symbols that relate directly to our human nature. The heart, for instance, stands out as the archetypal seal of all knowledge and feeling. It is the "seal" of the intelligence in the Islamic perspective as well as the sacred cave or niche of all higher emotion and noble sentiments. We refer here not to the physical heart of course, but the spiritual heart of each individual that serves as the central spiritual faculty and therefore must reside behind the physical projection of the pulsating heart pump. Allah knows what is in the human heart and He knows what lies at the heart of the cosmic universe. There are other powerful symbols that relate to the human body such as the Hand, Eye, and Face of God. "Allah's Hand is over their hand" (48:10); "Allah is the Hearer, the Seer" (40:20); "Wherever you turn, there is the Face of God" (2:115). These microcosmic symbols are powerful channels of insight that can lift the veil and cross the unbreachable isthmus (*barzakh*) that exists between the physical and spiritual planes of existence.

Finally, we should not overlook the fact that the phrases and verses of the Quran enter the daily life of the Muslims to the extent that the rhythm and texture of life itself becomes interwoven with prayers, epithets, litanies, and invocations that are derived expressly from the sacred text. "It is easy to understand the capital part played in the life of the Moslem by those sublime words which are the verses

[15] "Truly, the creation of the heavens and the earth is greater than the creation of man" (40:57).

[16] Titus Burckhardt, *Mirror of the Intellect* (Cambridge, UK: Quinta Essentia, 1987), pp. 244-245.

of the Quran; they are not merely sentences which transmit thoughts, but are in a way beings, powers, or talismans. The soul of the Moslem is as it were woven of sacred formulas; in these he works, in these he rests, in these he lives, and in these he dies."[17] The Quran is an integral part of a Muslim life, permeating every aspect of daily routine, shaping its parameters, providing its coloration, motivation, and ultimate goal. It is the first sound that is whispered into a newborn's ear, and, if one is blessed with a so-called "happy death," it the final sound that is uttered as one takes leave of this world, becoming a verbal bridge into another dimension.

Beyond these key moments, however, there is the language we use in our daily lives that is punctuated linguistically with Quranic epithets. Every formal action, such as beginning a work project or setting out on a journey, commences with the phrase "In the Name of God, the Compassionate, the Merciful." When a person sneezes, asks how another person is, or even finishes a meal, he praises God by way of thanks. When a disaster overtakes the Muslims, they immediately say that "there is no power except in God"; but when a thing of beauty presents itself, they are quick to say "glory be to God." When Muslims express the intention to accomplish something and have a future wish, they immediately invoke the will of Allah as the guiding principle to their every desire. They wish a thing to happen only if God wishes it.

Such epithets have their origins in the sacred Quranic text and become, through the use of everyday speech, expressions of sacred sentiments that are embedded within the very soul of the Muslim and emerge to the surface in the form of daily linguistic usage no matter what may be the mother tongue of the person. Turkomans, Iranians, Malays, Pakistanis, Bangladeshis, and Mongolian Muslims all employ these Quranic phrases in their Arabic formulation within their own mother languages, wherein these phrases function "as is," unchanged and original, Quranic at source and fully comprehensible as a form of communication. In return, these languages are sometimes referred to as Islamic languages.

[17] Frithjof Schuon, *Understanding Islam* (Bloomington, IN: World Wisdom Books, 1994), p. 60.

Quranic recitation also determines the very framework of a Muslim's spiritual life. Muslims draw on the language of the Quran to give a spiritual frame to their hopes, fears, sorrows, regrets, and aspirations. They use the Quran as a means of withdrawing for a few moments during the course of the day, whether it be in the early morning when the birds sing their own sacred verses, or after the sunset prayer when the calm of dusk merges into the stillness of night. The holy recitation relieves the mind, the psyche, and the soul of the reciter from the gravitational pull of this world with its implicit imbalance, disharmony, and lack of peace. When Muslims arise in the morning at the call to prayer, they have available the sacred book that contains all they need to know; they therefore possess the means to realize that knowledge in their daily lives. Small wonder then that devout Muslims turn to the Holy Quran for sustenance and strength on a daily basis throughout the course of their lives, a turning that preempts doubt and despair and leads them back to the center and source of their existence within the Divine Being.

At the dawn prayer, the shadowy rays of the saffron moon flow across the window sill. In the pre-dawn darkness, the night sky shines forth the light of ancient star dust with its message of an eternity within time and an infinity within space, before disappearing with the coming of the dawn. There is a hint of incense in the air whose assault on the senses captures a feeling of sacrality that becomes a moving force within the mind and heart. Heavenly scents accompany the two angels who descend to witness the Quranic recitations that occur every morning across the crescent of the Islamic world. Having performed the ritual ablution and prayer, Muslims in various corners of the globe sit cross-legged on a prayer carpet and reach for the Noble Quran, the Illuminated Book, a document that is "on a tablet well-preserved in heaven," as well as a printed book held in hand. They kiss it out of profound respect, place it on forehead and heart, and then commence to recite verses from the Holy Book. *Alif, Lam, Mim,* they chant sonorously the Arabic letters that commence the Quran's second chapter: "This is the Book, of which there is no doubt, and guidance for those who fear God" (2:1).

With the divine words of revelation, Muslims forever repeat the task of planting in the ground of their souls the seeds of a divine knowledge that brings guidance and certainty. When the mind becomes illuminated with knowledge, when the heart is on fire with desire, when the imagination paints dreams of mystery and beauty, and when the higher emotions are brimming with devotion and love, then do the seeds of the divine Mystery take root and grow. The early dawn light creeps cautiously across the windowpane while the out-sized autumn moon sinks heavily below the emerging horizon. As the words of revelation echo through the emerging dawn, the aspiring soul becomes a staging ground of a worship that rises through lower levels of conscious awareness in order to return to its origin in the universal consciousness that radiates from the Mind of God.

# 6. Living in the Presence

And recite the Quran with measured recitation. (73:4)
Allah cometh in between man and his own heart. (8:24)

Devout Muslims live with the Quran not as a book on a shelf to be perused at random, but as a miraculous presence waiting to be encountered and communicated with. Their attitude calls to mind a statement of the American transcendental philosopher Ralph Waldo Emerson: "Other men are lenses through which we read our own minds." In the minds and hearts of Muslims, the verses of the Quran serve as reflecting lenses through which the Muslims can see themselves as a mirror reflection of the Truth of the Supreme Being. The words of the book are beacons of light connecting existential truths with celestial realities. When Muslims read the Quran, the knowledge and light of a higher reality bursts in upon their ordinary consciousness, a profound and enlightening experience that is as unexpected as it is earth-shattering.

In chapter 5 I have endeavored to explain the mysterious value and import of the Quran, which Muslims see as a revelation from another, unseen dimension of reality. Contrary to the sentiments of the modernist mentality, with its rational and secular worldview, the verses of the Quran present a picture of the true reality and therefore the only reality worth taking seriously. Understanding the true nature of the Quran and what it sets out to accomplish is crucial in understanding the spirit of the ambiance and culture of the Islamic world, along with the so-called Muslim mentality that is the logical extension of that world.

On a fundamental level, the Quran needs to be understood as a sacred revelation from a higher dimension of reality. The book and its verses must first be accepted abstractly and in principle by the mind, then affirmed substantially by the heart with a faith that is ultimately based on the intuitive knowledge of God. In the previous chapter, we have explored the notion of the Quran as seed words of the Divinity, seeds of knowledge that are accepted—indeed affirmed—by the mind and planted within the ground of the human soul. If that were enough, we could wrap it in velvet cloth and set it on the mantelpiece in our living room as the universal book of knowledge to be respected as the *prima facie* exemplar of universal truth.

However, contrary to what the modern secularist worldview would have us believe, we are not just the mind. Inclusive within the higher faculties of the mind, we have the discerning mirror of the intellect, the broad field of the imagination, the sacred niche of the heart, and the heat of the emotions and higher sensitivities that give light to the intellect, wings to the imagination, mystery to a secret heart-knowledge, and burning embers to the higher sacred emotions that come together as the sublime experience of the Presence, the *sakinah* in traditional Islamic terminology. Like the words of revelation, the presence descends from above and settles upon the ground of the human soul from on high, representing none other than the ethereal presence of God Almighty, nurturing the seeds of the Quranic revelation within the ground of the human soul. In the spiritual state of consciousness aroused by a concentrated and devoted reading of the sacred Quranic text, the sound of a thousand thunders could not more effectively transform countless sacred syllables into a rhythmic force with the power to carry the human mind beyond the sorrows and tribulations of this world to an altogether higher plane of reality.

What did the Quran as a revelation from God mean to me thirty years ago as a fledgling Muslim convert? The short answer must be "not much"; because I was sitting on the edge of our modern-day secular wilderness, although I had not yet fallen into the abyss of absolute forgetfulness concerning my true origins and ultimate destiny. Still, no one had to convince me about the importance, indeed the necessity, of a divine revelation; I still retained some semblance of a fundamental belief in the existence of the Supreme Being and the need for some form of communication that could transcend the barriers that separate the Divine and human dimensions.

The idea of the Quran as a revelation from an Absolute Being to mortal humans captured my imagination and eventually seized the intellections—not to mention the reasoning and higher faculties—of my mind. Muslims would call it blessing (*baraka*) or mercy (*rahmah*); to my reckoning, it emerged out of nowhere, as though one day I had passed by a wintry bush shorn of any life-giving properties and saw reaching out to me from this bundle of dead vegetation a solitary bud closed tight and awaiting the process of self-awakening. If so, then the rest of my life has been a constant monitoring of that emerging bud, akin to watching the measured opening of a flower or the metamorphosis of a butterfly from a time-sequenced camera compacting eons of tedious observation into a breathtaking narrative of time-compressed seconds.

I also firmly accepted the logic that if I had faith in a Supreme Being, and if that Supreme Being has spoken in words to a humanity in need of guidance and mercy, then I should find out not only what the Divinity has chosen to relate to His thinking creation, but also the manner in which this revelation has been delivered. What secrets lie sequestered within the letters, syllables, and words that make up the verses of the Holy Book? What mysteries of the unknown lie waiting for the human mind to experience and absorb?

Indeed, I was soon to find out that the Quran is much more than just a body of knowledge preserved within the covers of a book. It offers a resolution to the perennial mysteries concerning the origin of the universe, the origin of life, and the mystery of human consciousness, as well as providing a spiritual framework for the understanding of the human entity. In addition to being a Book, a Word, a Recitation, a Guidance, a Mercy, and a Light, the Quran is an experience of a unique and otherworldly Presence brought down into the world of humanity through letters, words, phrases, and verses that amount to the calligraphic signature and divine disclosure of a Supreme Being.

My love for the Quran finds its source in a tiny spark that must have flown off the burning embers of some cosmic hearth and fallen down to earth to find its way into the mind and heart of this then fledgling believer who found himself living in the remnants of a traditional civilization, grimly trying to stand firm during an era dominated by such mythologies and illusions as secular humanism and material progress. This initial spark reignited the smoldering ruins of an uninspired life with its affirmation of truth based upon the idea of unity at the heart of creation. Indeed, I had a willingness to believe, but where was I prepared to go with this impulse, I wondered, and where did I expect it to lead me?

I had been brought up as a devout Christian in an Irish Catholic community just outside of Boston, Massachusetts. I was well familiar with the idea of a created Word Incarnate. The image of Christ was imprinted on my developing mind as the human revelation *par excel-*

*lence*. When I became Muslim,[1] I knew nothing of the Holy Quran, its contents, its history, and manner of delivery, or its role within the life of the Muslim; but I believed implicitly in the "idea" of revelation, namely that if a person accepts that a Supreme Being exists, then logic demands the acceptance of a revelation in which such a Supreme Being communicates the knowledge of His existence along with the means to respond to that knowledge in a meaningful and effective manner through effort and spiritual disciplines. That was one psychological hurdle I did not have to overcome, unlike many in the Western world today who have inherited no true understanding of the meaning of revelation and what it could mean to them and their lives. Only much later did I learn, not through knowledge but through experience, of the profound meaning of the *sakinah*, the blessed experience of the Presence of God, that accompanies the experience of either reciting the Quranic verses by heart or reading the verses from the depths of the heart.

The Quran states that: "Wherever you turn, there is the Face of God." Here "face" is symbolic of the all-pervasive and qualitative "personality"—for want of a better word—of the Divine Being Who is subject neither to place, time, nor any other earthly condition. Humans, on the other hand, are subject to place and time and live in a dimension in which the true nature of reality is veiled from their direct view. The knowledge of God must be made available to us by virtue of our humanity; but once the revelatory knowledge has been made available, we alone are to blame for not abiding by His guidance. The experience of the Presence, however, is earned through spiritual discipline and sacred practices of worship whose effect is to lift the veil that separates the human consciousness from the true face of the unseen Reality (*al-Ghaib*).

This question of the presence is crucial in understanding the true nature of Islamic worship and the spiritual disciplines, such as Quranic recitation, that together form the cornerstone of such worship. The words of the text are the sacred talismans of transmission. Muslims recognize that they have the words of God, words with which to

[1] My conversion and the reasons why I became a Muslim are documented in an earlier book of mine entitled *The Seeker and the Way: Reflections of a Muslim Convert* (Kuala Lumpur, Malaysia: Noordeen Publications, 1999).

speak and think and internalize the divine disclosure, words that reflect every virtue and every intimacy in life, words with which we can express sacred emotions and affinities that reside in the deepest well of our beings, words that tell of a primordial era when the story of the first man and woman began to unfold and that to this day capture the imagination of the receptive mind. By intoning through rhythmic breathing and chanting and establishing a rhythm of sacred vibration that courses through the body in waves of sacred evanescence, the worshipper is able to call himself back to a more authentic mode of being that finds its source in the spiritual verities. Through rigorous discipline and an absolute adherence to the laws of recitation (*tajwid*), we are able to recapture a genuine sense of the divine presence that accompanies the verses of the divine disclosure.

Of course, I knew none of this sacred intimacy that could be made possible through the recitation and chanting of the sacred Quranic text. Armed with the primal impulses of an affirmative faith that expressed a readiness to believe and that made me a repository of hope awaiting fulfillment, I set myself as a new Muslim convert on a course to come to terms with the Quran and overcome any and all obstacles that may get in my way. Call it determination, decisiveness, short-sightedness, or possibly a kind of holy madness, but I remember a spiritual conviction to my attitudes, which were tenacious and deep-rooted, although from whence they came, why they had arrived, and what form of expression they would take I had no clear idea.

Somehow, for I am a person who remembers the essence of an experience without necessarily remembering the details, I came in contact with a charming Kashmiri Indian while I was teaching at the University of Kuwait, whom I have referred to elsewhere as the "laughing Sufi." He was a merry fellow indeed, laughing his way through a minefield of philosophical speculation with a conviction and a certitude that left me dizzy with desire, anxious to rise above myself and my own limitations, and hopeful of his promises to raise my consciousness to a level of awareness not previously experienced that would change my perception of self and my experience of the world. To me at that time, this sounded hopelessly inviting. He explained at one point that he had a legendary aspiration to translate the Quran and he saw in me the perfect collaborator for such a project. Preposterous as it may sound, he made me a proposal that I could not easily refuse—namely to help him translate the Quran. He would orally transmit the meaning of the verses in English and I would later polish the language into a modern-day vernacular. As *tabula rasa* and virgin receptacle to the words of the Divine Pen, I could become the linguistic filter and wordsmith in this approximation of a translation from Arabic to English.[2]

It seemed to be the perfect opportunity of becoming acquainted, if not with the actual words of the sacred text, then its primordial knowledge and its sacred import. Its meaning would be delivered in the oral tradition out of which it was born. We embarked on this endeavor that ultimately took over one year to complete. Meanwhile, we had generated some interest in our "project" at the Saudi Embassy in Kuwait and were received by the Saudi ambassador amid all the pomp and splendor that comes to be associated with the princes and kings of such ruling elite classes in the Arab world. I was indeed astride the flying carpet of my childhood dreams and floating on a cloud of rarefied experience, half terrified and half in thrall of the visions of grandeur passing before me. When the project was completed after an unbelievable effort involving self-discipline and forbearance, we returned to the embassy and delivered the entire body of the work, all 600 pages or so bounded tightly together by a red ribbon squared in fours around the bundle of the manuscript.[3]

That was my first introduction to the meaning of the Quran in English, personally delivered to me by my "laughing Sufi" whose love of the text and whose faithfulness and devotion to its meaning and import passed into me with the words of his translation. As I suggested in Part One, in explaining the meaning of the Quranic text, his was the voice of the Prophet, the voice of those companions who first repeated the blessed word, the voice of the archangel and ultimately the Supreme Voice of Allah. My faithful friend, my earthly master and beloved benefactor, has since passed beyond the known horizon at the hem of this world; but I will always remember the image of his

[2] Of course, the Muslims say that technically speaking, it is impossible to translate the Quran in the same way that a work of literature may be translated. Because the essence of the Quran relies upon the literal Arabic letters as the formal representation of the revelation, the liturgical value of the text is lost in translation.

[3] Sadly, the then reigning King Faisal of Saudi Arabia was murdered in his palace by a nephew who had ostensibly come to greet him and offer his *salaams*. Official Saudi interest in our project died with his unexpected passing.

chubby, mirthful face as he delivered to me, if not the sacred words of the original text—for that privilege would come much later—then the translated meaning of the Noble Quran, verses and stories and a body of knowledge as from father to son, as from the messenger to his companions, as from the great Archangel Gabriel to the mind and consciousness of our beloved Prophet, upon whom blessings and peace, words and verses that sparkle on the tongue like sunlight on the bay and illuminate the great cave of the heart like the flickering light of a camp fire on a clear dark night. This was a rare and unique introduction, if not to the Quran itself and its very words, then to its meaning and import, amounting to being a very important first step for a non-Arabic speaking new Muslim in coming to terms with the Holy Book.

Through a *madrasah quraniyah* system of education in all traditional Islamic cultures, the study of the Quran begins in childhood at the age of reason, concentrating on the correct recitation of the Arabic letters, sound, words, phrases, and finally full verses of the Book in all Arabic-speaking countries, and also most notably in Islamic countries where Arabic is not the native tongue. Because the verses of the Quran are considered to be the absolute word of God, it is imperative that young children gain mastery of the fundamentals of Quranic recitation at an early age, a skill they will carry with them for the rest of their lives.

The tradition of the Quranic *madrasah* began with the first *madrasah* in the mosque of the Prophet Muhammad where the "Companions of the Bench" devoted themselves to the study of the Quran from the Prophet himself, in itself a privilege and a blessing that one can only pretend to appreciate. Many of these companions then traveled far and wide in the propagation of the newly emerging religion. Many of them established and settled in mosques in distant lands where they started to teach Quran and Hadith to students seeking knowledge of Islam. Thus, they initiated and perpetuated the tradition of the *madrasah* by carrying on the *isnad* or chain of transmission from the beloved Prophet himself.

I recently asked my faithful Pathan friend Farman Ullah about his *madrasah* experience as a child, wishing to hear firsthand the native impressions of a devoted, traditional, and conservative Muslim. "We study morning and evening at mosque after prayer and sit in a circle with imam." I asked him what he remembers learning. "We first learn the graded books that introduce the system of Arabic letters and their correct pronunciation." Coincidentally, these innocent exercise books are called *al-qaeda*, which in Arabic means "base" or "basic," a term that is now universally recognized as the name of Osama bin Laden's terrorist organization. "Did you know what you were reading," I asked my friend tentatively, not wishing to offend. "Of course," the Pathan shouts with good-humored indignation. "We know and love our holy book. What you thinking? We prepare ourselves to make reading with *wudhu*.[4] I doesn't touch book otherwise. We very respect Quran at that age and every time." And I think that his love of the Quran has its roots in a holy instinct that was born early in childhood as he studied with vigilance the letters, words, and phrases of his *qaeda* reader that to his young, innocent mind comprised the very words of Allah. There is no compromise when it comes to the Quran; it is instinctive and a matter of personal honor among devout Muslims to maintain a close and respectful relationship with the Holy Book of Islam.

I came to Islam as a grown man who had embraced the religion as a matter of decision and active choice, but this was only the first step on a long road of acclimatization and realization of what it truly means to be a Muslim—and what it means to me—an effort of self-discovery and consciousness-raising that is personal and unique to each individual. "For every soul," according to one well known tradition, "there is an individual path to follow." As such, I knew that I had to come to terms with the Arabic Quran if not now then later, the Noble Book being the alpha and omega of all Islamic spirituality, its source material and its means of expression and worship. The religion began with its first descent into the mind of the Prophet in the Cave of Light in Makkah, and will come to fruition through the sincere expression of each individual Muslim life faithful to its dictates and guidance. In my childhood, I never attended a traditional Quranic *madrasah* because I converted to Islam later in life, over thirty years ago. However, like

[4] The ritual ablution in Islam that not only precedes the prayer, but also Quran reading. Muslims cannot touch the Book unless they have ritually purified themselves, and this injunction is strictly adhered to by the faithful.

all serious devotees of the religion, I very soon set about learning the intricacies of Quranic recitation, without which Islamic worship in the form of prayer, which uses Quranic verses as part of its ritual or Quranic recitation, would be impossible.

I do not like to measure these things in months and years and prefer the concept of an uninterrupted continuum of the present moment bathed in some perspective of eternity, but sometime after familiarizing myself with the meaning of the Quran in translation with the aid of my Sufi friend Haneef, I set myself the task of learning the basics of the Arabic script. Of course as a Westerner, even though I had a focused interest in other languages as an English teacher and spoke French and German with ease, I had great difficulty initially with the Arabic letters. Yet there was an appealing magic to the formation of the letters that radiated a whimsical quality of arabesques and changing profiles that seemed to spread across the page like untied knots leaving behind a bold air of incoherent mystery. Once thoroughly familiar with the alien letters, however, I set about familiarizing myself with the words and phrases of the sacred text.

Eventually, I felt comfortable enough with the letters to enable me to begin mouthing the sacred speech. It is one thing to be a child and undergo the demanding rigors of learning the basics of one's mother language letter for letter and sound for sound; quite another to be a grown adult in the throes of an alien wilderness of symbols and sounds patched together with an exact science of pronunciation (*tajwid*) with fixed rules and regulations that require the intonation of a chanted psalmody as a natural rhythm of sound emergent from within the sacred text and given life by the human voice. How was I to learn this on my own? I couldn't very well sit myself down next to the seven-year-olds of a Quranic *madrasah*; at least my state of development at the time would not have permitted such recourse. Nor could I sit myself down amid the faithful who often gather after the early morning *fajr* prayer in many a mosque across the Islamic crescent to fine-tune their Quranic recitation skills. Any genuine attempt to read the Quran at that stage would have proved to be scandalous. Somehow, I needed to develop a reasonable amount of skill and accuracy before gathering the courage to join the circle of worshippers after the dawn or sunset prayer.

The next phase in this process of familiarization with the physical demands of the text in terms of pronunciation, intonation, and the rhythmic tonal qualities implicit in correct psalmody led me to the convenience of a newly developed technology at that time in the mid-70s, the walkman tape player. The Quran is available in its entirety on a series of tapes; some of the traditional Egyptian and Syrian sheikhs who are adept at the fine art of Quranic recitation are legendary. There are of course different styles of psalmody; I followed the advice of a Muslim friend and purchased the entire Quran recited by an Egyptian sheikh known for the quality of his "sound" and the perfection, accuracy, and clarity of his pronunciation. The entire Quran came to thirty different tapes that coincided with the thirty equal parts (*juz*) that the Quran is divided into.[5]

After the *maghreb* prayer at sunset, I would set aside a half hour's time and listen to the tape while reading aloud and meticulously following the progress of the text. In this way, I was able to detect whether I was making a mistake or not, and I read along while simultaneously listening to the sheikh's pronunciation through earphones. The tonal clarity and the vibratory resonance of the sound of the human voice intoning the sacred verses rang through my head with the clarity of a resounding bell, echoing the famous comment of the Prophet when he told his wife Khadijah that when he heard the first verses of the revelation being recited to him by the Archangel Gabriel, they had the clarity of a clarion bell, and later he was to say: "It was as though the words were written on my heart." I spent about a year in this process of becoming more familiar with the text until I felt that the words were somehow written on my mind as resonant echoes from some distant, higher plane; but they were yet to be written on my heart.

One lesson had already come clear to my novitiate mind: the Quran is by name a recitation rather than a reading *per se*, meaning

[5] According to the tradition of Quran recitation, the Quran is divided into various sections and parts and are usually read in accordance with one of these divisions. The thirty equal parts remain the traditional and standard length for a routine recitation because it coincides with the length of a single month. Devout Muslims make efforts to read a *juz* a day as a matter of routine and inculcate this habit into their daily life. Reading the entire Quran during the holy month of Ramadan is considered standard practice by all Muslims. Other divisions are three, seven, and ten—all sacred numbers in the science of numerology—but these take considerably more time to perform and are sometimes attempted as part of a night vigil or during the holy month of Ramadan.

predominantly an oral tradition in commemoration of earlier revelations delivered to peoples of other time periods and recalling the universal quality of legends and myths whose knowledge and meaning conveyed truths delivered orally and intended to be transmitted orally. As such, the Quran is yet another manifestation in a long history of oral traditions that have been passed down through time as sacred forms of communication that are direct and immediate between people, rather than being relegated only to some fixed place on a page, lying closed in and sequestered within the covers of a book. The symbolic value of an oral text conveys meaning effectively and economically to the mind without necessarily having the intermediary of a formal script whose practical value now serves us well but that does not supersede or enhance the intuitive directness that takes place orally between people. The written page contains a kind of nostalgia for the time when the words on a page were spoken as a kind of poetry or solar speech, whose meaning transcends dimensions as well as distance. These oral revelations were as intangible and invisible as the Spirit their words convey and as eternal as the Cosmic Mind out of which they were born.

I was yet another recipient vessel among generations of humanity poured full of knowledge and blessing, but I still couldn't claim to have gotten inside the words of God any more than they have gotten inside me. In truth, as a vessel of the Divine Spirit, I felt as hard and brittle as glass, ready to be broken and shattered into pieces at the slightest whim of destiny and at the merest contingency of this world. How I needed these words of revelation to fill me up and cast me to the spirit of the wind that "bloweth where it listeth." I was gradually becoming more familiar with the formalities of the text; but its inimitable spirit and the higher consciousness made available through the intonation of the text still eluded me. Where was the "holy presence," the descent of the *sakinah,* I had read about in all the traditional books that I so eagerly devoured? Where was the beloved presence that creates within the human mind a sparkling consciousness cracking open with fresh awareness like the report of river ice in a raw winter dawn? Was I only a dense and tightly woven sieve leaving the thick film of sweet nectar behind at the doorstep of my being? I continued to search for the living reality of the book that would not come easy and without care, and I continued to work at the process of internalization of its knowledge and blessing that would hopefully set me truly on the quickest and surest path of return to God until reaching the spiritual station of no return.

Only when I felt sufficiently comfortable with listening to the tape-recorded text did I consider myself qualified to enter, not a *madrasah quraniyah* as such, but a Quranic circle of the type held after the early morning (*fajr*) or evening (*maghreb*) prayer in many mosques throughout the Islamic crescent for reasons that have hopefully been made clear. For one full year, I sat in a small group of Muslims with the imam of a mosque who guided us through the intricacies of learning the science of *tajwid* mentioned earlier to facilitate correct reading. It is a complicated reading discipline designed to enhance and stylize the forward movement of the text with well defined rules that involve correct pronunciation of each letter, the elongation of certain vowels, the use of ellipses, indications to pause and stop in the reading to facilitate breathing and to enhance meaning, to name only a few of the ritual complexities required in order to achieve correct recitation. This is not even to mention the psalmodic chanting that the voice eventually assumes, a skill that comes with practice and time. It takes diligent effort to become adept at Quranic recitation, but having once passed through the rigors of this well-specified discipline, it becomes an aspect of sacred ritual that every Muslim takes very seriously, not wishing to misread and distort the sacred flow of the text. Any interruption in the flow of the text and any misreading or mispronunciation is immediately repeated correctly to preserve the integrity of the meaning and out of deference to the integrity of the sacred text.

I feared that this kind of public Quranic recitation would take on the character of a trial by fire that I was not prepared for. As a foreigner and non-Arab, I would obviously be subject to rigorous attention, a novice subject to close scrutiny among a den of wolves. This however proved to be an uncalled-for fantasy that found no place in the reality of the experience. The Sheikh exhibited infinite patience as well as an infinite rigor appropriate to the demands of the task. One did not make mistakes in reading and reciting the text without close censure, as even the slightest errors of pronunciation, intonation, and rhythm were not overlooked. Certain Arabic letters such as *ayn* (ع), *ghayn* (غ), *sad* (ص), and *dhad* (ض) do not exist in the Western alphabet and are extremely difficult to approximate, much less pronounce like a native speaker; but with practice, I soon learned that anything is possible.

I discovered to my surprise that Arabs themselves have difficulty reading the Quran without making errors of some kind. Either a lack of habit in routinely reciting the text or perhaps occasional over-familiarity with the Arabic language and a tendency to resort to colloquial pronunciations sometimes hindered an accurate delivery. In fact, my slavish devotion to the literal text and my conscious effort at the correct reading of letter for letter gave me an edge over those native-speaking Arabs who felt lulled into a false familiarity with the classical Arabic of the text that they had not truly mastered. I took nothing for granted and worked hard at becoming adept at recreating every letter and sound with precision and accuracy.

Had I arrived at the "holy gate" of some cosmic ocean whose majestic sound could sweep the mind and heart of our singular humanity across eternities of cosmic awareness and infinitudes of cosmic space? The answer must be a resounding "no!" One does not approach the book with the intention of shattering cosmic barriers and arriving on the shores of some vast enlightenment. It was enough for me to get the text right, taking care not to betray the integrity of the sacred speech and to fulfill the mandate of its ritualistic discipline and worship. I would leave the rest to God.

At some point within this time frame—it must have been nearly a decade into my experience as a Muslim living in the Islamic world—I decided it was time to carve the words of some of the verses onto the encasement of my stone heart. I still did not feel the softening of the heart that I had read about in some of the mystic literature of the Islamic tradition, and still less the expansion of some cosmic awareness raising my consciousness above the mundane level of my own immediate concerns. Where was the burning desire to transcend my limitations; when would the melting of the heart take place before it could flow through some alchemical metamorphosis into the realms of the higher sentiments and spiritual emotions? I decided to learn some of the verses and *surahs* (chapters) so that I could recite them from memory. I wanted to learn some of the Quran "by heart," as the idiom goes. In other words, like the Prophet, I wanted to learn them to the extent that they were "written on my heart."

There is a well known and strong tradition in Islam of committing large portions of the Quran—if not the entire Quran—to memory, a tradition that goes back to the Prophet himself and most of his original companions. To become *hafez al-Quran*—preserver in memory of the

Quran—remains a deep aspiration for many devout Muslims. We can only imagine the incredible intensity of the people of that time, not only living in close proximity to the Prophet himself, but also listening firsthand from his holy person to the very words of Allah as they were revealed to him. It is small wonder to imagine the fire and the determination to internalize these words in whatever manner possible, not the least being their full memorization. The tradition has lasted down through the centuries to this day, when young children still learn large portions of the Quran by heart. It is an on-going commitment that must be maintained through a systematic process of daily repetition and review, a process that amounts to continually living in the presence of the Noble Book.

Once I had committed my mind to the task and set myself on the road of memorization of certain of the shorter "Makkan" chapters of the Quran that traditionally come in the last several parts (*juz*) of the book, I began the slow and meticulous process of committing to memory verse by verse of one, then a second and a third chapter, until I had finally accumulated a goodly number of *surahs* within easy reach of my mind. I had set myself the task of learning the verses "by heart" and ended up learning them "with the heart." It is interesting that in the Islamic perspective, the Muslims refer to the heart when explaining such matters rather than the mind. Indeed, the heart is the "seat" of the intelligence according to Islamic scholars, the place where the fusion of knowledge and sacred emotion takes place in order to bring about the complete realization of the truth that lies embedded within every aspect of existence. As the symbolic pulse of the human entity, it is knowledge of the heart that will lead us out of ourselves on the road to union with the Supreme Being.

The process of learning something by heart implies first of all the realization of how true learning takes place. Wanting to understand and have some knowledge internalized within one's being as an applied wisdom is not enough. Before truly understanding a thing, the simplicity of true learning is required. Using the senses, first the eyes are engaged in reading the letters and words, then the tongue is engaged to give voice to the words as they were intended to be heard and whose resonance moves out into the atmosphere like ripples on a placid sea. Repetition is the key: The fervent and continuous perfecting of the words through the repetition of the syllables, far from eroding the language and wearing it down into platitude, actually energizes and revives the words, making them real on the tongue and then sacred within the heart. I repeated syllable by syllable, phoneme by phoneme, word by word, phrase by phrase, verse by verse, backward and forward if you will, until I felt that it was committed to memory. The next day, I would review what I had learned to make sure it was still a part of me and if it wasn't, I repeated the process until it was firmly embedded in my mind. There were of course advances and retreats, peaks and valleys, slow conquests and persistent failures, until such moment arrives when the verses are engraved upon the heart. To this day, there are verses written on my heart in indelible ink that I memorized thirty years ago. They are with me now forever, Lord willing.

In truth, what happens is that the mind falls down into the well of this learning process; one feels awash in the sacred text partly because it opens onto a world of transcendence and enlightenment and partly because of the harmonious effect the vibratory sound has on the physical body. Oftentimes, you will see Muslims in the mosque swaying from side to side during a Quranic recitation, a habit that I found myself taking to as well, if for no other reason than that it felt right; the entire body seemed to want to take part in this sacred adventure in learning. The end result is that the doctrine is not learned mentally as we are accustomed to learning things in the West, imposing so many facts onto the plate of the mind. The living experience of the Quran is engraved on the heart as a prelude to becoming a part of the person's entire being, internalized as it were as part of the fabric that makes a person what they truly are in their essence, and ready to be drawn upon for guidance and support during the course of a person's life, as the need arises. Being able to summon the words of revelation and draw them out of the well of one's inner being without the aid of a book gathers together the spirit and the voice from what a person has internalized rather than calling upon some reasoned or intellectualized meaning from the mind alone.

The art of memorization has been lost in the Western world. Even as a child over half a century ago, I used to memorize portions of the catechism and learn poems and nursery rhymes by heart. Being able to recite them at will was considered a high accomplishment, representing a kind of internalization of the poetic ambiance and mind of the poet himself and in this way the creative process he went through remains a living reality through the force of the words imprinted on the memory. People in the West have nearly forgotten the value of reciting sacred verses from memory in the tradition of Quranic recitation or as in the Hindu tradition of repeating sutras in the Vedic scriptures. In their need for mobility, speed, and continual change, the idea of repeating a sacred scripture, a consecrated mantra, or one of the Names of God seems tedious, repetitious, and without value. We have lost the realization that through such repetition of the sacred Name and/or memorization of revelatory verses of scripture, a person comes to identify him or herself with the divine name and consequently with God Himself. According to Ramakrishna "God and His Name are identical." In Christianity, the Hesychastic "Prayer of the Heart" continues the Brahman tradition of repetition of the Name by repeating the name of Jesus over and over again until it becomes "second nature." They are exercises in concentration and application of principial knowledge that bring about an appeasement of the mind and a strengthening of the spirit. Who could ask for anything more?

Still I asked myself what else I could do to take leave of the borderland of an ego-entrenched psyche and climb inside the text, wrap it around my heart like a warm woolen cloak, and attain the proximity as well as the warmth of its sacred presence. How could I give up the familiarity of my own human voice for the grandiloquence of the single sovereign voice of the sacred text whose power knows no bounds and whose energy contains modes of transcendence. It is a voice of a million years, the voice of eloquent silence that resounds within the cave of the heart in search of a suitable resting place. After much contemplation, I resolved to leave behind temporarily the vocalizations and verbalism of the original form and turn to the written script of the text whose calligraphic ornateness and alien majesty as a sacred Islamic art called upon the sense of sight. I hoped that the engagement of all the senses of the body would allow them to serve their rightful function as effective instruments to facilitate the internalization and realization of the spirit within the text within the mind if not the higher consciousness of my wandering, modern-day soul.

The gifted writer and story-teller Somerset Maugham recounted in his revealing work entitled *The Writer's Notebook* that he taught himself how to write by sitting down and copying out classical essays and sections from the great works of literature "by hand." He theorized that by using his eyes and nose, hands and fingers, by touching the paper, copying the letters and words sentence by sentence, and by using as many of his senses as possible, since they are the very portals of experience, he could get under the skin and venture forth into the mind of the writer. He wished to recreate for himself the act and experience of creation and what it means to capture in words the essence of a meaning that originates in the mind but that must be translated from abstract thought to concrete words that convincingly convey a meaning as they lie upon the page. Of course nowadays, people do not write with feathered plumes and indigo ink, preferring instead the speed and facility of the word processor; but that did not preclude my taking Maugham's advice to approach on a more intimate level the actual mind of the writer and the creative process involved in the writing. In the case of a sacred revelation, I wondered where this would lead me.

As a prototype of language, the Quran itself is the product of both an oral and written tradition. As mentioned earlier, the Quran is primarily a recitation and the Prophet himself was instructed by the Archangel Gabriel to "recite in the name of your Lord," this verse being the very first verse revealed to the Prophet of Islam. However the *sakinah* or spiritual presence is to be found in the written as well as the recited Quran. According to a Holy Tradition, God wrote with a Mystic Pen that symbolizes the Universal Intellect, the inner reality of all things that is preserved on the Guarded Tablet before the creation of the world.[6] The Supreme Pen (*al-Qalam al-a'la*) has traditionally been identified with the Universal Intellect, while the ink is the reflection of All-Possibility and results in the possibility of the manifestation of the creation, recalling the Quranic verse: "And if all the trees on earth were pens and the sea—with seven seas added—[were ink] yet the words of Allah could not be exhausted" (31:27). The Pen therefore

[6] "The first of the things Allah created is the Pen (*Qalam*) which He created of Light (*Nur*), and which is made of white pearl; its length is equal to the distance between the sky and the earth. Then He created the Tablet (*Lawh*, or *Lawh al-mahfuz*, the 'guarded tablet'), and it is made of white pearl and its surfaces are of red rubies; its length is equal to the distance between the sky and the earth and its width stretches from the East to the West."

has an important significance as a universal symbol of the creation of the Word, the Logos, and the revelation, while the Guarded Tablet "preserved in the Paradise" maintains the record of universal manifestation[7] and sets the precedent for the significance of the written word.

Needless to say, the Quran as book and written document (*al-kitab*) for future generations needed to be written down.[8] The act of writing the text of the Quran ultimately became the sacred art of calligraphy which is central to the Islamic civilization. What oral Quranic recitation signified as a sacred sonoral art found its counterpart within the written tradition as the sacred art of Quranic calligraphy. According to Ali ibn Abu Talib: "The beauty of writing is the tongue of the hand and the elegance of thought." The imagined, spoken, and written word complemented the essential meaning through different mediums of expression. This was the origin of the tradition that I then turned to in my endeavor to wrestle with the complexities of the Quran and more fully come to terms with all its sublime aspects.

It is one thing to passively regard the written word on the page and quite another to actively engage oneself in the writing of a particular text.[9] The experience becomes a challenge when the letters, words, and phrases are derived from an alien alphabet that needs to be scripted and learned as a child learns to write. Having set myself the task, I bought a special notebook and pen to use as my calamus and blessed reed, in order to faithfully execute my sacred endeavor. I began with the seven-verse opening statement of the initial *surah* appropriately entitled *al-Fatihah*, the Opening. I did not concern

[7] Another tradition, reported by Ibn Abbas, says that "Allah created the Pen before He created the Creation." Also, "the Pen burst open and the Ink flows from it until the Day of the Resurrection."

[8] The text of the Holy Quran as it is extant today is exactly the same as the text delivered by the holy Prophet to the world as the Word of God. After his death, the first Caliph Abu Bakr collected the written records and gathered together all those who had memorized the Book and with their help had the whole text written in Book form. In the time of Uthman copies of this original version were made and officially dispatched to the capitals of the Islamic World at that time. Two of these copies exist in the world today, one in Istanbul and the other in Tashkent.

[9] There are 6,234 verses in the entire Quran. Copying 12 verses a day on average would produce a completed manuscript in about a year and a half. It took me roughly two years of sporadic work on the project to complete the task.

myself with the length, scope, and breadth of this challenge; had I done so, I might have developed a fear that I was not up to the challenge. When dealing with the Quran, it does not matter whether you are occupied with the verses for a few minutes or an entire lifetime. Like a true friend, the book does not count the hours and days; it is enough to be there, together and entwined in a holy relationship that becomes a continuum of the ever-present eternal moment striking a vertical sword across the horizontal axis of earthly time. The ethereal and timeless power of the text is persistent and will not freely and easily give up its secrets. If a person is fortunate enough to partake of the sacred blessing (*baraka*), it reaches inside to touch the pulse of the heart and one must decide one way or another what it means and what to do about it.

Whenever I could find the time, but preferably at least once a day, I sat myself down in a state of ritual ablution to copy the sacred text in the humble tradition, if not the accomplished style, of the traditional Quranic calligraphers and illuminationists. The words and verses multiplied on the page, pages multiplied upon pages, as I worked my sacred reed through the contours and curves that make up the physical formation of the Arabic letters. The formation of the Roman alphabet relies predominantly on its straight and angular lines and has a forward movement from left to right down the page. The letters seem to have clearness and efficiency as their primary motivation, but they do not inspire as do Chinese pictograms or as does the arabesque and fluid style of the Arabic script. In the traditional Islamic setting, everything commences from the right: People leave elevators from the right side first, greetings and salutations occur from the right and hand-writing has a forward movement from right to left down the page. Within the world of the Roman alphabet one would look in vain for the flexible, complex, and gentle ornateness offered by the letters *noon*, *sheen*, and *lam* (ن, ش, ل) of the Arabic alphabet. While Western landscape art is full of space, and light, the sonorous and calligraphic arts in Islam are full of sound and stroke.

Consider the bold, vertical stroke of the *alif* (ا), statuesque and statesmanlike as if in commemoration of the vertical stance of *Homo sapiens*. The letters *noon* (ن), *ba* (ب), *ta* (ت), and *tha* (ث)—differentiated only by dots resting either above or below the form of the letter—contain all the suggestive, symbolic, and sensuous curvature of a cup ready to contain the nectar of some sublime meaning. Like shapely crescent moons and spiraling galaxy clusters that harbor within their sublime forms the darkness of night and the silence of the universe, the letters spread out across the page as silent sentinels to the underlying sense of mystery that pervades all of existence, just as the trees and texture of a solemn forest create a sense of sacrality through the ambiance that emanates from their presence. It is almost as if the symbolic images of the letters contain metaphors of meaning even before they constitute the totality of a word. In writing stroke for stroke and letter for letter, the traditional calligrapher virtually stepped inside the written text and in so doing was able to create within himself the sense of a larger presence beyond the very horizon of the self.

You enter a revelatory text through the medium of copying as you might enter into the lost valley of Shangri-la. In doing so, you enter a realm that transcends the limits of the individual self, taking you far beyond snow-capped mountains and the puffed elegance of the cumulus clouds that gather at their summit. It takes you beyond the trite sensibilities of the human mind, beyond the horizon of one's limited cognitive world, indeed beyond the contoured and shapely elegance of the Arabic script and the florid manner in which the words and verses of the Quranic text are written, beyond and into a world where the great mystery envelopes and becomes a part of us by virtue of our symbolic participation in the actual writing of the sacred words of God. Imagine if you could walk to the very edge of the horizon, sit yourself down, and examine the broad panorama before you revealing what lies beyond the horizon. Before your eyes and beyond your wildest dreams, there is spread out before you a wilderness landscape seemingly beyond the continuum of time and space in which the primordial spirit hovers amid gnarled millennium trees and divinely sculptured rock formations. There is a primitive aspect to the shape of the letters and their emergence as words whose primordial quality weaves arabesques of symbols and shapes that actually trace a kind of spiritual presence onto the terrain of the blank white page, a page that by filling up with verse after verse of the sacred discourse becomes a calligraphic map whose terrain veils in secrecy an actual spiritual presence.

The experience of copying the Quran created a spiritual discipline within me that spilled over into untold areas in the experience of my daily life. You cannot spend days of your life writing down the words of revelation without becoming touched by some indelible mark of mystery and sacrality permeating other aspects of one's daily routine. Emotions become raw and facts become bold. There is a truth and a reality to every created thing, from the atom with its elemental building particles to the spiraling galaxies with their uncounted billions of stars. Everything takes on symbolic value and therefore everything has meaning and significance, creating a kind of vibratory confluence of power and energy that makes itself known through sounding rhythms and symbolic strokes of the Arabic alphabet. Reciting the text or writing down its verses becomes an intimate private encounter with the sounds and symbols that reveal the meaning of the universe. The personal ego fades away and what takes its place is the sublime experience of the truth of the Noble Book before you, with its message of the oneness and unity of the Reality, the very message and summative height of the entire religion, contained within the primordial point that commences the formation of any written word.

To step into the text you become a part of it and it becomes a part of you. In participating in the sound, the memorized texture and hand-scripted formation of the letters and words, the text then touches you with its energy and power. You and the text are one and the same for those moments that you take up the book in hand, recite the sacred verses, or copy them down and fill a blank page with their extravagant beauty. The largeness of the revelation, which encompasses all mystery that is to be resolved and all knowledge worth knowing, allows you to come to an understanding of yourself that would not otherwise be accessible in our daily existence. In a strange sense, the knowledge itself is secondary: Knowledge goes nowhere if it is not realized and internalized within your being as wisdom that shines out through behavior and good works. The experience of worship is so haunting and so elevating, indeed so entrancing an experience that it makes you cry sometimes in spite of your sensible, rational, and modern mentality and in spite of the hard shell that surrounds the viewfinder that filters the perceptions of our minds and shapes our conscious world. There is an archaic affinity to the experience that is so strange and beautiful it also makes you feel afraid of being unable to live up to the moment once it passes. When you take leave of the Book, just as when you take leave of your prayer carpet and re-enter the contingencies of daily life, you take the experience with you because it has become a part of your being by virtue of the participation in the sacred discipline.

In this way, and over the course of over thirty years as a Muslim, I have attempted to come to terms with the beloved, the holy, the noble Quran. Have I succeeded or failed? It is not for me to speculate on such matters, and who can measure such things? It is enough to know that I have grown to love the Quran as I have grown to love the Prophet Muhammad who delivered it to humanity and can no longer conceive of living without it any more than I can conceive of living without the pulse of my heart or the ground of my soul. When I sit down after the dawn prayer, I read and recite the verses with familiarity and ease, to the extent that coming to the Book and reciting its verses feels like coming home. When I close the book and walk away from a session, I feel refreshed and complete, like having visited some far distant country whose vistas put things in perspective and whose language gives voice to a knowledge of the stars.

In having recited the words of God, I have invoked His presence. I have filled multiple notebooks over the years with my hand-written verses, perennially adding to and complementing the first primer that initiated my child-like attempts to get closer to the Divine Revelation by copying down the verses letter for letter and word for word. I realize now that it is not the having done it but the doing it that fills me with joy. In keeping with my namesake, the Prophet Yahya, I have followed the guidance he was given when one of the verses of the Quran admonishes him to: "Seize the Book with (conviction and) strength." I have been living all these years in the presence of a revelation whose truth and light fills my advancing years with the same Truth and Light that has filled the universe since time immemorial. In remembrance of that Truth and Light, I hope to continue to "seize the Book" until the end of my days.

In our quest for the essence of a truth that we can weave within the fabric of our being as a golden thread connecting us with the unity of the universe, it may come as a surprise for some people in today's world to learn that Truth speaks to humanity in one of our own human languages, in this case the consecrated language of Arabic. These seed words contain a knowledge, a blessing, and a presence—true, innocent, and absolute—both in their physical representation and their substantive deployment as guidance for humanity: Knowledge because the universal mystery that underlies all of existence must have a resolution to the enigma at the heart of the human condition; blessing because we humans need divine compensation for the intrinsic drag and weightiness of "this world"; and presence because the human mind, heart, and soul find satisfaction and peace through an intimacy that is born through the interaction of love and truth. When planted within the ground of the human soul, these seeds take root and grow, inspiring the human entity in unexpected ways and leading toward a destiny that finds its fulfillment in reading and reciting the open book of one's true being through the revealed Book of the Supreme Being.

# PART IV

# THE ASCENT

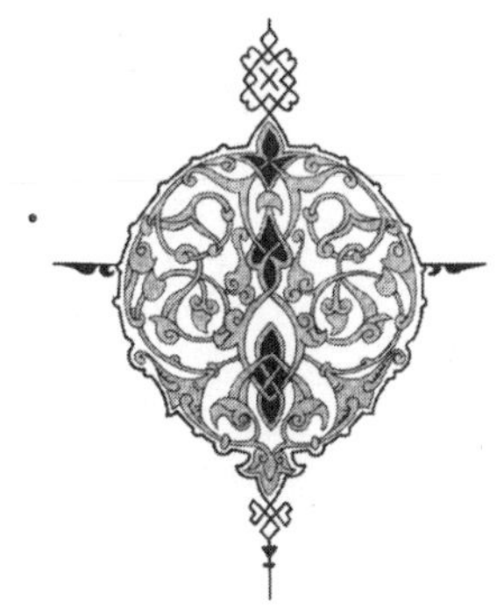

# 7. Prayer as Ritual

> All thinking is a form of prayer, and there is one and only one prayer: For right understanding of reality and for relating to it with courage and dignity.
>
> —Awadh Kishore Saran

The Religion of Islam has established human communication with the Divinity through a prayer ritual that combines a formalized ceremony with an individualized statement of devotion and worship that emanates from the Muslim soul. In commemoration of the Prophet Muhammad, peace be upon him, who learned the ritual of prayer from the Archangel Gabriel—the angelic messenger *Jibra'il* of the Quranic text—all Muslims learn the formalities of the prayer ritual when they come to the age of reason, although many very young children from around the age of two feel at ease amid the rows of worshippers in the mosque and often mimic the movements of their elders in a spontaneous outpouring of their innocent souls. Indeed a lifelong habit of the ceremony of prayer represents a spontaneous outpouring of the Muslim soul that reflects an instinctive faith in a Supreme Being, the beloved Lord and Master of the universe, Allah, whose very name awakens the *sakinah* or Holy Presence of God within the human heart.

The ritual form of worship strikes at the very heart of the Muslim psyche and gives both shape and substance to the Muslim mentality. In the previous section on "the descent" we dealt with the sudden irruption of the divine words of revelation onto the human plane of existence; in the present section on "the ascent" we propose to deal with the emotive and heart-inspired expression of one's deepest and most secret intimacies through a ritualized form of worship and praise that represents the highest human expression of acknowledgement of the truth of one's being and the truth of the one reality. In an era that values the seen over the unseen, that seeks to explain the origin of the universe from within the natural order itself rather than from the supra-natural order that is the origin and source of its laws and harmonies; that understands the human entity to be the result of an evolutionary process that began as some spontaneous effusion of dead matter, with that mysterious spark we know as "life" resulting from the fortuitous interplay of chemistry and lightning whose modern counterpart lies in the birth of Frankenstein; and, finally, in an era that through a secular, humanistic worldview offers possibility and promise to the notion of perpetual human progress, the notion of a formalized and sacred ritual that addresses the Hidden, the Unseen, and the Mysterious in life requires some explanation.

To the Muslim soul, however, prayer is the natural ascendant response to the revelatory "sword of a divine knowledge" that has come down to humanity, not as a cosmic flash of lightning across the heart of darkness, but as the wellspring of the essential knowledge and vertical wand of Heaven intersecting the horizontal plane of earthly time with the conscious awareness of the eternal moment, and the Truth that fills that moment. Our existence in time pulls us away from the timeless and the eternal; but the higher faculties of intellect and intelligence, the higher emotions and sentiments, the intelligence of the heart, and the human soul that is the ground of our spiritual identity, do not belong to this world or to time as we know and experience it. There is nothing that our hands can hold onto that is worth having. They cannot hold a moonbeam or seize a rainbow. The beauty of an eagle in flight eludes our grasp as well as our common sense. It is only who we are in our essence, what we believe in and how, through prayer, that we communicate with a higher order of existence that lifts us out of the deep well within ourselves and sets us back on the path toward the true spiritual destiny of the human race.

To pray is in effect to step neither backward nor forward but out of time completely for a few moments. Once again, we remember our primordial origins, as the human soul, awash in a sea of multiplicity and afloat amid the turgid currents of a dark *Kali Yuga* era,[1] is infused with the "breath" of the Divine Spirit. Beyond individual worship, prayer recreates the optimum conditions of body, mind, and heart for the awakening and raising of human consciousness to the point that it "sees God everywhere"; not with the human eye of course, but with the inner eye of a consciousness that sparkles with the remembrance

[1] The fourth and last cycle in the Hindu measurement of earthly time that begins with the *Krita* (or *Satya Yuga*) and ends with *Kali Yuga*, no less than the present Age of Darkness.

of God, just as the waters of a restless bay shimmer in the sunlight of a late afternoon.

In order to better understand life's mystery, Islam makes possible a private and intimate relationship with God. The encounter between the human and the Divine is direct and immediate; there are no clerical "go-betweens" such as one finds in other religions. The earth is God's mosque and conscious awareness fused with an instinctive faith and good works supported by right intentions become the weft and woof of the inner being just as the thread on a loom becomes the prayer carpet ready to be spread wherever one walks. While there are always parents and relatives as mentors and guides, leaders in the community who maintain the integrity of the social fabric, imams in the mosque to lead the faithful in prayer, and sheikhs and walis who set the standard of holiness and sanctity, in the end every Muslim stands alone with his Maker, and when he stands on his prayer carpet, he brings this awareness with him. This gives a sacerdotal quality to the Islamic character: each Muslim is a virtual celebrant enjoined to perform his own rituals of praise and worship. Standing on his prayer carpet, nothing comes between a Muslim and his Lord. The sacred communication is formal, direct, and surprisingly real. The Muslim is in the presence of God and the presence of God is within him. For those few moments of focused remembrance of all that is sacred and true, the mystery that governs the human worldview and colors it with insecurity and doubt fades away like morning mist, making the prayer ritual a bridge between knowledge and faith in God's enduring Reality.

Complementing the first duty to affirm the testimony of faith in the one God, the prayer ritual is the second earthly duty and the very cornerstone of all spirituality in the Islamic cosmos. Five times a day, the Muslims interrupt their daily routine. After making their clear intention, they perform the ritual ablution, which is an inner as well as an outer purification, then throw down their prayer carpet or walk to the mosque, in order to take their stand for a few minutes on the symbolic terrain of sacred ground, at the disposition of the Divine. Through the prayer, as a matter of principle, Muslims turn their mind, heart, and soul inward in order to communicate on an intimate level with God. Each performance of the ritual of prayer reminds the Muslim of God, while the rhythm of prayer rituals aids in maintaining this God remembrance throughout the day; thus it is that the spiritual benefits of the prayer last throughout the entire day. Prayer is not only a communication with the Divine, but a state of mind that awakens a spiritual consciousness fully responsive not only to the call of the prayer but that the faithful take with them when they leave their prayer carpet and must meet the demands of life.

The Quran enjoins the Muslim to "establish regular prayers" (17:78) at five established times during the day. Beyond the formal and ceremonial prayer, however, lies the inner prayer of the heart. "And celebrate the Name of thy Lord in the morning and in the evening" (76:25). The name of course is none other than the name Allah as the Name of names, but also includes the other 99 names and qualities of the Divinity mentioned in the Quran that characterize the divine essence. The Quran goes on to exemplify a more intense kind of prayer in the form of nocturnal vigils: "And part of the night prostrate thyself to Him, and glorify Him throughout the long night" (76:26). The pursuit of the way encourages this kind of spiritual dedication and anticipates a higher spiritual station. "Soon will thy Lord raise thee to a station of praise and glory" (17:79).

For devout Muslims, vigilance and watchfulness of soul are the keys to the way of return to God, qualities distinguished by their intimation of vision and readiness. The pursuit of the way becomes a journey through all phases of personal and spiritual identity toward a consciousness of self that finds its natural and only true complement in its unity in the absolute Consciousness of God. The believer offers his limited individual soul in exchange for the embrace of the Supreme Self. If the beginning of this process is human aspiration to reach beyond individual limits, the destination and end is always God. The life experience of the human individual is the very heart of the way, the human offering in expectation of the divine promise of salvation in the Divine Beatitude.

One key component of the prayer that is perhaps not well understood among non-Muslims is what takes place before the prayer, namely the ritual of ablution. Purity has such importance within this perspective that it is reported that the Prophet has said: "Cleanliness is half of the religion." The ablution is important, not only because it highlights purification, but also because it lays emphasis on certain aspects of the body that undergo the ritual washing. Islam stresses both outward and inward purity and has made the ablution a necessary ritual prior to the prayer. Humanity is instinctively spiritual, but it is not instinctively pure. Humans must work on themselves at every level before they can hope to achieve a purity of being that allows admittance into the divine presence. In Islam, the very foundation of all peace rests on purity. A traditional Islamic writer has reflected on purity in this way: "Knowing the divine Unity is not for dust and water. It requires something more, and that something is a clean heart and a pure soul."

The Islamic traditions (*hadith*) relate that the Archangel Gabriel taught the Prophet not only the details of the ritual prayer, but also the ritual ablution, both of which have remained in their original form down to the present day. Muslims everywhere continue to perform the purification ritual—known in Arabic as *wudhu*—and the prayer ritual in the same way that Gabriel originally instructed the Prophet.

The Quran goes into the specific details of the ablution ritual: "All those who believe! When you prepare for prayer, wash your face and hands to the elbows. Rub your heads and wash your feet to the ankles. Allah doesn't wish to place you in any hardship, but rather He wishes to make you clean and to complete His favor upon you, so that you may be grateful" (5:7). The *wudhu* purification ritual is a symbolic and externalized ritual, but its implications and effect reach deep into the inner person. The Muslims are not just washing their face and hands as a token gesture to the command of God. Rather they go through the motions of washing specific parts of the body with the hope that what they wash on the external level will also be purified on the inner level. Five different areas of the body are singled out for special attention. They are the hands and arms, the face including the mouth and nose, the head, the ears, and finally the feet. Let us consider the symbolic implications of these corporeal regions for a moment.

**The Hands**

Washing the hands three times opens the ablution ritual. Behind the symbolic image of the hand lies all good works, all honest labor, all the traditional art and craft skills, all creativity and power, all aid and generosity. According to the Quran, all actions are sent forward into eternity by man's own hands. "Who is more unjust than the one who is reminded of the signs of his Lord, but who turns away by forgetting the actions that his hands have sent forth?" (18:57). When the Muslims gather together "in rows" on the Day of Judgment, their hands will speak for them concerning what they had accomplished on earth: "That day We shall set a seal on their mouths, but their hands will speak to Us" (36:65). Hands are portrayed in the Quranic narrative as powerless when confronted with the truth. "Certain men formed a design to stretch out their hands against you, but God held back their hands against you" (5:12). Those who encourage evil and forbid what is just are called "close-fisted. They have forgotten God and so God has forgotten them" (9:67).

The image of the hand can, in addition, symbolize power and strength. "When you exert your strong hand, do you do it like men with absolute power?" (26:130). Furthermore, hands are also subject to abuse by the unjust who "shall bite at their own hands in anguish and fear" (25:27). Finally, the Quran likens belief in God and the rejection of evil over the good as the firmest of handshakes: "Whoever rejects evil and believes in God has grasped the most trustworthy handhold that never breaks" (2:256). The hand also implies beauty of shape, elegance of form, and dexterity of movement. The thumb provides agility; the fingers express precision, creativity, and skill; open palms traditionally mean friendship and good will. The creative spirit of the fine arts flows through the artful dexterity of the hands, including painting, sculpture, and especially music, without forgetting to mention the traditional crafts that in earlier times were considered a skill with a sacred meaning. Friendship passes between people through the shaking of the hands. The raised hand bears witness to the truth, a hand on the scripture confirms the truth, while a hand over the heart confers commitment, friendship, and promise.

Beyond the symbolic meaning of the human hand, however, must lie the implications of the divine hand of God, of which the human hand is but a mere image and reflection in form. The Quran refers many times to the Hand of God, but once again this does not mean to imply that God has an actual hand. The divine Hand symbolizes the powers of creativity, possession and ownership, beneficence, and guidance. God asks Satan in the Quran: "What prevents you from prostrating before the one whom I have created with my own hands?" (38:75). In addition to having the name of Creator (*al-Khaaliq*), God is also referred to as the King of the Supreme Dominion (*al-Malik al-Mulk*), a name which attributes all possession and ownership to Him alone. "The entire earth will be but His handful and the heavens will be rolled up like a scroll in His right hand" (39:67).

With regard to His beneficence and mercy, the Quran tells us that all blessing originates in the hand of God, who is also the Originator (*al-Mubdi'*) and the Merciful (*ar-Rahman*). "They have no power whatever over the bounty of Allah. His bounty is entirely in His hands, to bestow upon whom He wills" (57:2). Finally, the Muslim never feels abandoned and can never taste the full bitterness of human despair, because "the hand of Allah is over their hands" (48:10). God is the source of all power and all power rests in His hand. "Say: In whose hand is the governance of all things? Who protects, but who is not Himself protected? Say if you know!" (23: 88).

### The Five Senses

Muslims wash the organs of the five senses prior to the prayer ritual. On the outer level, the eyes, ears, nose, mouth and fingers may need rinsing; on the inner level, the senses are the doors and windows of the human form and require periodic purification on a deeper, more symbolic level. The powers of the senses affect more than the body alone. One experiences the world through the five senses, for the sake either of salvation or of damnation, depending on how one uses these gifts of God. Desires speak so demandingly through the senses that they can be the portals through which people separate themselves from God rather than instruments that can lead them back to God. Through ritual purification, Muslims can open the door of their inner senses to the inner purification and heighten their awareness of the implicit wisdom that lies embedded within the sense experience. In the Quran, part of the paradisal promise is through its appeal to the senses. The faithful will smell the heavenly scent of musk. They will taste the divine waters of *sansabil* and will see reflected in the heavenly world a world of divine lights. The external senses prove the reality of this world. The inner senses yearn for the promises of the Divine Reality and the paradisal milieu of that Reality.

### The Head

The head marks the extreme limit of the human physical form, with the crown of the head pointing heavenward. Sitting atop the human torso on the shelf of the shoulders, the head is all intelligence and nobility projected through physical form. As such, it is the most direct reference to the Absolute that resides in the pictorial image of the human frame. Human beings consent with a nod and can deny their own mystery with a shake of the head. The ennobling crown is the house of the cognitive mind, while the cranium supports the cerebral brain, which is itself a miraculous mystery to modern science, as it sends functional messages throughout the nervous system with decisiveness and alacrity. The brain is man's personal cosmic computer as it stores an infinite amount of neural impulses that are ready to be used as the need arises. The Muslims pass their water-drenched hands over their heads during the ritual ablution, but they are symbolically purifying all that the head contains.

**The Feet**

While the head points heavenward at one end of the human body, the feet firmly connect man with the earth. Just as the Quran speaks of "strengthening the heart," it also refers to the firmness and stability of the feet, "to plant your feet firmly therewith" (8:11), just as roots give firmness to a tree. Moreover, the feet make possible the journey through life. Will the feet move the believer forward along the straight path, or will they lead backward along the path of hypocrisy? Will his feet lead him to the right or the left, down a crooked path, or will he wander aimlessly around without direction or purpose? "Have they feet to walk with? Have they hands to lay hold with?" (7:195).

The faithful wash their feet five times a day, partly to clean them from the accumulated dust in desert climates or from the sweaty odor accumulated from shoes in colder climates, and partly for the inner remembrance that will advance them along the way to God with determination and purpose. With the feet, the Muslims make their way to Makkah for the sacred pilgrimage in the ultimate expression of the earthly journey, wherein life itself becomes the journey. "The feet will bear witness to all that they did" (36:65). In anticipation of this journey, they make their way daily to the mosque, and in so doing every footstep promises a blessing in return for the intention and the effort.

Finally, the feet support the human torso, providing locomotion. The feet give humans an erect stature, so that they may not only stand alone and unaided, but upright as *Homo sapiens*, God's thinking creature, the human *alif*, who has been fashioned and shaped by the Hand of God (*al-yad Allah*) and vivified with His Spirit (*ar-ruh*). With his feet, the believer makes his journey through life, a journey that moves from the outward to the inward level of reality, and a way for the human soul to rise above itself.

**The Face**

The face of humanity openly reflects the human soul and expresses the story of a life that is unceremoniously carved within its flesh and folds. The human countenance projects an image of the person that reveals a ghostly presence of the human theophany that lies behind the physical mask. "On their faces are the marks and the traces of their prostrations" (48:29). The full range of emotions passes across the face and projects their impressions for the world of humanity to witness and observe. The face can project clarity, intelligence, and human goodness or it can project confusion, ignorance, and evil. Darkness can cloud the face with the stuff that shadows are made of as much as an inner light can illuminate the face with the rays of an unearthly presence that needs no introduction. Anger, hate, frustration, and despair can distort the face, as much as hope, patience, serenity, and wisdom can create a picture of an individual in harmony with a presence greater than anything this world can produce. At the moment of death, a person will have earned his face as much as he will have earned the Fire or the Paradise. "The fire will burn their faces; they will grimace and grin with twisted lips" (23:104).

The soul passes out into the world of humankind through the face, and more specifically through the eyes. In a variety of Quranic verses, we read that faces will reflect light, shadow, and darkness in this life and in the next life. "On that day, some faces will be black: It will be said to them 'Did you reject faith after you accepted it? Then taste the penalty for rejecting faith.' But those whose faces are white, they will be in the light of Allah's mercy, where they will dwell forever" (3:106-107). The faces of those who prefer the evil alternative will be painted the blackest black of night. "Faces will be covered with pieces from the depths of the darkness of night" (10:27). Some faces at the final hour will be humiliated in the dust: "We shall gather them together, prone on their faces, deaf, dumb, and blind" (12:97). Some faces will be sorrowful, others will be grieving: "Is one who walks headlong, with his face groveling, better guided; or the one who walks evenly along the straight path?" (67:22).

Finally, the face summarizes in an image the quasi-divine majesty of man who, through the pursuit of the truth, achieves a feeling of peace through surrender unto the one Reality. "Set thy face towards the meaning of religion with true piety" (10:105). Indeed, religion itself stems from this surrender of the self to God, while the self is summed up once again in the image of the face. "Say: I have submitted my face to God" (3:20). Surrender is the ultimate spiritual expression made available to man through the religion; as such, surrender becomes the face of a person's religion just as the human face is the composite physical form that expresses both humanity and spirituality. "Indeed, whoever surrenders his face to God and performs all that is good, his reward is with his Lord" (2:112).

When the Muslims perform the ceremony of prayer, they bow down and make the full prostration, putting their face and forehead to the earth in a self-effacing expression of submission to the highest Reality, a surrender that the body itself gives expression to. Symbolically, they surrender their inner self through the action of putting the face to the ground. Once they have adopted this process of surrender symbolically through the ritual of prayer, they can then begin the long process of inner spiritual evolution that is expressed in the Quran as seeking after the Face of God, a spiritual evolution that can only be realized through the hard, earthly struggle known as the battle of the soul, or the *jihad al-nafs.* "And keep thy soul content with those who call on their Lord morning and evening, seeking his Face" (18:28). The true battle finds its field of encounter within the soul. The spiritual motivation is the vision of God; the human process is a surrender of self; the final purpose of humanity is transcendence of soul that amounts to a unity with the Divine Being in which "everything perishes except His Face" (28:88).

The hidden messages of the Spirit continue to find their way into the souls of men and women through the very simplicity and utter profundity of the words and images of the revelation. The value of the symbol is always that it creates not only a formal but a meaningful image with the power to illuminate the knowledge and truth that could not be known otherwise. The symbol of the Face of God articulates in a verbal sound an abstract quality of pure Being that might otherwise be inaccessible to the human heart. There is no knowledge of God without remembering the Face of His all-encompassing wisdom. There is no human personality without the spark of the living and eternal Personality of God. There can be no human face without the projection of the divine Face into the world of manifestation and form. Nor would the human self be meaningful without the expression of the Divine Self. There is only one Supreme Being and that being is God. The human messages of surrender, hope, and intimacy through prayer and worship are written within the body, mind, and heart of man; but the saving message of Truth, the very object of the human search for meaning, must reside within the image of the Face of God. "All that is on the earth will perish, but the Face of God will abide, full of majesty, bounty, and honor" (55:27).

If prayer is a compass—and indeed in the Islamic tradition the ceremony of prayer focuses on the center of the earth, the Kaaba in Makkah, before soaring vertically toward the mysterious empyrean of the Spirit—then its four coordinators of north-south-east-west are good intention, thought, word, and action. This is especially true for the prayers that conform to a specified liturgy, as in the religion of Islam. A person resolves to pray through a good intention, thinks about and communicates prayerful thoughts, using the sacramental and ritual words—in Islam the words of revelation—and performs prayer through a formal ceremony. Canonical prayer that conforms to a specific liturgy permits the practitioner to participate existentially in the life of the spirit and connects the world here below with the Reality from above. The *Pater Noster* ("Our Father"), commonly known as the Lord's Prayer in Christianity, and the ceremony of prayer in the Islamic tradition are two forms of canonical prayer that are still viable and living traditions available to modern man, although the Islamic ritual is a ceremony whose forms and actions—such as the bowing and prostrations—contain their own significance and blessing.

Each of these two traditions represents a different aspect of canonical prayer. The *Pater Noster* permits the cognitive processing and visualization of sacred symbols through a formalized prayer whose very form has an interior dimension as well as an aspect of universality that has the capacity to touch the souls of all men unconditionally. The Islamic prayer ritual, which features the first seven verses of the Quran—its opening chapter, called *al-Fatihah*—embodies and formalizes sacred symbols, evocative sounds, auditory symbols, symbolic gestures, and movements that set in motion the quintessential alchemy of the soul within the Islamic setting.[2] Both of these forms of canonical prayer lead from the world of outwardness and separation to a world of inwardness and union. They permit the practitioner to place him or herself within the center of the self, namely the heart, and establish a rhythm that can influence all aspects of the life experience.

The *Pater Noster*, along with the *Ave Maria*, are used by Christians in association with the recitation of the rosary, a spiritual practice that—through its ritualistic pattern and formulaic method—establishes an internal rhythm that makes an enduring impact on the soul of the practitioner. As a small child, I remember being dragged from behind trees and the top of flower trellises in the summer evening twilight to gather together with the rest of my siblings and our parents to recite the rosary that was broadcast every night at 7:00 by the then Cardinal Cushing of Boston.[3] It represented a sobering interlude from the frenzy of our childhood play; yet it established a pattern of discipline and remembrance that I have preserved to this day and that serves me well in the pursuit of my Islamic spiritual disciplines. Similarly, the Islamic prayer ritual, with its emphasis on a practice of five appointed prayer times, literally seals a person's daily existence with the hot wax of a sacred routine, identifies and quantifies the day's external rhythms, and provides a refuge from the vicissitudes of

[2] "Mental activity is capable not only of thought but also of imagination, thus of visualizing a symbolic form; in like manner, the spirit is sensitive not only to concepts but also to evocative sounds, to auditory symbols; and in like manner again, the body is capable not only of movements that are necessary or useful, but also of symbolic gestures. . . . The visual image *a priori* addresses the mind, thus it pertains to the region of the forehead; sound is in connection with our center, the heart; and symbolic movement, quite evidently, concerns the body" (Frithjof. Schuon, *To Have a Center* [Bloomington, Ind: World Wisdom Books, 1990] p. 144).

[3] Cardinal Cushing was a crusty old priest with a gravelly voice. He was a source of terror among the children of the diocese of Boston because of how he looked and the manner in which he conducted the sacramental confirmations of the children of the diocese. At one point in the ceremony of confirmation, the cardinal struck the child on the cheek as a symbolic gesture of toughening the wayward child for the long road in life ahead. We all lived in terror of this beloved and saintly cardinal on our day of confirmation because the symbolism contained a reality that was hard to ignore. Cardinal Cushing was a friend of the Kennedy family and officiated at the inauguration of John F. Kennedy in 1960.

life and its inevitable evil possibilities. The prayer ritual performed by Muslims the world over leaves its imprint not only on the soul, but on the Islamic society generally.

It is worth highlighting the symbolic imagery of both of these prayers since they play such a significant part in awakening the mind not only to the key, fundamental concepts of Christianity and Islam, but also because they both create a feeling and an ambience that awakens the imagination to higher levels of spiritual experience. The Lord's Prayer, replete with its sacred, symbolic imagery and its corresponding universal themes, reads as follows:

| | |
|---|---|
| *Pater Noster,* | Our Father, |
| *qui es in caelis:* | Who art in heaven, |
| *sanctificetur Nomen Tuum;* | Hallowed be Thy name; |
| *Adveniat Regnum Tuum;* | Thy kingdom come; |
| *fiat voluntas Tua* | Thy will be done, |
| *sicut in caelo, et in terra.* | On earth as it is in heaven. |
| | |
| *Panem nostrum cotidianum* | Give us this day |
| *da nobis hodie;* | Our daily bread. |
| *et dimitte nobis debita nostra,* | And forgive us our trespasses, |
| *sicut et nos dimittimus* | As we forgive those |
| *debitoribus nostris;* | who trespass against us. |
| *et ne nos inducas in tentationem;* | And lead us not into temptation; |
| *sed libera nos a malo.* | But deliver us from evil. |
| *Amen* | Amen |

| | |
|---|---|
| Lord: | *Our Father* |
| Paradise: | *Who art in Heaven* |
| Holy Name: | *Hallowed be Thy Name* |
| The Divine Coming: | *Thy Kingdom come* |
| The Divine Will: | *Thy will be done* |
| Heaven and Earth: | *On earth as it is in Heaven.* |
| | |
| Sustenance: | *Give us this day our daily bread* |
| Forgiveness: | *And forgive us our trespasses* |
| Forgiving: | *As we forgive those who trespass against us* |

| | |
|---|---|
| Evil: | *And lead us not into temptation* |
| Deliverance: | *But deliver us from evil.* |
| Resolution: | *Amen.* |

Of the twelve elements identified here, the first six refer directly to the divine perspective in the identification of God as father, His heavenly abode, His sacred name, the divine coming and the divine will, with reference to the polarities of earth and heaven in commemoration of the existential reality. The second six elements of the prayer refer more specifically to humanity as such, with reference to their earthly and human condition, including their sustenance, forgiveness, and ultimately their deliverance.

"Our Father" identifies the human mentality with the patriarchal persona of the Divine Being, resorting to familiar familial terminology in coming to terms with the concept of a Supreme Being as the progenitor of the human soul. Within the symbolic imagery of this perspective, the sacred psychology is such that God is referred to as father in keeping with the Biblical figure of the ancient and stern patriarch of which the prophets were the human counterparts. "Who art in Heaven" locates the other-dimensional and other-worldly kingdom that promises the human entity transcendence of the limitations of his earthly condition, although Christians are reminded elsewhere in the New Testament that "the Kingdom of God is within you." "Hallowed be Thy Name" recalls the sacredness of the absolute Name of God, and if it be hallowed, then it becomes the medium of human worship and praise, thus the holy Name becomes the basis and focal point for the prayer.

"Thy kingdom come, Thy will be done." Contingent upon the human impulse to pray is the response of the Divine Being, manifested as the coming of the kingdom and the perfection of His will. Once again, we have been told that the kingdom is within and therefore directly associated with the perfection of the human will in perfect harmony with the Divine will through surrender. "On earth as it is in Heaven" links once again the created earth with the other-worldly paradise, offering possibilities that can be achieved on earth that will ultimately lead to promises that the Lord's Prayer merely hints at through symbolic language without further elaboration. It is appropriate that the faithful remind themselves of the immanent blessing of the "Father" and the divine recompense for the human response of devotion and worship.

"Give us this day our daily bread" reminds the faithful of their dependence on God for their daily sustenance. Bread is of course symbolic of life itself; in Arabic the word for bread is *aish*, which is the colloquial word for the verb "to live," emphasizing through the spoken language that bread and life are one. Obviously, humans owe their ultimate sustenance to the Divine Being, who provides the human sustenance necessary for survival, including the cycles of seasons, agriculture, and weather, universal cycles that highlight the fundamental reliance on God for His provision of mankind.

"And forgive us our trespasses." We need to ask forgiveness for our transgressions as a matter of spiritual routine. Because we are human, we suffer the fault of our own limitations and weaknesses. Our deliberate sins and evils take us outside the norm and alienate us from the beatitude of the divine presence. We ask forgiveness because of who we are and what we have done.

"As we forgive those who trespass against us." We cannot ask of God that which we are not prepared to ask of ourselves. If we ask for divine forgiveness, we must be prepared to express our own humanity in light of the divine example and forgive those who trespass against us. Otherwise, on what basis can we rightfully expect that we ourselves should be forgiven?

"And lead us not into temptation" because temptation is the prelude and forerunner of all that leads us away from the Divine Beatitude. We must rely on the Divine Being to keep us out of harm's way, and that must include the way of temptation that can only lead to further separation from the Divine Being.

"But deliver us from evil." After the divine forgiveness, after the promise to forgive those who trespass against us, and after the heart-felt entreaty to keep us far from temptation, the Lord's Prayer concludes with the petition to the Lord that He may deliver us from evil, and the inclinations that will lead us into further evil. Deliverance from evil means none other than deliverance from Satan, the great corrupter, seducer, and whisperer into the ears of mankind.

Finally, "amen" is the sound word that concludes the prayer and seals the communication. Its sonorous cadence and prolonged vocalization approximates in some way the utterance of a sigh. "Amen" actually means "so be it" with the implication "so be it as truth and certainty" and contains within its utterance a definitive and conclusive air. Therefore it resolves in a word the heart-felt entreaties of the prayer and brings the sacred communication to its logical conclusion. "Amen" closes once again the envelope to eternity that had been opened by the commencement of the formal prayer.

I include this extensive mapping of the Lord's Prayer and refer to other Christian prayers such as the familiar Hail Mary because the sacred Latinate words "*Pater Noster qui es in caelis*" and "*Ave Maria gratia plena*" found a place in my heart many years ago when I was a young child. This childhood experience has remained a kind of measuring stick of native and instinctive spirituality that I hold up to myself even now and whose spiritual force continues to perpetuate the fragrance of childhood innocence within the adult mind.

As a modest young child, and much to my dismay, the nuns who saw to my education singled me out from the pack because they discovered I had a sweet boy soprano voice. It was not something that I was proud of and I had a natural aversion to singing in the presence of others; even though when I was alone, I sang to my heart's content, happy to have a voice that could express the inexpressible melodies in my heart. I loved the sober elegance of the sacred church songs that accompany the liturgy, the Christmas songs, and the well known *Ave Maria* of Schubert and Gounod that every tenor attempts to render with majesty and verve. Something indescribably holy and otherworldly in these melodies appealed to my simple, innocent mind and lifted me out of the routine of my everyday world.

The small suburban town where I grew up outside of Boston had a church named St. Agnes. I remember the massive stone stairs that led up into the spacious nave of the church. On Sunday morning, however, I always entered through the sacristy disguised as a virtual angel bedecked in my purple gown and white surplice. I was one of a hundred children in the boy's choir that had a reputation in the area; people came from miles around on a Sunday morning to hear the sacred songs of the boy's choir that accompanied the popular 10:30 High Mass. Much to my chagrin I was singled out from this group for two reasons, firstly because I was the shortest of the entire lot and therefore led the line as we filed into the nave of the church and took our places in the passageway behind the main altar. Secondly, I had been selected as the premier soloist for the choir, the boy selected to stand out from the pack and deliver the important solo parts during the Mass. I sang such sacred songs as the Schubert's well known *Ave Maria* (Hail Mary full of grace) and the sober and majestic *Panis Angelicus* (The Bread of Heaven). The prospect of stepping out from the shadows of the high altar and the restless group of boys who had the luxury of singing in anonymity struck my tender young heart with a unique combination of terror and sublimity, yet in spite of the fear my pounding heart betrayed, I stepped out every Sunday morning during the course of the liturgy and sang, as if in a trance, a variety of sacred songs for that particular celebration of the Mass. This was prayer at its most enchanting and sublime moment, giving voice to the pious entreaties and intimate expressions of love that reach by natural inclination for the heavens.

Amid the ethereal shadows of the altar, dressed in the traditional vestments of the boy's choir, the air filled with the aromatic flavors of burning candles and heavily scented church incense that wafted their arabesques of smoke through the latticework and arches, I remember the experience as the externalization of my soul through the sound of my innocent voice. I was no longer myself as a body, a person, or even a thinking animal; I had somehow transcended the normal course of events to meet the demands of the moment, the voice becoming and being an active presence with its own truth and its own form of praise, unburdened by physical form and soaring into places on high not normally accessible to people on earth. Birdlike and from the cavern of my small fluttering chest there emerged a melody that I could only recognize as some God-given gift which I had not earned but was mine to employ and enjoy. Out of some deep well in my being, I poured forth all the raw emotion and my confused desire for God into the music of the composer, the sound of my voice riding the melody as if it were riding an unruly tiger, wild, thrilling, and uplifting beyond belief. The song emerged from my depths as a voice from Heaven rather than from the breath and vocal cords of a terrorized child. This was prayer at its sweetest and most profound moment, emerging through the pure voice of innocence and passing through the ears and hearts of the faithful as it made its way through the rafters and trellises of the church, through the open door and out into the sky, where all song melodies unite with the celestial rhythms of the spheres and ultimately mingle with the voices of the angels to be listened to by the cohorts that roam the empyrean of Heaven.

As I commit these thoughts and images to paper, I listen to the echo of a child's voice and reminisce on the experience of beatitude that in these restless and heavy times is difficult to imagine and almost impossible to recreate, except through savoring the fragrance of a distant time and place when a young child's prayerful song was no doubt listened to and heard.

Muslims recite the opening seven verses of the Quran,[4] the *Surat al-Fatihah*, as the key component of the Islamic prayer ritual. The seven verses are recited a minimum of seventeen times a day throughout the course of the five prayers, and this does not include supererogatory prayers related to the *Sunnah* or the practice of the Prophet—additional prayers that accompany the five ceremonial prayers at the "appointed time"—which would include even more repetitions of these seven "opening" verses. In terms both of doctrine and method, these verses are of paramount importance to every Muslim because, in the first place, they represent the quintessence of the meaning of the entire Quran and because, in the second place, they are repeated between twenty and thirty times a day by the practicing faithful depending on their vigilance in following the practice of the Prophet. Without a doubt, these seven verses have the power on physical, psychic, and spiritual levels to transform the practitioner and to soften the human heart.

Once again, we are reminded of the three aspects of prayer generally: thought, word, and action. Much is made in Islam of a person's intentions. In fact, a celebrated saying of the Prophet relates that actions will be judged according to their intentions. Prayer must begin with the proper intention, and this is assisted in Islam through the action of the ablution (*wudhu*) ritual. A Muslim goes through the motions of a ritual washing with its literal and symbolic significance for outer and inner purification—"He who makes ablution afresh

[4] The opening seven verses of the Quran are described by the Quran itself as seven of the oft-repeated verses (*sab'an min al-mathani*) in the following verse: "We have given thee (the Prophet) seven of the oft-repeated (verses), and the mighty Quran" (15:87). Scholars have often referred to these seven verses as the quintessence of the whole of the Quran.

revives and refreshes his faith"—and this in turn sets in motion a thought pattern that leads directly to the words and actions contained within the Islamic prayer ritual. The words are none other than the seven verses that open the Quran together with a number of Quranic epithets such as "God is great" (*Allahu akbar*) and "glory be to God" (*subhan Allah*), while the actions are the gestures of bowing and full prostration that make the ritual so distinctively Islamic.

As we have attempted with the Lord's Prayer, it is worth highlighting the symbolic imagery of the seven verses of the *Fatihah*.

| | |
|---|---|
| Praise: | Praise be to God, Lord of the worlds |
| Names: | The Infinitely Good, the Ever Merciful |
| Judgment: | King of the Day of Judgment |
| Worship: | It is Thee we worship and<br>it is in Thee we seek refuge |
| Guidance: | Guide us on the straight path |
| Beatitude: | The path of those on whom is Thy Grace |
| Damnation: | Not of those on whom is Thy Wrath,<br>nor of those who are lost. |

"Praise be to God" opens the Islamic prayer with formal praise of God as the most fitting spiritual attitude that not only men and women but every living creature can offer the Divinity. Praise is the most elementary as well as necessary human response to the spiritual truth of the Divinity, especially for human beings, who must give voice to their praise through deliberate intention and prayer, unlike the other animals who praise the Divine Being by simply *being* what they are instinctively.

"Lord of the worlds" highlights the fact that the universe is made up of multiple worlds both outer and inner, microcosmic and macrocosmic, but that there is only one Divinity who is the Lord of the metacosmic universe that is inclusive of all the worlds.

"The Infinitely Good, the Ever Merciful" are alternative names of God, and express variations of His divine qualities and attributes of which the human qualities are but reflections. God gives us our daily bread as the Lord's Prayer has stated and this is only one of the infinite mercies that emanate from the Divinity, our very existence being the ultimate mercy.

"King of the Day of Judgment" is one of the names of God directly identified in the *Fatihah*, perhaps to indicate that God is not only Lord of all the worlds, but also master of the end of finite time. We by contrast are slaves of the King, just as the relative must defer to the absolute and will ultimately disappear in the Face of the Absolute.

"It is Thee we worship and it is in Thee we seek refuge" completes the praise initiated in the opening verse. Praise is the initial, instinctive impulse as a prelude to the systematic worship of the Divine Being because "no one compares with Him." Worship recognizes God for what He is and provides us the opportunity to escape from the confines of our own limited mentality for the sake of the Beloved who becomes the object of all worship. Refuge then complements the concept of the Lord of all the worlds and is the natural response of the human lover for the Divine Beloved. Refuge is possible because of the sacred trust between the human and the Divine. God is infinitely Good and Merciful and therefore the only refuge lies in returning to that goodness and mercy.

"Guide us on the straight path" represents the saving entreaty of human beings who know their place in the hierarchy of being and know the condition of their inner being, namely as entities in desperate need of guidance along a path that is straight and direct and that leads to a clear destination. The straight path is ultimately the path of hope and the path of ascent represented by the vertical dimension that intersects the horizontal plane of existence with its projection of universal truth, and thus the reference in the following verse to the path of grace.

"The path of those on whom is Thy grace" is available as part of the Divine Mercy and the overflowing beatitude that has the power to attract and draw us upwards. Humans need to open themselves up to that grace and respond with an affirmation of the Truth through intelligence and free will.

"Not of those on whom is Thy Wrath and those who are lost." Those people who do not pursue the path of grace and blessing are susceptible to the Divine Anger and the separation that is implicit in that wrath. By opposing the Divine Unity, they become separated into a realm of endless multiplicity and ultimately suffer damnation by virtue of the fact that, with their free will, they have separated themselves from the Divinity.

Needless to say, every Muslim gladly closes the verses of the *Fatihah* with the firm conviction to take the path of those who receive the Divine Favor and avoid at all cost the path of those who receive the Divine Wrath, while remembering the well-known inscription that is said to be written at the base of the throne (*al-arsh*) of Allah: "My Mercy precedes My Wrath." The prayer concludes as in the Christian prayer with the sonorous word *Ameen*, intoned by all the faithful in congregational prayer as a means of setting the seal on their prayer to the Divine Being with whom they wish to communicate.

A review of the respective contents of the Lord's Prayer and the *Fatihah* highlights the distinctive, and at the same time similar, character of the two spiritual traditions. Both prayers identify the Divinity and give Him various Names, the Lord's Prayer paternal, the *Fatihah* regal and qualitative. The Lord's Prayer makes reference to the coming of the (second) Kingdom which implies a day of judgment—a day that the *Fatihah* refers to expressly. The Christian prayer mentions sustenance in the form of "daily bread" while the Islamic prayer focuses on worship and the trust between the human and the Divine. Finally, the Lord's Prayer focuses on forgiveness and deliverance from evil while the Islamic prayer employs the imagery of a path (*tariq*) leading in two directions, the one vertical and transcending, bound for the beatitude and blessings of the Paradise, the other horizontal and potentially downward, bound for the netherland of unspeakable separation and loss characteristic of damnation. Both prayers find their resolution and are sealed by the word "Amen," a statement of certainty and an affirmation of the Truth.

There remains one final note to sound in this exposition of the Islamic prayer as ritual remembrance of our true Origin and final Abode, and that is none other than the sonorous and captivating call to prayer that emanates five times a day from the minarets of mosques clear across the Islamic crescent from the Maghreb (the place where the sun sets) in the West to the Khyber Pass (a natural passageway linking Afghanistan with Pakistan) in the East. Indeed the call to prayer is both a collective and individual summons that makes its way through the streets and by-ways of a city or town, steals through open windows, down passageways, across unsuspecting rooftops, through ears, into minds and finally down into the hearts and souls of humanity to resurrect a memory and a remembrance of the "one thing needful" amid the pressure and turmoil of daily life and its pressing demands.

The role of the Islamic *adhan* (the person who calls the faithful to prayer) is a rarefied and honored duty of a selected member of the faithful. When Muslims hear the cry of the *adhan*, they remember the clear and courageous call of Bilal, the black African former slave famous as a faithful believer who suffered torture[5] at the hands of the enemies of Islam and whose clear voice reflected and emulated the intensity of his faith. The call that signals the appointed prayer time continues to sound down through the ages as a cry in the wilderness of modernity and a clarion call to spirituality. Its intonation throughout the day and its interaction with the structure and pace of life weaves a texture of spirituality into the fabric of life, highlighting the primordial and the preternatural that overlays all of existence and that lies also within the soul as a primal summons to remembrance.

When I traveled to the Islamic world for the first time to take a post as a lecturer in English at Kuwait University in the Arabian Gulf, one of the first things that I noticed as distinctively Islamic was the ubiquitous call of the *adhan* five times a day, a thoroughly unexpected artefact of traditional spirituality that transported me back in time to earlier fantasies of flying carpets and Turkish bashas sitting on oriental prayer carpets awaiting the call to prayer. Bilal's original call has broken over time into countless pieces to become the call of a multitude of sacred voices galvanizing cities and towns across the Islamic crescent toward the remembrance of God, voices that struggle for supremacy in the mind of the faithful amidst the cacophony of today's city life. The echoing voices of the *adhan* all come together to beckon the heart to withdraw for a few minutes of the day and return through the prayer ritual to that abode we are promised in revelation.

The Islamic prayer ritual is existential, intimate, and revelatory. As an existential phenomenon, it happens in the here and now five

[5] Umayyah, one of the leaders of the Quraish tribe in Makkah at that time, would take Bilal out at high noon into an open space and have him pinned down to the ground with a large rock on his chest, inciting him to renounce Muhammad and worship the false gods al-Lat and al-Uzzah. While he endured his suffering, Bilal is reported in the traditional sources to have simply repeated: "One, One."

times a day. The Muslims live with this routine of spiritual practice and in return this discipline of remembrance becomes a part of them. As a phenomenon of intimacy, it fulfils the fundamental and instinctive urge of believers to express their thoughts and desires to their Creator and Lord. As a revelatory phenomenon, the experience of the prayer becomes a mirror reflection of the total essence of the human soul. It brings together the primordial mystique that accompanies the descent of the divine revelation with the human spirit that ascends on high with the whispers of the prayer ritual. As such, it completes the process of descent and return to that source of knowledge and blessing that has created life in the first place and that empowers all of the created universe to exist as a mirror of light in reflection of the one true Reality.

## 8. Prayer as Communication

For the Great Spirit is everywhere,
He hears whatever is in our minds and hearts,
It is not necessary to speak to him in a loud voice.
—Black Elk

When it comes to addressing the great questions that confront all humanity, questions that strike at the core of the fundamental mystery that pervades the very nature of reality, the human being stands between the two most disparate kingdoms on earth: the world of matter and the world of the spirit. It seems as though the universal mystery is designed to haunt the human psyche like a wind blowing through trees, just as the resolution to the mystery lingers in the background of the mind as a stirring sap of motivation and promise to come to terms with the meaning of life on earth. A secret has been whispered into the human soul that awaits discovery and unfolding. Humanity is confronted in this life with a locked door within the mind that requires the choice of the right key to unlock it. We grasp at symbol images of universal import that can stir the imagination to higher levels of thinking, giving breadth and depth to a choice that will determine the course of life and become its defining characteristic.

All journeys start with a choice of destination and an affirming first step. I became a Muslim over thirty years ago when I saw that the Islamic tradition led in a direction I wanted to go. But it is not enough to have chosen a path and purpose in life; there must be a means of communication with this farther shore, a way of listening and a way of being heard in return. Like the sea lion who roams out of the murky depths toward the sunlight that shines down near the shore, so do human beings attempt to take leave of the shallows of their own mind by crossing into a borderland of sunlit meadows where their world is changed from the finite to the infinite, from the imperfect to the perfected, from the relative to the absolute, and where opportunities for communication and fulfillment of self are made available to the aspiring soul. As we stand at the sun door of the spirit, leading back into the realms of the infinite and the eternal out of which we are born, we need the key of communication to open the door and lead us within. It is "the universe," according the Henry David Thoreau, "that will not wait to be explained." We need to communicate with it as it passes us by.

As an effective form of communication from the human to the Divine, prayer has represented the heartfelt expression of billions of human beings across the great span of recorded millennia and will continue to remain the hidden connection with a higher dimension of reality as long as people preserve the kernel of true spirituality within their hearts and free-willingly disclose that profound sense of intimacy as the outward expression of an inner reality.

The history of prayer is represented in time through multiple forms including private and individual prayer, spontaneous prayer uttered because of shock or crisis, canonical and liturgical prayer, contemplative or meditative prayer, and finally the prayer of the heart, or the invocation and remembrance of the sacred Name of names, creating within the individual a heightened consciousness of God and the holy sentiments that must accompany such focused awareness.

As a precise method of spirituality and as a formal means of communication with the Divinity, prayer always and forever helps people center themselves within their own timeless center and permits them to escape the prison of their own mentalities by reaching out beyond the individual ego to the Supreme Self. Prayer has centered upon ceremonies, rites and rituals, private whisperings, intimacies and entreaties, or unconscious (subconscious) cries for help, and has employed the spiritual artefacts such as prayer wheels,[1] prayer beads, and prayer carpets to aid and support the routine required to maintain the spiritual discipline of prayer. Prayer has provided the equilibrium and balance in an unpredictable world whose fundamental mystery

[1] In Tibetan Buddhism the prayer wheel, *mani-khorlo*, is used as a means of concentration. It is turned in the direction of the movement of the sun, thus a clockwise direction. It must be kept in motion. When the attention of the practitioner is directed to something else, the movement will stop. Therefore the use of the prayer wheel is nothing mechanical for it is accompanied by a movement of the mind and is reminiscent of the Buddha's first sermon in the Deer Park, the *Dharma-chakra-pravartana*, the "Setting in Motion the Wheel of the Dharma." Similarly, prayer beads are used in a number of religious traditions, for instance in the rosary of both the Catholic and Orthodox Churches, and in Islam where they are called by the Arabic *subha*, and where once again their use is an aid in the remembrance of God, creating a verbal theophany in which there is a psalmonized recitation of epithets from the revealed Quranic text.

refuses to disclose itself, permitting human beings down through history to speak from the depths of their hearts the genuine sentiments that lie grounded within their souls and enter the mind as expressions of aspiration and hope.

Prayer emerged as the *modus operandi* of the primordial man of the Golden Era, represented by the Adamic Garden of Eden, a time in which human existence itself was a living prayer, and the primordial man and woman walked and spoke directly with God. After the fall from the paradise at the end of the Golden Era, prayer emerged within the minds and hearts of individuals living during more traditional times as the fundamental mode of spiritual expression. The prayers of the Prophets recorded in sacred scripture[2] provided the models that could recapture the drive of primitive spiritual instincts to escape the dark cave of the individual self and transcend human limitations. Without prayer, the human species would exist in much the same manner as animals exist, namely without the mirror of a higher consciousness that reflects the truth of the one Reality that humans identify in words they can understand as Lord, Creator, Master, Father, King, and Holy Spirit.

The future of prayer, with regard to the inner life of modern man, commences with a number of questions that summarize the tenor of the times: Why do people pray? Is prayer necessary? Where does prayer lead us? These are contemporary rather than perennial questions. They are asked when people everywhere have abandoned the spiritual perspective for the sake of a secular and materialistic perception of reality, and lead lives that embrace the promises of this world only. Such questions would not have been asked during more traditional times when prayer was instinctive within the heart, a spiritual

[2] All of the prophets were men of prayer, but the Prophet David in particular could be characterized as the quintessential man of prayer. The great Psalms passed through the Prophet David, referred to in the Quran as the Zubur scriptures. The dialogue that we hear between creature and Creator gives us a direct insight into the normative substance of prayer. Psalm 139: "O Lord, thou hast searched me, and known me. Thou knowest my downsitting and mine uprising, thou understandest my thought afar off. . . ." And later: "For there is not a word in my tongue, but lo, O Lord, thou knowest it altogether. Thou hast beset me behind and before, and laid thine hand upon me. Such knowledge is too wonderful for me; it is high, I cannot attain unto it." This was David, the great prophet-king and slayer of giants.

instinct whose efficacy was never cast into doubt.[3] Prayer for more traditional peoples was the natural and instinctive attempt to communicate with the higher Being whose Intellect infuses the human mind with its knowledge and light. The essence of prayer, as St. John Damascene and many other saints have said, is "to elevate the soul to God." Prayer was always directed towards God, who while present in the "everlasting now," as the German mystic Meister Eckhart used to say, is neither ancient, modern, nor futuristic, but rather eternally now in the present moment.

Perhaps we should articulate what life would really be like without the support system of prayer and without the possibility, much less the challenge, to communicate with a Supreme Intelligence who is also the unknown Mystery that lies at the center of our very being as well as within the heart of the cosmic universe. Without prayer, there would be no true means of centering ourselves and even no way of identifying our center. There would be no process of interiorization to counterbalance the hard and brittle process of exteriorization we now experience. There would be no effective means of transcending human limitations, except by vague aspirations of wanting to be good without having any control over the process of inner desire that can seek the evil alternative as well as the desire to be good. There would be no outlet for the higher emotions and sacred sentiments that emerge from our being as signature statements of our inner life. Ultimately, there would be no means of communication with the Divine Being who is the Source and Origin of all truth and all reality, a truth and a reality that is one and that unites the manifested universe into a totality that encompasses and harmonizes the macrocosm into a unified Whole in keeping with the central theme of *al-Tawhid* (unity) in Islam.

The modernist spirit does not appreciate the power of prayer to change, purify, and perfect the heart and thus the inner essence of humanity. Action has become the by-word of the modern person, action that is no longer based on a traditional worldview much less on pious contemplation. The simple truth is often forgotten today that correct action depends on the correct mode of being. People today want to perform good works without actual *being* good, to reform

[3] The medieval description of the Anti-Christ is one of a man whose knee-joints are formed "backwards," thus one who cannot kneel down to pray.

the world without attempting to reform themselves, to exalt action above all without a supportive contemplation to shape the contours of that action.

We are living in a time when all kinds of explanations, proofs, and testimonies are demanded. In the new millennium, we are fast moving toward the concept of a global society. We are proud, as a civilization, of our pursuit of the knowledge of reality through science, which, however, thereby defines the parameters of the existing human reality. Modern society is intrigued by an ever more sophisticated technology that can smash atoms to create nuclear fusion, send space probes into far distant space, build computers that can perform prodigious feats of calculation, and communications and information systems that connect people at the speed of light. In our pursuit of a knowledge concerning the heavens, the heart of the atom, and the distant reaches of the stars, we have lost the meaning behind the symbolic image of the infinitude of the heavens, the heart of the atom and the city of God that we behold in the stars. As a consequence, we have lost the meaning of ourselves as microcosmic beings within a macrocosmic universe that is one and indivisible. Traditional man would have prayed, for that reason alone if for no other, since his prayer created the invisible threads that connected incomprehensible worlds and communicated heart-felt messages between those worlds that made sense and were effective in putting life in perspective.

People living in a traditional society would never have asked why Heaven existed, nor would they have risked their own identity by questioning the prevailing traditional views of man, God, destiny, judgment, and the promises of the paradise. Traditional peoples concerned themselves with the true nature of reality and were primarily concerned with how to respond to that reality rather than question why that reality existed. The traditional framework encouraged the acceptance of a divinely ordained Reality as foundational and fundamental to all of existence and the religious forms provided the doctrine and above all the methodology so that the faithful could not only know, but also "taste" that reality, as the Sufi mystics would say, through direct personal experience.

The true meaning of the concept of religion has been lost in the shadows of time as an outmoded and archaic artefact of earlier civilizations, leaving behind form without substance and knowledge without scientific proofs. Similarly, the instinctive habit of turning to God in prayer has been abandoned from the routine of peoples' daily lives as the bedtime habit of children and the elderly. Previously, prayer for traditional peoples was the formal and valid means of communication between the human and the Divine Being to the point that it was second nature for individuals to turn to God in prayer. Now the majority of people the world over no longer pray on a regular basis and therefore no longer enjoy the blessings, the security, and the peace of mind that accompany an individual's holy efforts to communicate with the Divine Being through acts of prayer and supplication.

In the modern era, certain individuals continue to pray instinctively, partly because no matter how pressing the desire to deny God and the reality of the Spirit through the assertion of the ego and the mind-altering sentiments of today's modern, secularist culture, they know deep down in their own helplessness and spiritual loneliness that they need God and that prayer is the principal means of communicating that need. All human beings know in their heart of hearts, namely in their soul, that they are alone without the Divine Benefactor in a solitude that would be intolerable if its true import were brought to bear on the human mentality.[4] Plainly and simply, man prays because he *has* a soul, a soul that lives and breathes and is fused with the very Spirit of God; therefore a soul that yearns to be reunited with that Spirit in the course of fulfilling its sacred vocation here on earth, no matter how atrophied the soul's expression may be during this dark *Kali Yuga* era in which we live.

Prayer has profound implications. To have a relationship with the Divinity and to establish communication with Heaven must give a particular shape and coloration to the kind of relationship that people will have among themselves and with the world. It is worth recalling at this point the philosophical maxim of Descartes, "I think, therefore

[4] It is perhaps part of the mystery of the Divine Being as well as the subtlety of the divine design that man is not crushed by his denial of God and reduced by his pretensions of being alone and on his own in this world. As part of that design, human beings are free to deny the Absolute and are given a little time, as the Quran affirms, "to play," even if they will have all eternity to suffer the consequences of that misguided and arrogant denial.

I am" (*cogito ergo sum*). It was considered revolutionary when it was proclaimed in the 17th century and was eventually incorporated into the growing wave of a philosophic movement that has thoroughly indoctrinated the mentality of the modern era with its expressed reliance on the powers of ratiocination, even to the point of stating that we can prove our own existence by virtue of our ability to think. If we understand the manifestation of the purely visible world and our corporeal beings to be shaped by our ability to think and reason things to perfection, then we have little use for communication with a Divinity who represents the supreme object of human desire.

The human instinct for prayer as a communication with the Supreme Reality suggests the need for the soul, as holy ground, to act as a purifying sieve through which pass all human desires and aspirations from the individual self to the Supreme Self, much like ground water passes through earth to become purified, sub-surface table water. Prayer implies the need for a mind to articulate the desires, the doubts, and the aspirations that move out of the subjective being in search of the Objective Truth. Prayer implies the need for a heart to sing the praise, the worship, the holy sentiments that elevate the individual to a plane of consciousness that recalls the primordial era when Adamic humanity's very existence was a prayer and primordial man could have proclaimed, "I exist, therefore I pray" (*sum ergo oro*). The traditional attitude portrays human beings in prayer because their very existence calls for this, an existence that virtually becomes the outward manifestation of an inner prayer. As primordial man, existence itself was a living prayer, while the traditional and thus the fallen man prays precisely because his existence represents a separation from God. Traditional man prays, therefore, by way of compensation for this separation, in order to create the possibility of re-establishing the communication that was a matter of second nature to the primordial man.

Prayer offers a direct means of escape beyond the confines of the human subjectivity. It is the formal means to withdraw temporarily from our earthly ego-persona for the sake of a direct, indeed intimate communication with the Divine Being, an act of communication that transcends the abilities of normal intelligence by connecting the human mind with the Supreme Intellect. Prayer provides a means of spiritual ascent that is verified by the messenger Muhammad, upon him blessings and peace, when he is reported in the *hadith* literature as saying to his companions: "Prayer is ascent (*mi'raj*) for the faithful (*mu'min*)." The practitioner can withdraw for a few minutes from the strictly horizontal plane of earthly existence with its downward attraction and enter the holy realm of the vertical ascent whose axis intersects the horizontal plane and virtually injects the spiritual perception into every aspect of what would otherwise be a purely secularized form of human life.

Because prayer shapes the contours and atmosphere of the heart and soul with its overlay of divine Objectivity and holy Presence, it is the spiritual discipline *par excellence* of the spiritual life of the human being. When people pray, all the key elements of their being come into play, and not just the physical body with its folded hands, bowed head, and downcast eyes, even though the body language itself bespeaks of a moment that transcends the physical and timely plane for a spirituality that is virtually timeless and other-worldly. The mind responds to a consciousness of God; the will is shaped and strengthened by its resolution to pray; the prayer activates itself as virtue within the soul and serves as a lingering presence long after the prayer is finished. In fact, prayer permits people to interiorize a fully manifested and external existence. "To interiorize life itself and to become aware of the inward dimension, man must have recourse to rites whose very nature it is to cast a sacred form upon the waves of the ocean of multiplicity in order to save man and bring him back to the shores of Unity. The major rites or pillars . . . are all means of sanctifying man's terrestrial life and enabling him to live and to die as a central being destined for beatitude."[5]

If the sacred testimony of the *shahadah* represents the quintessential summary of the religion of Islam imprinted indelibly upon the heart of Muslims, then prayer is a kind of existential statement of all that a person is at a given moment in time. Prayer is the expression of the immediate, momentary, and spontaneous self with all of the hopes, fears, frustrations, weaknesses, and human needs that only a divine Being in His full plenitude and unlimited beatitude could address with true credibility and ultimately satisfy.

[5] Seyyed Hossein Nasr, *Islamic Life and Thought* (Albany, NY: SUNY Press, 1981), p. 193.

Prayer establishes the meeting of the Divine with the human, and makes ready the sacred encounter between man and God, with its ambiance of humility, fear, awe, reverence, and miraculous wonder at its possibilities and its challenge. A progression of moments in prayer can be identified as follows:

the moment of meeting
the moment of acknowledgment
the moment of heightened consciousness
the moment of communication
the moment of promise
the moment of fulfillment

Whenever a person enters a temple or church and kneels down to pray, whenever he enters a mosque or lays down a prayer carpet and raises cupped hands or open arms to salute the Divinity, *the moment of meeting* has arrived. The celebrant can withdraw for a few moments from the march of time to arrive at an atemporal way station in which God is near and man is not alone. As a verse of the Quran poignantly acknowledges: "I come between man and his own heart" (8:24). All the elements of truth, including certitude, knowledge, higher emotion, and sacred expectation, come together to form the meeting ground and ambiance of the sacred encounter.

The intention to pray presupposes the realization and acceptance that God exists and is the Object of all desire, thus bringing about *the moment of acknowledgment.* Human intelligence and free will have brought the individual to this moment in time and the intention to pray reaffirms the Islamic witnessing that there is no divinity but the one Divinity. The choice of the real over the illusory and the acceptance of knowledge over ignorance can become vivid for a few moments and ultimately internalized within the very soul of the individual as a truly human resonance of the spirit, creating an echo of the Real and the Truth that reverberates through a person's being and sets the stage for a sacred dialogue, for God is the Listener and the One Who Responds to the prayer of His thinking human creation.

The moment of acknowledgment then becomes immediately overlaid and absorbed into *the moment of heightened consciousness* in which the self-absorbed ego consciousness identified as "I" can resolve its fundamental dilemma of identity and its own personal enigma through the certitude of "You" and "Him" reminiscent of God's affirmation of Himself in the Quranic "there is no god but You" (21:87) and "there is no god but Him" (2:255). The crisis of self-confidence is resolved, at least in principle, and the Muslim can comfortably express the inner feelings of the true self rather than continue to be the victim of an ill-defined and unpredictable ego adrift on a sea of incertitude.

*The moment of communication* is actually the *raison d'être* of the prayer, its reference point and door. It permits a person to depart from the confines of the individual ego and express through sincerity his or her inmost needs to a Divine Being who has the capacity to listen and respond as no other being conceivably could, and who is Himself available to us as the spiritual Mentor, Lord, and Master. Through this sacred communication, the full range of human expression is made possible, including the low point of a personal despair, petitions and entreaties, and ultimately the gratitude and thankfulness that are the natural response to the divine blessings received in life.

Prayer culminates as a *moment of promise* in which those who find themselves in the act of prayer can rest content that what they have communicated will be heard. In the loneliness of the earthly setting, awash in multiplicity, on one's own and confronted with a mystery with seemingly no resolution, the human entity can take comfort from the promise that all prayer is ultimately heard. The close companion of the Prophet, Ali, once said: "Those who know the world live alone," while Allah has promised in a well-known verse of the Quran: "Call upon Me and I will hear you" (40:60). Prayer offers unlimited promise for those with the devotion to make their prayerful remembrance of God.

When a Muslim takes leave of his prayer carpet and completes the formal prayer ritual, he or she takes *the moment of fulfillment* back out into the world. The world remains the same, but the person has changed, made different by virtue of the experience of the eternal "now" that the moment of prayer has produced. The moment of prayer opens onto the only Reality worth knowing and creates in return a reality of the eternal present within the context of earthly time, shattering its illusion. The Psalms (XC:2, 4) beautifully relate of the supra-natural concept of time in earthly terms: "From everlasting to everlasting, thou art God. . . . A thousand years in thy sight are but as yesterday," while the Quran echoes the Psalms with the verse: "Verily a day in the sight of thy Lord is like a thousand years of your reckoning" (22:47), and makes reference to celestial time in human terms: "The angels and the Spirit ascend unto Him in a Day the measure whereof is (as) fifty thousand years" (70:4).

Ultimately, the impulse to pray is a cycle that perpetuates itself unto eternity. The feelings of fulfillment generated by the prayer will lead the aspirant back to the original impulse to pray, in order once again to experience those moments of meeting, acknowledgment, heightened consciousness, communication, and promise that the prayer initiates and leads to fruition, bringing together into one sublime circle the complementarity of reasoned intention and spiritual fulfillment.

As we have come to realize over the years being Muslim within the Islamic traditional world, prayer has many modes of expression. Existence itself is a prayer as is the search for knowledge. All acts of generosity, courage, and patience are forms of prayer as are all good works and actions performed with sincerity of intent and consciousness of the higher reality. In addition, everything in the creation prays and praises the mighty Creator of the universe, from the song of the lark to the buzzing of the bee, producing in effect a cosmic prayer that unites all living things through instinct, worship, and praise. "The seven heavens and the earth and all beings therein declare His glory; there is not a thing but celebrates His praise; and yet you understand not how they declare His glory! Verily He is Oft-Forbearing, Most Forgiving" (17:44). As the face of the sunflower naturally follows the movement of the sun, so do all things within nature instinctively offer praise and prayer to the Absolute Being, simply by fulfilling the demands of their own true nature. "Hast thou not seen that Allah, He it is whom all who are in the heavens and the earth praise, and the birds in their flight? Of each He knoweth verily the worship and the praise, and Allah is aware of what they do" (24:41). Humans, however, praise and pray knowingly and willingly, and it is their ability to conceptualize the Supreme Consciousness and their desire to connect with that higher consciousness that makes them the most eminent of the earthly creatures. We are *Homo sapiens* because of our intelligence and free will and *Homo spiritualis* because of our intellect and heart, with the capacity to formalize and externalize our minds and hearts through thoughts, words, and actions.

Prayer takes on many forms of expression, but can be categorized for the sake of convenience into three distinct modalities: individual prayer, canonical prayer, and inner prayer. Distinctions can be made first of all between individual and canonical prayer. In canonical prayer, which has a universal character, God is the author and man the subject; not individual man but man as such. In principle, canonical prayer contains in its formal liturgical expression everything that concerns men and women in all places and at all times. In other words, it contains all possible individual prayers in a summary form and addresses the universal concerns of humanity with respect to the Divinity. As we mentioned in an earlier section, the *Pater Noster* ("Our Father") and the *Ave Maria* ("Hail Mary") are Christian examples of canonical prayers. In the Religion of Islam, the *salat*, the prayer ritual with its repetition of the opening seven verses of the Quran, is the canonical prayer specified to be performed five times a day.

Individual prayer necessarily has a more private and personal character. Not universal man but the individual practitioner is its author and God is not the subject but rather the object of the prayer. We can make further distinctions within individual prayer between spontaneous and private prayer. When we are shocked by a death, a sudden sickness, or a disaster, we instinctively call out to God for protection and/or release. Such spontaneous prayer is drawn from the well of some proto-instinct that lies within our depths as a natural reserve of intuitive spirituality. For those who still have the habit of individual prayer, this prayer arises out of their very nature and is as distinctive and individual as are the different destinies, desires, and needs of people around the world, whose prayer comes from the heart and whose message corresponds to the personal needs of the individual.

The most immediate aim of individual prayer must be communication with the Divinity, whether it be spontaneous or simply the heart-felt overflow of gratitude for the blessings we receive. Arising out of the needs of our individual nature, private prayer permits the practitioner first of all to release the psychological knots and inner complexes that are so characteristic of modern-day mentalities. Prayer helps to dissolve the subconscious aberrations that develop because of the ego acting as the seat of human pride that initiates the forgetfulness of God and the subordination of the inner Self to the externalized ego. Sincere prayer helps to drain away the secret poisons that build within the individual from a lifetime of unconscious living, poisons that permeate a person's judgments and emotions with their dark and malevolent perceptions acting in disguise as beneficial urges. Finally, private prayer externalizes and makes known to individuals their weaknesses and failures and permits them to give voice to these limitations or distortions in thought, word, and deed through a human projection of humility and intimacy with the Divine Being.

Private prayer has a commonality of characteristics, even if its individual content and substance alternates with individual needs and temperaments. Most people bring with them into the prayer a range of emotive feelings and holy sentiments that create the overall ambiance of the prayer. These modalities of consciousness and feeling can be listed as follows:

Humility–Realization
Piety–Sincerity
Fear–Reverence
Will–Love

Firstly, people bring to the prayer the complementarity of humility–realization in which they realize immediately that they would be "a thing unremembered until I remembered you." Humility is none other than the knowledge of one's place in the scheme of things and in the hierarchy of being and to know that one is completely dependent upon the Divinity for both life and destiny. Humility is a prolongation of realization; fraternal brothers in the proximity of the Divinity.

The interaction of humility and realization then leads to piety–sincerity in which piety represents a knowledge of who man is and who God is—referred to as *taqwa* in the Quranic revelation—while sincerity complements piety's knowledge with its forthright sentiment. Piety represents an appreciation of the knowledge of God and a willingness to assume an attitude of piousness in the relationship with God; sincerity fills the prayerful person with an ever-increasing presentiment of God and opens wide the door of the heart for the Presence of the Divinity.

The modalities of fear–reverence complement each other within the heart of the individual and create a balance between the absolute terror of the unknown and the uplifting awe of that which begins to be known through effort and aspiration. Fear brings us face to face with the Divine Mystery, while reverence responds to that mystery with awe in the face of the Divine Disclosure. In every prayerful encounter, there must be an element of fear in which the unknown will never be revealed or resolved, while there must also be the accompanying reverential awe when the human entity is permitted glimpses of the divine secret through a revelatory experience of the presence.

Finally, the modalities of will–love bring the aspiring Muslim soul to the prayer carpet in the first place and permit the overflow of spiritual emotion to instill the inner person with feelings of equilibrium and inner serenity. The will permits humanity to turn to God on an individual basis, to call upon, entreat, beg, petition, and thank the Divine Being for the gift of life. Love must be the final emotion of a heart overflowing with gratitude and thankfulness for the beatitude of the life experience. As an encircling spiral ascending upward, love fuels the will to turn again and again through prayer to the Divinity for succor and support.

Through the attitudes of humility, piety, fear, and desire, and their corresponding modes of realization, sincerity, reverence, and love, the soul can universalize the individual prayer with higher emotions and holy sentiments that create an ambiance that is both fitting and appropriate to any encounter with God.

In addition, individual prayer generally contains a combination of the following characteristics: resignation, regret, resolution, acceptance, trust, petition, gratitude, and praise. Resignation represents a fundamental surrender of the human will to the Divine Will of God. It accepts the human will as limited and recognizes the need for the will to be supported by the all-knowing and all-willing guidance of the Divine Being. Regret represents knowledge of what we have done and who we are as a consequence of our actions. We cannot forge through life without coming to the realization that we have weaknesses, limitations, and evils that need to be given their rightful name and recognized for what they are. These realizations manifest themselves as regret within the conscientious individual in prayer. Resolution follows regret and bespeaks the desire to avoid evil, to change our limitations, and to turn our weaknesses into strengths of character. With resolution comes acceptance, not only of who we are and the potential that we can become, but also implies an acceptance of our own destiny as rightfully ours, a destiny that must come to us by virtue of who we are and what we accomplish during the course of a life.

In a word, we put our trust in God because He is who He is, and we are who we are. The sacred trust has been established between the human and the Divine and there is therefore no need for fear or uncertainty that what comes to us belongs to any other. As such, we have the right in private prayer to petition the divine Being for that which we need or desire to accomplish our purpose in life. Once provided with what we need, gratitude is the natural sentiment of the faithful soul. Thankfulness is crucial to the inner dialogue between the human and the Divine for it represents a consciousness of the good and a fundamental awareness of the blessings that we have been granted. Thankfulness gives form to and expresses the knowledge that what we have has come from God and from none other than Him. As the Noble Quran relates: "We come from God and to Him we will return" (2:156).

God is identified across a number of religious traditions as Lord (*rabb*). Our minds conceive of God as the absolute and supreme Being, but when in prayer His humble servant address his God as Lord, He immediately enters the soul. He inhabits this sacred sanctuary of prayer as the Supreme Listener who gives ear to our troubles and hardships with understanding and benevolence. From his lofty abode, God maintains the integrity and harmony of the metacosmos, dispensing with justice and mercy, yet as Lord He is our personal and intimate friend (*wali*).

Through prayer, practitioners can lift for a few moments the false mask that they show to the world in order to reveal the true *Homo spiritualis* that exists within. In a world that loves to psychologize, prayer's psychological component is, perhaps, increasingly significant. Prayer has the power to dissolve inconsistencies of human character, release psychological knots, disperse human complexes, and shed human weaknesses. Even after we leave the prayer carpet to re-enter daily life,  the effects of prayer allow us to be who we truly are..

Prayer conveys an experience of spirituality that cannot be denied. We experience this reality, of course, not by the outer senses which can only verify the external world, but through the inner senses which can verify the internal, non-tangible world of the spirit. The Islamic mystics often refer to the "tasting" (*dhawq*) of truth and of the reality of God. Tasting is only one of the inner senses, along with seeing, hearing, feeling, and smelling, that approximate an experience of a reality that is other-dimensional and other-worldly. This does not mean that the inner eye will see God, angels, or other spirits of the non-tangible world, any more than it means that God, one of whose names is the All-Seeing (*al-basir*), sees the world with a physical eye. Rather, because the human being is modeled in the image of God, we can fine-tune our inner senses through prayer and other spiritual disciplines so that the faculties can become modes of perception for inner worlds of experience.

In order to heighten the perception of the inner senses, the religions have always encouraged the use of certain traditional supports that stimulate the external senses in order to affect the inner senses. For example one closes the eyes during the prayer, deliberately *not* to see the external world in order that one may better view with the inner eye the universe that is within. Physical postures and clothing both also create a sacred feeling that activates the inner psyche through these outer forms. Physical postures such as bowing and prostration, folded hands, the lotus posture in yoga, even the extended hands upward in open embrace practiced by the Plains Indians of North America have always accompanied sincere prayer. All these gestures create sacred feelings and enlarge the dimensions of the inner experience through the outward forms of sacred gesture and movement in prayer. Similarly, the clothing of traditional societies invariably facilitates the movements of the prayer ritual, in addition to being "culturally comfortable" to their mentality and suitable to the climate and environs.

Finally, the sense of smell acts as an aid in the remembrance of God. Joseph, according to the Quranic narrative, sent a shirt to his father Jacob as proof that he was still alive and as a sign of the joyous news of his impending return. When Joseph's brothers arrived home, Jacob said: "I do indeed scent the presence (*rih*) of Joseph." To "scent the presence" literally means to sense the scent, air, atmosphere, even the breath of Joseph, for the word *rih* has all these implications and is a close derivative of the word spirit (*ruh*) in Arabic, the very same *ruh* that God breathed into the body of man in order to create a *living being*.

Both incense and perfume create a particular atmosphere that is generally associated with the spiritual practices of religion. Incense has been used through the centuries in mosques, churches, and temples to refresh the mind and body while inwardly refreshing the spirit. Musk is identified in the Quran (83:26) as a scent of the Paradise and is traditionally applied to the body, especially the hands and head, before the prayer in Muslim countries. The profound and penetrating scents of musk and incense remind Muslims of their divine connections and serve as direct remembrances (*dhikr*) of God, so powerful is the association of these holy smells with the Islamic prayer ritual. In this way, the outer forms of the senses possess psycho-spiritual properties that can lead the mentality of man beyond mere forms in the direction of the celestial realities that lie at the heart of all forms. It is not surprising that aromatherapy has begun to take hold of the imagination of many people within modern societies today as an alternative therapy to sickness and depression, a therapy that has long been the mainstay of traditional societies who knew the value of sacred smells and used these smells not only to ward off temptation and misery, but also to raise their consciousness and enhance their spirits with the spirits of these enriching scents.

If the Islamic witnessing (*shahadah*) signifies knowledge and discernment, then the ritual prayer signifies experience and union. The sacred formula, as God's gift to man through a divine descent, conveys a theoretical knowledge of the Reality and a practical means of discernment between the Real and the unreal. Prayer, as man's response to God and as a formal means for the human ascent, translates the knowledge that we have of God into a true experience of the Divine Presence. To resolve to pray is to turn to God in one's heart; to assume a prayerful attitude is to enter into the Presence in order to reunite oneself with the Divinity; to actually recite the prayer is to communicate the human aspiration to the Divine Listener, the One Who Hears and Answers Prayer (*al-mujib*). Thus God, man, the meeting, and the eternal moment become a part of the human as well as the celestial reality, while the world and all that it contains including man, his wealth, his possessions and his fame, even life itself assume an air of unreality, a passing cloud or a feather in the wind. "What is the world if not the outflowing of forms, and what is life if not a bowl which seemingly is emptied between one night and another? And what is prayer, if not the sole stable point—a point of peace and of light—in this dream universe, and the straight gate leading to all that the world and life have sought in vain?"[6]

Prayer is the pause in life's progression within this world, a moment that shatters earthly time in order to recreate the broken pieces within the totality of the eternal moment. The experience of the prayer with its message of the one Reality permits the human being to escape from the implicit limitations of the earthly context and sphere. As a formalized and spiritualized mode of action, prayer permits the faithful to depart, however briefly, from the world of thought and action into the world of pure communication from the human to the Divine. Through prayer faithful believers everywhere can take leave of themselves and shed the density of their earthly persona with the words "Lord, hear my voice; Lord, listen to my entreaty; Lord, answer my prayer with the Mercy of Thy Self." In return, the Divinity shines down upon the human soul penetrating rays of beatitude and light.

[6] *The Essential Writings of Frithjof Schuon*, ed. Seyyed Hossein Nasr, p. 444.

# PART V

# THE JOURNEY

# 9. Breakfast in the City of Light

> One prayer in my mosque is better than one thousand prayers in any other mosque excepting al-Masjid al-Haram. (Bukhari: 2/157; Chap. 37, 282)

In the previous parts of this work, we have reflected upon and explored the significance of four key ideas that summarize the essence of the religion of Islam. "Awakening" addresses the question of the perennial mystery that confronts everyone in life and describes the process of a person's surrender to the unity of the one Reality and the one God that Islam has come to proclaim. "Foundation" lays the groundwork of the spiritual experience that begins with the mystery of faith, passes through the certitude of a knowledge of God, and ultimately arrives at realization of the heart which reflects back out into the world through the light of virtue. "Descent" captures the encounter of the Divine with the human through the revelatory words of God, making available for humanity the essential knowledge that gives meaning and purpose to the life process. "Ascent" sets out to portray the encounter of the human with the Divine through the prayers, aspirations, and entreaties of the human soul in communication with its Lord and Master.

This final part calls upon the image of the journey to evoke the feeling of departure and return that lies at the heart of the human condition. Once the human soul had accepted the sacred trust of God by responding to the question "Am I not your Lord" with witnessing and surrender ("Yes, we witnes s you" [7:172]), it began its sacred journey of return to God, which was prefigured at the beginning of creation and comes to fruition in the journey through life that is allotted to each individual soul. Islam has ritualized the image of the journey into the fifth and final pillar of the religion, when every Muslim once in his or her life makes the sacred journey to Makkah. Not only do the Muslims face the Kaaba in Makkah every time they recite the canonical prayers, but they also perform a physical and indeed symbolic journey to the very center of the Muslim world and in doing so actually journey to the Kaaba of their own heart, evoking in the process a spiritual experience beyond compare.

The following account highlights certain impressions that resulted from my visit to the two holy cities of Makkah and Madinah in Saudi Arabia during the holy month of Ramadan,[1] impressions that hopefully belie the ignorant and often false notions that now predominate across the globe about Muslims and their beliefs, impressions that may begin to sketch a narrative event of the fast of Ramadan in the holy places as an expression of faith and spirituality by millions of Muslims the world over in light of their true meaning and significance.

As the chartered Saudia flight, packed with a contingent of pilgrims, circles for a landing on this predawn mid-November morning, I notice in the distance a luminous glow of light reaching vertically into the overcast heavens. The *Masjid al-Nabawi* (The Prophet's Mosque) announces its location at the very center and heart of the city of Madinah in a brilliant display of light. Visible from outer space even, this beacon of light is certainly the most obvious landmark in the darkness of the desert plane. As if in counterpoint to this unexpected radiance, a pale harvest moon descends soberly toward the Eastern horizon, drenching the desert landscape with its silvery incandescent moonbeams. I have returned once again to the City of Light after an interval of 15 years.

The airport itself is small and unpretentious and I pass through customs without much ado. No one seems to notice or care that I am an American Muslim of Boston Irish ancestry, perhaps because I am dressed incognito in the Pathan native cloth consisting of baggy pantaloons tied together with a cloth rope and an overhead shirt that flows down to the knees. I am wearing it because more comfortable attire could not be found that is so well suited to the Islamic prayer rituals and the other demands of the lesser (*umrah*) pilgrimage. That, together with a white skullcap, allows me the luxury of being anonymous as I blend into the surroundings with the other eager pilgrims. The Saudi Government pilgrim visa stamped across a full page of my passport will gain me entry into the Kingdom even if it may raise some eyebrows and questions later when I return to the US.

The bus ride into town could have been anywhere in the Middle East, the dry and dusty desert landscape by the side of the road, the

[1] "Ramadan is the (month) in which was sent down the Quran, as a guide to mankind, also clear (signs) for guidance and judgment (between right and wrong)" (2:185).

invading billboard signs advertising things people don't need and shouldn't want, the craggy rocky hills silhouetted against the horizon, the dingy cement houses and cluttered shops huddled together in close proximity as if for protection from some unknown force. We pass a traffic light here, turn a corner there, when suddenly we emerge onto the grand concourse of the sacred mosque of Madinah, called the Prophet's Mosque because the Prophet himself is buried in one corner called the Sacred Chamber in an area that originally comprised the rooms where he lived with his wife 'Aishah. The first mosque of Islam[2] was an extension of the house of the Prophet.

The sight of this magnificent edifice is overwhelming, to say the least, for its mammoth size and stately presence. For sheer bulk and magnitude, this architectural wonder strikes awe in the beholder. The entire structure rests serenely amid an open expanse of plaza that extends perhaps 500 meters on each side of the mosque and whose surface is covered with alabaster and marble.[3] Everything about this broad setting bespeaks of openness, air, and light and provides striking views of the mosque from any angle of approach. This is the very center and heart of the city. Everything beyond the sacred enclosure immediately becomes an afterthought to the necessities of daily life. A grand avenue leads down from the mountains beyond the edge of the small city to the five grand portals that distinguish the front side of the mosque. At a glance as you approach from the grand promenade, the building seems monumental. Like a photo that simply refuses to contain the image you wish to capture, the sight of the mosque simply refuses to be contained in a single glance. You have to span your vision from left to right, right to left, to take it all in, and even then, it seems incomprehensible to fully grasp in all its magnificence.

For all the value of this stately structure, the setting comes alive with the sheer numbers of people that are moving in and out and around the mosque. Much like witnessing the celestial bodies or calculating the astronomical numbers of stars and galaxies, the numbers

[2] The dimensions of the original structure were 2,450 square meters with three doors on the south side, and in the eastern and western wall.

[3] The total plaza area is 235,000 square meters and accommodates 400,000 additional worshippers. The mosque itself may now accommodate approximately one million worshippers during peak times of crowding.

of people range beyond the scope of clear comprehension and only because you are there with the rest of this vast congregation can you begin to believe what you appear to be experiencing. For the sheer force of its impression, this is like no other moment in time. There seems to be a secret here worth exploring. Indeed the secret lies in the intention of those who have joined me on this pilgrimage, all of whom have a single-minded focus and a purpose that is absolute and beyond any doubt. The sheer numbers of people bring a reality to the situation that might otherwise be lost. It is the supreme example of humanity giving rise to the expression of their deepest yearning and nothing and no one is going to come between them and their aspirations.

The day is punctuated of course by the five devotional prayers of Islam and at any given moment vast crowds of people are either moving toward or away from the imposing sanctuary of the mosque. As I arrive in the early morning after my night flight to greet the Prophet and extend my *salaams* as is the Islamic custom, I find myself moving against a sea of humanity who are now exiting the holy mosque after the early morning prayer and the commencement of the fast. The entire concourse is bathed in light amidst the otherwise still darkened night within the city and this light no doubt shines heavenward as a vertical symbol of human aspiration and a love for God like no other love, while grand colonnades bedecked with gilded lamps that are harmoniously dispersed across the concourse illuminate the marble-floored forecourt like silent sentinels watching over the faithful. In the distance in the eastern sky, the promise of dawn begins to emerge over the horizon behind the rocky Madinah hills just outside the city.

Once inside the imposing stone structure of the mosque, the building gives way to endless archways, pillars, and colonnades that extend disbelievingly in every direction and seemingly for miles. The archways receding into the distant areas of the mosque give a feeling of infinity of space while the rows of carpets, and the rows of worshippers standing upon them, give a feeling of an eternity of time, for the ritual prayer captures for the mind of the devotees a moment of eternity within the present moment. The pillars and colonnades, marble bedecked and with glittering brass frames containing shimmering lamps at their crown give a feeling of open expansiveness and light that is breathtaking to behold. The endless rows of carpets left to right, row upon row, extend all the way from back to front of the mosque, which however cannot be seen from the front entranceway.

The faithful have now settled into their routines following the prayer. It is nearing six in the morning and some people have rendered themselves supine in various postures of repose, no doubt through the sheer exhaustion of having spent most of the night in prayer and night vigils within the sanctuary of the mosque as is the custom during the holy month of Ramadan. It is clear that they are either exhausted or accustomed to sleeping on the floor. Some roll up the carpets to use as a pillow. Others have pulled a length of carpet over themselves like a makeshift blanket. They are all in various attires of Islamic dress including *jalabiyas*, kaftans, *thobes*, and the Pakistani *badla* (suit) that I am wearing, complete with shawls, scarves, skullcaps, Gulf-style headdresses, and turbans. Many of them have wrapped themselves in their long shawls or unraveled turbans and resemble shrouds wrapped for burial, recalling sleep as the "lesser death." The mosque in principle is nothing but open, extended space, with no furniture or marking points, containing only floor carpets for the faithful to sit on and the *mihrab* or sacred niche that indicates the direction of Makkah and provides the setting and enclosure for the imam to lead the prayers.

The mosque is a sacred sanctuary as well as the venue for prayer; in Islam it is the sacred architecture *par excellence* and therefore is often considered a work of art. Upon entering the mosque, the Muslim returns to that harmony, order, and inner peace that is the cornerstone of all spirituality. As such, the building gives way to become a primordial symbol of the sacrality associated with a house of worship. Indeed, in the Islamic worldview, the earth itself is a sacred mosque where men and women of all types and generations express their fullest sense of worship through living and working within the sanctions of the Divine Priority, in keeping with the *hadith* which states that "the earth was placed for me as a mosque and purifier."

I intend to make my way through this magnificent place of worship deep into the inner sanctum of the original mosque, which became the extension of the family quarters of the Prophet highlighting the concept of the mosque as the logical extension of the home. It is here along the original southeasterly section of the mosque that the Prophet lies buried, together with his Companions and first Caliphs Abu Bakr al-Saddiq and Omar bin al-Khattaab. It is customary to visit the tomb of the Prophet and greet him with *salaams* upon first entering the sacred enclosure of the mosque. I make my way slowly amid the multitude and savor every moment. The mosque is still jam packed with people of every race and nationality. Old and young intermingle; many are lying supine, others are gathered in groups or sitting in circles sharing their impressions. People are moving about as I am, deferring to the space of others, careful to step over those who are resting on the floor without a care in the world.

As I move deeper into the mosque, I notice that the upper walls and ceiling are embellished with geometric forms, arabesques, Quranic calligraphy, and mini domes hand-carved from wood in remembrance of the traditional era when the handcrafts represented a form of art. Given the size and dimensions of the mosque, it is quite a trek from front to back. Deep within the well of the enclosure, I come upon an inner open courtyard that gives rise to the heavens. It comes upon you unexpectedly and already the dawn light is bathing the inner courtyard in beams of early morning daylight. I take note, however, of a group of huge, light-colored sunshades that have been cleverly designed to open at the push of a remote controlled button and fan out overhead in perfect symmetry to protect the worshippers from the onslaught of the mid-day desert sun that promises to fill the courtyard open to the elements. I am told that the opening of these gigantic mechanical umbrellas is a sight to behold.

I know I am nearing the tomb of the Prophet through two pieces of evidence, the architectural change of the building which has a smaller, more crowded, and less grandiose aspect and dates back many centuries to the time of the Prophet and the early Caliphate era and by the density of the crowds of people all vying for proximity to the resting place of the Prophet. There is a section of the mosque cordoned off and positioned adjacent to the wall of the Prophet's tomb that is referred to and revered as the *al-riyadh al-jannah*, which roughly translates as a "garden" of the Paradise. The Prophet has referred to this part of the mosque by saying: "What is between my house and my *minbar* is a garden from the gardens of Paradise." It is an area that according to the traditions of the Prophet is actually a part of the Paradise that will rise upward and return to its original home on the Day of Judgment, which in Islam is alternatively referred to as the Day of Accounting and the Day of Religion.

Many years ago when I first became Muslim, I remember quietly entering this section of the mosque and ensconcing myself on the light blue carpet distinguished from the red oriental carpets spread through the rest of the mosque. There was indeed not only a special quality of serenity and calm there that one would come to expect in the paradise, but I felt as I sat cross-legged on the carpet as if I had come home at last and that there was nowhere else I needed to go. An otherworldly fragrance seemed to unexpectedly permeate the air and I remember considering what that scent reminded me of until I had to confess that it reminded me of nothing related to this world, that it had an otherworldly quality that seemed exquisite and heavenly.

As I sat in this "garden of Paradise," my mind took on wings and I began to fly. Call it autosuggestion of the tradition if you like, but a dream quality seemed to emerge like dawn mist over the waters of a lake. The strange, otherworldly scent began to raise my level of consciousness from the mundane to the sublime in some unconscious manner, and I felt I was entering another dimension virtually impossible to describe. Then, without warning, I felt a surge of emotion well up inside me from depths I didn't know existed, an emotive feeling so strong and satiating that I could do nothing but surrender to the power of these sacred emotions and I began to sob a storm of hot tears for all I was worth. At first, I did not know why I was crying, except that I realized that the place, the moment, and the overall ambiance were powerful enough to evoke such an unexpected, powerful reaction. The outburst was not convulsive or hectic; it was sheer weeping without an obvious catalyst. It was not the kind of grief caused by the death of a loved one or the loss of a valued treasure; instead it was an emotive collapse without hill or valley, a release from the rigidity that holds us together in life, vast and inconsolable at first as a child's first confrontation with the unknown. The hot tears came as a soothing balm for the trials and tribulations of my life, the frustrations and the shattered hopes, the dreams, the remorse, the failures and perhaps even the successes. I sobbed for the person I had been and the person I might well become. The sobbing slowly died within me throb by throb until a wave as cool as spring water flowed across the shore of my being and an abiding peace streamed through my mind and body. I had received the gift of tears spoken of in the traditions of Islam in which the soul uses the mind and body to free itself of certain complexes of the psyche and psychological knots of the spirit as a form of liberation from the lower self and as a means of purification.

On this occasion fifteen years later, however, I had to forgo scaling the heights of such an elevated spiritual emotion that I experienced on that former occasion—or so I thought—because the section of the mosque called the *riyadh al-jannah* was simply a teeming cauldron of wide-eyed humanity all in contest for a piece in this "paradise" on earth. I therefore joined the more sober, turgid throng making its way down the aisle that passes in front of the three tombs of the Prophet and his beloved companions Abu Bakr and Omar. It was slow going indeed, and except for the occasional shove or elbow in the ribs, perhaps it was a good thing, because as one approaches the front doors of the tombs, with their silver encrusted plating covered with Quranic verses, the realization suddenly dawns with an expectation brimming beyond belief that one is approaching the very presence of the Prophet. Here is where he lived, where he prayed, and where he died. Here lies the man that Allah chose to receive His revelation and to deliver it as the Holy Quran to future generations of humanity. Through his mind passed the very words of God and from him, they passed out into the world of humanity down to the present time. Muslims spend a lifetime attempting to find ways to express their love of God, but their love of the Prophet comes naturally and spontaneously because he is the vehicle and the path through which the love of God is possible.

As I turn a corner and approach the aisle that passes in front of the enclosed rooms containing the various tombs, the dense but still orderly crowd thickens considerably. People with cupped or extended hands in an attitude of prayer are moving slowly forward at the pace of molasses and everyone proceeds deferentially, concerned for the comfort of their Muslim brothers and not wishing to create an undue stir. Then I am there and I send forth my *salaams* to the beloved Prophet, upon him blessings and peace. Neither the hectic throng nor the imposing and unexpected presence of military guards at the doors of the tombs can disturb the surging feeling of humility and awe that begins in the pit of my stomach and rises to the tip of my cognitive consciousness lifting me off my feet and beyond the gravity limits of this world. As I shuffle myself along as only one of a surging crowd of worshippers, I feel lost in the wave of a deep and abiding emotion and I think: We remember the Prophet Muhammad every day in our prayers and we invoke his name and sayings as a matter of course, but now I am here at his tomb, visiting his ancient home and place of earthly investiture. I have presented myself here in person to make my holy *salaams* to the memory of his sacred person and his exemplary life. Together with all Muslims, I feel a deep and overwhelming love for the Prophet to the extent that the evocation of his memory creates a feeling of melting in the heart and brings tears to the eyes. It is a powerful, indeed an overwhelming moment. In the presence of greatness, I utter my humble prayer as intercession to God through the Prophet as I remember all those in need within the circle of my life, a dying brother on life support, my diabetic friend, and all those who asked me to intercede on their behalf.

A moment whose quality will be remembered for years to come has passed me by, just as the slow-moving sea of humanity I am part of has passed by the tomb enclosure. Before I fully realize what has happened, the crowd has deposited me outside the mosque again like a piece of driftwood thrown ashore by the sea. I gaze distractedly and a little disoriented at the luminous glow on the eastern horizon as the sun announces its arrival and bathes the eastern face of the mosque with its harsh light without any thought or mercy for the faithful.

Later in the day, after the mid-afternoon prayer whose timing occurs when "the shadow equals the man," I strolled through the open concourse within the forecourt of the Prophet's mosque to witness the late afternoon activities and the preparations taking place for the breaking of the fast, the eagerly anticipated and communal occasion that commences precisely at the call of the *adhan* (the call to prayer) just after the descent of the sun beyond the perimeter of the horizon.

The swarm of pilgrims has dispersed somewhat but the place is still teeming with life and activity. The crowds proclaim endless movement in, out, and around the mosque. The *suk* or marketplace at the edge of the concourse begins to come to life with the dying rays of the relentless desert sun that even on this mid-November afternoon has drawn temperatures up to 100 degrees. I hear the grating sound of metal as the shopkeepers open the metal shutters protecting their shops. I espy a small ledge or shelf by a fountain that marks the end of the grand promenade and the beginning of the concourse leading to the five front portals of the mosque. It looks like an opportune place to observe the late afternoon activity around the main square in front of the mosque. Once ensconced on this narrow, uncomfortable shelf, I observe the goings-on.

The grand promenade leading up to the mosque ends here, circling the fountain and returning whence it came. All traffic is blocked, but I notice that certain cars are allowed through the police barriers, especially vehicles that are delivering food to the mosque. It is clear that people have shifted gear from the sluggish ambiance of the hot mid-afternoon. A great number of local people from Madinah are now in full preparation for the breaking of the fast. Across the great expanse of the forecourt, long mats have been laid down row upon row. The rows seem to number in the thousands. Upon this matting is laid a makeshift plastic tablecloth in length-wise strips. Trucks pull up, trolleys appear out of nowhere, and great cartons of oranges and bananas, large boxes of yogurt and dates, are unloaded by determined and efficient townspeople. Soon thereafter, I notice great vats of briyani[4] being unloaded from various trucks, this being a tasty favorite dish made of meat and rice pungently seasoned with fried tomatoes, onions, and a multitude of spices. The trucks swing in around the fountain, people jump out of the vehicles, and download these great containers onto trolleys, which are rolled away in the direction of the mosque.

Meanwhile, all manner of humanity are making their way somewhere round about the mosque precinct. I notice a group of women moving with stately grace through the swirling masses, several of them bearing cartons of goods on their heads, a small rounded cloth separating box from head as a concession to good sense. They look as if they would not be able to walk without them. I see invalids being pushed around in wheelchairs; a man is driving his own motorized chair, an obese person is being pushed around in a make-shift vehicle large enough to accommodate him; there are even one or two people who pass by being carried in overhead litters. Parents with children, husbands and wives, rowdy street urchins who greet me boldly in Arabic with the words "How are you Papa?"

An elderly man with a sculptured beard who was supporting himself heavily on a hand-carved branch of a tree ploddingly makes

[4] A culinary favorite of Indians, Pakistanis and Gulf Arabs by way of association, consisting of highly seasoned rice cooked with meat and its juices.

his way up to me and sits himself down with a tired smile. Our two different worlds meet briefly on this occasion. He greets me with the traditional Islamic greeting that every Muslim understands: *Salaam alaykum* (peace be upon you), and I return his greeting. We exchange smiles and hand gestures in the spirit of communal friendship, brought together here for these few moments in this time and this place in the name of the one God that binds us together. Then, with a sigh, he takes his leave and with the support of the makeshift cane, makes his slow way back into the mosque. My heart goes with him for a few moments in my mind's eye before he disappears from my world once again in the dense crowd.

It is time to give up my treasured shelf by the fountain and prepare myself for the great event of the breaking of the fast and the evening prayer. Interspersed through the great concourse are pavilions with signs indicating that the *hammam* (bathroom facilities) and parking lie below the upper concourse. A set of escalators leads deep into the cavernous underground where there are endless batteries of parking available that can accommodate up to 5,000 vehicles. I observe the curious surreal quality of the sight of various crowds of people serenely availing themselves of these swift moving stairs. On an intermediary level lie the *hammam* areas accessed through a traditional stairway. I proceed there to take care of the necessary natural functions along with a great many other people and once completed proceed to the ablution stations which are well appointed with a stone seat in front of a faucet well placed to accommodate both hands and feet. A small shelf is there for eye glasses, watches, caps, and other paraphernalia that people have with them. The facilities of the *hammam* are marked by convenience and cleanliness and seem very spacious.

It may seem awkward to even mention these things, but to the harried pilgrim, many of whom have no real place to stay, these conveniences make a huge difference in the ease and comfort in which they perform their spiritual duties. To the outsider the ablution may seem like an inconvenience and a test of ritual fastidiousness, but to the Muslim it is a pleasant interlude in addition to having a practical as well as symbolic meaning. I eventually find a free ablution station and sit myself down to perform the Islamic *wudhu*, a ritual cleansing that must precede every prayer and Quranic recitation. Most people have now come to know that it involves the washing of the hands, nose and mouth three times, the arms to the elbow, the head, ears and feet to the ankle. What they may not realize is that after trudging through the dust and heat of this desert clime, the *wudhu* ritual is unexpectedly refreshing and gives pause to the perspicacity of the divine command to undergo this preliminary ritual to wash away not only the sweat and dust and sometimes sleep of the individual, but also on some symbolic level to cleanse the inner human world of the impurities that have crossed the threshold of the mind and heart during the intervals of forgetfulness between the prayers.

When I emerge from the underground *hammam* quarters, the scene has altered considerably. Across the great concourse and forecourt of the Prophet's mosque, a vast crowd now sits politely row upon row that number in the thousands on matting and carpets that extend from east to west across the forecourt. It is a mythical sight that is incredible to behold. The dying sun casts its late afternoon rays across the court, bathing the open plaza and the multitude of pilgrims sitting there in the foreglow of sunset. The expectant people, who have been fasting since the early morning call to prayer, sit cross-legged in front of their simple break-fast fare patiently awaiting the first call of the *adhan* that marks the end of the fast.

There is still a half hour before the call of the sunset prayer and I am determined to brave the crowds within the mosque and find a place in anticipation of breaking the fast and saying the prayer within the mosque enclosure. I make my way toward the great central portal, weaving discreetly through the vast crowd of people either sitting on the ground or moving up and down the aisles that give access to the doors of the mosque.[5] As I take off my sandals[6] and pass through the mighty doorway, I notice a Quranic verse (15:46) chiseled into the stone lintel over the door: "Enter therein, (Paradise) in peace and security."

I am stunned by an insistent echo as I cross the threshold, "Come, come, come, sit here! Tofaddal!" This is the Arabic greeting of invi-

[5] The mosque now has 85 doors composed of fine, rare teak spread across 41 wide gates. Covering the surfaces of the doors are brass arabesque medallions that are gold-coated. Inscribed in the center of each are the words "Muhammad, the Messenger of Allah, peace be upon him."

[6] Pilgrims take measures to safeguard their footwear. Many people carry a plastic bag with them, and tuck their sandals under their arm when they enter the mosque. There are shelves scattered throughout the mosque where these sandals can be stored and later secured. Losing one's footwear is a practical problem worth taking note of.

tation to join a repast. Somebody has taken me by the arm and is escorting me through the maze of legs and feet to what seems like the sole remaining place in the otherwise cavernous and body-packed enclosure, roofed with cascading archways in descending order as far as the eye can see. I feel dazed by the sudden good fortune and glad to have a place inside the mosque where I can break the fast and say the prayer. How this was actually going to happen in the next few minutes however was anyone's guess.

As I settled myself onto the carpet in front of my place setting, I see around me that bee hive activity that has made the breaking of the fast possible in the first place. Local citizens of Madinah have commandeered the mosque to create perhaps the largest breakfast place setting in the world. Row upon row of carpets as far as the eye can see and extending across the broad concourse of the inner mosque from east to west have been equipped with food and drink so that the faithful may break their fast. Lengthy strips of cellophane have been laid length-wise. My own place setting represents a microcosm that mirrors perhaps tens of thousands of place settings now existent throughout the mosque. There is an appetizing ring loaf of bread, freshly baked and sprinkled with tasty sesame seeds that radiate an odor of wholesome goodness in the style of true bread that one seldom finds today. There are a number of fruits, including an orange and a banana and a handful of Madinah dates at each place setting. There is a full milk cup of yoghurt accompanied by a small tray of freshly ground *zattar* that Arabs favor and like to sprinkle into the yogurt. Every place setting has a small plastic spoon to stir and eat the yoghurt. It is a magnificent if not unbelievable display of planning and forethought. Of course feeding the faithful during Ramadan is incumbent upon the Muslims and brings with it special blessings that are highly favored. Minutes before the call of the *adhan* and the momentous breaking of the fast, *Zamzam* water[7] is poured and passed along the rows from large thermo containers situated along the aisles of the mosque.

In a final gesture of generosity, I am quickly passed a small plastic cup of Arabic coffee pungent with the spice cardamom, which I set down in front of me amid the array of delicacies that await my con-

[7] From the Zamzam well at the Grand Mosque in Makkah. The Zamzam water is transported daily to the mosque in special tanker trucks from Makkah, 430 kilometers away.

sumption. Then I hear the piercing cry of the *adhan. Allahu Akbar, Allahu Akbar*, followed by the profession of faith that there is no god but the one God and Muhammad is the Messenger of God, magnified tenfold and cutting through the silence like a piercing cry from beyond the known world. The vast congregation consisting of some astronomical number beyond reckoning or comprehension, but certainly approaching perhaps a million Muslims, paused for a brief second as if the loud report of a bullet had unexpectedly sounded, then everyone to the individual invoked the name of God and broke his fast with water and fresh dates in the traditional manner of the Prophet some fourteen hundred years ago.

I break my fast on a date and proceed with my makeshift repast, washing it down with a shot of Arabic coffee and refreshing gulps of the beloved Zamzam water whose purity and crystalline taste cannot be matched from any other well in the world. The thought crosses my mind that saying the prayer amidst this wreckage of food and drink, orange rinds and plastic cups, could be a problem. I had not accounted, however, for the planning and ingenuity of those responsible for this brief repast. Within minutes, our host for this little section of the mosque and his aids descend upon the rows depositing the leftover bread, dates, and fruit into great plastic bags reserved for the task. Once done, the entire assemblage of waste is carefully gathered up within the folds of the plastic floor cloth, which summarily disappears down the row and out of sight of the worshippers. The entire mosque had been restored to an ordered cleanliness in less than the minute it took me to dislodge my aging bones from the floor and stand together with the other worshippers in well defined rows to offer our sunset prayer.

If the world and all that it contains is woven from the stuff of which shadows are made, and if man is a transient and exile disconnected from his true self—a prodigal in search of his ancestral hearth—then this journey to the holy places that begins sitting cross-legged on a carpet with a million other aspirants and breakfasting together on water and dates becomes transformed into the true journey to that final abode of which the revelation speaks. In partaking of a revealed tradition, one gains entry into a world of vision and light; it is a reality woven of the stuff of which not shadows but threads of light are made. It makes demands on us as in the discipline of the Ramadan fast, but in compensation, its vision and light becomes a part of one's inner world and leads a person beyond the borders of his or her natural shadow self.

I look around at the sea of humanity surrounding me and think to myself: there is power here. The other earthly duties of Islam recall certain qualities and principles unique to each particular duty. The basic testament of faith recalls the serenity that accompanies the knowledge of God. Prayer remembers communication with the Divinity as well as a means of expressing one's innermost thoughts and aspirations. Charity or *zakat* emphasizes the need to remember the poor and needy, while the *hajj* or pilgrimage recreates in a formal ritual the journey of a lifetime. The bodily fast, however, in which the physical senses are tamed through the sheer force of a person's will, contains a subtle message of latent potential power that is impossible to ignore. It is a raw and natural power whose force emerges out of its own defining quality. It is the defining power of wind over water, of water against stone, of fire against wood. It is the creative power of the bud to become the bloom or the transformative power of the caterpillar to become the butterfly, a power whose force is to absorb and potentialize everything that runs to meet it and fall under its sway. It is the power of the word to stir the mind, of the voice to move the emotions, of the feathers of a wing to lift the bird. What, then, of the potential power behind the collective whole to bring themselves together and unite under a single unifying truth with a presence of mind and a determination of spirit, with a strength not only to climb but to move mountains?

As I glance across the carpet at the people around me, words simply fail. There is an aura of silence that underscores the general hubbub produced by such a vast congregation that speaks more than words can possibly convey. Facial expressions and body language, friendly eyes and broad open smiles, a nod of the head, a gesture of offering, these become the modes of expression that cut across all language barriers, culture, race, or nationality. I feel an outpouring of warmth and an emotive melting of the heart, a brotherliness and camaraderie that is impossible to explain or describe. A brief vision crosses my mind of New York and Paris and Kuala Lumpur and Sydney, for I am a well-traveled person and familiar with most of the major cities of the world. I have seen New York's Statue of Liberty and Paris' Eiffel Tower. I have climbed the Petronas Towers in Kuala Lumpur and listened to the arias of the Sydney Opera House echo across the Sydney harbor. Nothing, however, can match this staggering spectacle for its sheer magnitude, for the raw projection of a mass of humanity as a single spirit, and the sense of sacred purposefulness that emanates through the broad expanse of the mosque.

Having finished the sunset prayer in congregation with the fellow worshippers, I take my leave of the Prophet's mosque and proceed back out into the grand concourse together with the other streams of humanity who are now set on going about their business at hand. As I disappear back into the vast throng from whence I came, I notice once again the pale and ponderous moon climbing back over the horizon; a full moon, no less, for this is the mid-point of Ramadan, wearily raising its saffron face beyond the broad porch of the horizon to set up vigil once again over the faithful. It is a breezy mid-November evening, one day in the *ayam Allah* (the days of Allah), in the holy month of Ramadan 1424 A.H.[8] (2003 A.D.), in Madinah al-Munawwarah, the City of Light.

[8] The Muslims begin their lunar calendar from the year of the Hegira, when the Prophet Muhammad fled Makkah for Madinah seeking refuge from members of the Quraish Tribe who were his avowed persecutor and enemy.

# 10. Swept Away in the City of Peace

> And when We made the House a pilgrimage for men and a (place of) security, and appoint for yourselves a place of prayer on the station of Abraham. And We enjoined Abraham and Ishmael saying: Purify My House for those who visit (it) and those who abide (in it) for devotion and those who bow down (and) those who prostrate themselves. (2:125)

On a mid-November morning during the holy month of Ramadan in the year of the Hegira 1424 (2003 A.D.), I made the final leg of my *umrah* (lesser pilgrimage) journey overland through the black hills of Northern Saudi Arabia. By the time I arrived in Makkah that afternoon, a terrorist bomb had blasted its way through a residential area of Riyadh, destroying an apartment block housing expatriate Arab nationals and killing scores of people including many women and children. Under normal circumstances, if such a concept as normality can be invoked within this context of random terrorism, it is difficult to take in and fully appreciate the enormity of such an atrocity. Under the circumstances of that afternoon as I entered what the Quran refers to as the city of peace and security (3:96) in addition to being the "mother of all cities," it was difficult to reconcile the tragic slaughter and random violence in Riyadh and the prayers and aspirations of those circumambulating the Kaaba, the central focus of the Grand Mosque in Makkah.

In Islam, there are powerful indications concerning what are called in the Islamic Traditions (*Hadith*) the "signs of the hour" (*alamat as-sa'a*), meaning signs of the end of the world as we know it. Surely the image of suicide killers invoking scriptural justifications of a religion for their own diabolic purposes and acting in the name of God by boldly murdering innocent victims for some kind of political or social agenda has got to be a sign of the hour and a warning that the end of a world order as we know it is near, if not already at hand? Interestingly, one of the signs of the very end will be a cessation of the circumambulation around the sacred house in the sanctuary known in Arabic as the *Haram*. One of the *Hadith* forewarns, "Know that the world has come to an end when no one will circumambulate the holy Kaaba."

When my companions and I climbed onto the bus early that Saturday morning to make our way from Madinah to Makkah, a journey that the Prophet himself made with his companions, upon them blessings and peace, when they made their own first pilgrimage toward the end of his life, we had no idea of the devastation that had taken place many miles away in the capital of Saudi Arabia. Most of us had already had a foretaste of trouble, however, in a recent news item in which a shootout had taken place in Makkah where a number of terrorists were killed by the Saudi militia and a large cache of weapons had been discovered. In Makkah no less, the beloved "mother of all cities" of the Muslims and the city referred to as *al-Mukarramah*, "the Generous," security was very tight and 5,000 military personnel had been sent to further protect the pilgrims from any further outrage. It is a far different world now than the world I knew many years ago when I visited the holy places of Islam and first laid virgin eyes on the Grand Mosque and the central issue of the Kaaba. According to a verse of the Quran, "Allah hath appointed the Kaaba, the Sacred House, as a standard for mankind" (5:97).

Just as one greets the Prophet and sends forth one's *salaams* as the first gesture of respect on a visit to *al-Masjid al-Nabawi* in Madinah, so also I return to the tomb of the Prophet on the morning of my departure for Makkah, to send forth once again my sincere *salaams* together with the final prayers and intercessions on behalf of my close friends and loved ones. It is a melancholy leave-taking indeed. Once again, I make my way through the densely packed mosque after the early morning *fajr* prayer, deep into the inner sanctum of the original mosque that was once the actual living quarters of the Prophet. The visit here in this mosque and at the tomb of the beloved Messenger of Allah has become such a personal encounter that it is difficult to bid farewell without feeling some deep inner melancholy, as if leaving behind a valued treasure or taking leave of someone you know you will never see again, even though Muslims try to carry an awareness of the Prophet in their hearts by actively following his example in their own lives. I feel close to him here as never before and have experienced on this visit a deep inner connection that somehow transcends the normal course of life. It is a nearness and proximity to the Messenger who is the "friend" of God that I hope to take with me and preserve as a treasured remembrance after I leave.

Typically, the start of any journey always involves some kind of separation and loss intermingled with the sweet anticipation of departure and journeying, and this leave-taking is no exception. Back in the hotel, my companions and I don the traditional garment (*ihram*) worm by the pilgrims to Makkah either in the *hajj* season or at any other time of year when the "lesser pilgrimage" (*umrah*) is made. The distance between Madinah and Makkah is roughly 430 kilometers, a mere 260 miles by Western standards, but it is an overland journey through rough and harsh terrain. The makeshift plan of our guides organizing the bus trip calls for an early morning departure in order to arrive in Makkah in due time to fulfill the pilgrimage duties before the breaking of the fast and the sunset prayer.

The sense of timing, the pace and the rhythm in the Arab world, however, does not abide by the fixed and firm rigidity of time, place, and movement that one finds in the Western world. Flexibility is the name of the day among Arabs and one learns to flow with the contingencies of the moment and place. As for myself, I had donned the *ihram* garment, a seamless two piece cloth that was towel-like in texture, a kind of makeshift shawl for the upper torso that is thrown over the shoulders, and a kind of wrap-around sarong for the lower torso. Nothing else can or may be worn as one enters the sacred precinct in the pure condition of birth, having of course made the ritual ablution and announced his or her intentions beforehand. For reasons of safety and practicality, a special belt may be worn with secret pockets for money and identity cards that firmly secures the lower portion of the garment against untoward accidents. They say that clothes make the man, but as I sat in the front lobby of the Sheraton Hotel in Madinah early that morning awaiting the other pilgrims to meet the appointed hour of departure, bundled together in my shaggy cloth towels, I felt altogether a man of serenity and repose filling these traditional garments. In some strange sense, it seemed as if the garments themselves, steeped in tradition and symbolic of the neutrality of any kind of fashion, were wearing the man.

The modern overland coach departed around 9:00 am, several hours after the early morning appointment scheduled for 6:00 am, but who could possibly care about establishing a fixity in the fluid nature of time? We were together and on our way, sacred wanderers on an ancient pilgrimage taking us back in time to the house that Allah built, not fourteen centuries ago during the time of the Prophet, but several millennia back during the time of Abraham. According to the Quran (2:125), the Kaaba is the house that Abraham himself built, although apocryphal traditions suggest that Adam was the original architect of this "first sanctuary" (3:96) of worship. Here in the heart of a craggy desert wasteland lies the symbolic nucleus of the Islamic religion and the very direction and focal point of all prayer. The sense of direction and place plays an important role in the liturgy of Islam as well as in the human dynamic of its spirituality. The Messenger is the prototype exile as well as the model Muslim and this gives added intensity to the concept that man himself is an exile from his true abode and a transient in search of a final destination. The *mihrab* or sacred niche of every mosque worldwide points in the direction of the Kaaba in the Grand Mosque in Makkah. All prayer makes a symbolic horizontal journey across the globe to the very center of the earth whence the universal aspiration and worship of the Muslims makes an abrupt vertical ascent heavenward, reaching beyond the stars and galaxies toward the celestial horizon of the known universe.

We had hardly left the ragged edges of the city behind and not yet entered the famous hills surrounding Madinah when we made our first stop at the mosque that is traditionally considered the traditional changing ground into the pilgrim's *ihram* cloth. These traditions go back to the time of the Prophet who put on his *ihram* at this stage of the journey. The group I was with dispersed and people made their own way to the mosque to make the ritual of two prostrations in anticipation of the journey ahead. Once this was accomplished, the bus began to make its way into the black hills of Northern Arabia in earnest. It is a stark landscape indeed, uninviting, harsh, and blindingly bright. There is something hypnotic and mesmerizing about the austere setting of the desert. Its arid, uncompromising starkness is set in sharp contrast to the pristine purity and clarity of vision that the bleak landscape affords in compensation. One cannot ignore the sublime signposts and symbols of nature along the way: the infernal bright sun halfway up the heavens already—even the winter sun in the desert makes no compromises and sends its relentless rays of light down onto the open dusty plain without mercy; a dying full moon that was losing its pale early morning edge; the meta-symbolic image of the horizon itself, encircling everything within the envelope of a bi-polar universe of Heaven and earth and containing the message of an inscrutable mystery in what lies "beyond." Across the distinctive and seemingly endless desert landscape, the horizon traces a thin line between Heaven and Earth and marks the defining edge of the known world; beyond lies the mystique of a deep, dark secret.

We have made our intentions to perform the lesser pilgrimage, flown to Saudi Arabia, visited the Prophet's Mosque in Madinah, and journeyed across the heartland of Arabia in remembrance of the journey of the Prophet 1400 years ago, but nothing truly prepares the mind and heart for the overwhelming sight of the Grand Mosque in Makkah on physical, emotional, and spiritual levels of experience. Makkah itself is an ancient, craggy landscape of jagged, rocky, and uncompromising hills. The road leading into the city feels like a roller coaster ride and the view of cascading hills, houses, and shops precariously lodged along the cliffs is unexpected and disorienting. Then suddenly, the bus crests the top of a craggy knoll and the vision of the gray, white, and pink marbled edifice comes into view like a mirage from some heavenly realm. It is difficult to take in the colossal edifice all at once: its multiple minarets soaring toward the heavens, the massive three-storied structure that has been renovated and enlarged over recent decades in a monumental effort by the Saudi government to accommodate hundreds of millions of pilgrims every year, its incredible bulk wedged uncomfortably within the crowded central valley of Makkah. Surely there is no other physical edifice now existing on earth that can measure up to and compete with this incredible feat of architecture and the symbolic meaning it intends to serve?

A higher reality predominates over the physical reality of the Grand Mosque. Herein lies the very center and heart of the Islamic cosmos. This simple cube of masonry,[1] a form of proto-art that traces its roots through Abraham back to the primordial era of Adam, is the central axis where Heaven meets earth and where the Divine meets the human. Across the globe, the Islamic rites and spiritual practices, in every mosque and in the hearts of every devout Muslim, form a directional pattern that leads directly to the Kaaba in Makkah, which is the earthly reflection of a celestial shrine, which is also reflected

[1] The Kaaba is a small square building made of stones, about 60 feet long, 60 feet wide and 60 feet high. The four corners roughly face the four directions of the compass. The building, made from gray-blue stones from the nearby hills of Makkah, is covered with the Kiswa, a black brocade cloth that has the Islamic testament of faith (*shahadah*) woven into its fabric and embossed gold-lettered calligraphy as adornment.

within the heart of man. The inherent symbolism of the Kaaba as center of the human being and vertical axis beyond the earthly dimension, creates a feeling of sacred space and sacred time, a coming into the Presence through the sacralization of space. The circumambulation of the Sacred House as a physical reality raises the consciousness of a person to a rarefied spiritual universe as the Kaaba of the human heart meets the central Kaaba of the Divine Reality.

The many-sided circular structure of the Grand Mosque itself gives way to an open-air concourse that is touched by heaven and encircled by the angels, at least so it seems but Allah knows best. The symbolism of the building bespeaks of centrality and the primordial point. At the very center of this sublime nexus rests the Kaaba, while ecstatic pilgrims circumambulate the ancient house like stars circumambulating around the nexus of a galaxy in magisterial procession.[2] The house is the sacred symbolic structure here on the earth that mirrors the empyrean above, with devout pilgrims forever swirling in a steady stream of praise to the one God. To enter this circumambulating vortex of humanity is like no other earthly experience imaginable.

Upon arrival in Makkah, we exit the comfort of the bus and are brusquely thrust into a horde of pilgrims milling outside the mosque. Unexpectedly, we hear the call of the *adhan* pierce through the dull murmur of the crowd like a cosmic cry from heaven signifying the mid-afternoon prayer as we make our way into the mosque through the *Bab al-Salaam*, the portal through which the Prophet traditionally entered the sacred sanctuary. I write "we," not as a literary convention or reference to the group I was with, but as a gesture of conciliation to my faithful companion, Amr, an Egyptian Lab Technician and colleague who had adopted me as his trusted friend on the pilgrimage. Many years living in the Arab world has taught me the wisdom of never doing anything alone, unlike the tendency in the Western world where people maintain a fierce sense of individuality and tend to follow an independent line of action on their own if at all possible. I

[2] A point of interest: the circumambulation is in an anti-clockwise direction. This is in keeping with a similar pattern found in nature, including the electrons around the nucleus, the movement of the earth around the sun, and the movement of the stars around the central core of the galaxy.

have learned from Arabs the joys of companionship. They make an emotional commitment once they accept you as one of their own, and I have learned to give of myself in return, something which does not come naturally to me, possibly as a result of my upbringing in the West with its emphasis on independence and self-reliance. While I was the senior in age and rank—and according to the hyperbolic Amr a person who would gain immediate access to the Paradise on the Day of Judgment due to my status as "Muslim convert"—I still deferred to his judgment and common sense, not to mention the kind generosity of self and protective brotherliness that he freely extended to me. I don't think he realized just how reliant a person I really was in this situation, a stranger in a strange land, and dependent on his good will and friendship to help me through the challenging rituals before us.

As we entered the mosque and made our way toward the magnetic draw of the rhythmic mass of people circumambulating the Kaaba, I was becoming increasingly alarmed. The crowds were overwhelming and I was beginning to wonder, as I wrestled with my unfamiliar and ill-fitting garments, whether we would be able to find a place, indeed some special place in the shadow of the Kaaba, where we could say the afternoon prayer with serenity before performing the *umrah.* Various aisles were still open to people moving in and around the sanctuary and Amr suggested that we position ourselves right there in the aisle in view of the Kaaba when in a matter of minutes all motion would stop and the prayer would commence. In fact, the mosque was jam-packed with not a free space to be found. The heat even in November can be oppressive and I thought of those in the open courtyard under the intensity of the late afternoon desert sun. There in the shade, as I made my prostrations during the prayer (*salat al-asr*), I was sweating profusely and my heart began to beat erratically. I had been fasting since predawn with no food or water and felt a little dehydrated, dizzy, and concerned about my ability to fulfill the requirements of the rites; but the motions of the ritual prayer and the intensity of the situation, together with the presence of my friend nearby, guided me through the difficulties of the moment.

Amr's broad, respectful, village-boy smile greeted me upon the completion of the prayer. We were now to perform the sacred rituals of the "lesser pilgrimage" that date back to the time of the Prophet fourteen hundred years ago. It is interesting to note that the rituals themselves transcend the time of the Islamic Messenger and refer in their essence and symbolism to the Abrahamic era, shifting the focus of the rites beyond the inception of the religion of Islam proper to a more universal setting and significance with the patriarch Abraham as the symbolic father of the prophets.[3] Essentially there are three main duties to be performed according to the dictates of the lesser pilgrimage and these include the circumambulation seven times around the Kaaba in an anti-clockwise direction with the Kaaba on the left, followed by prayer at the Station (*maqam*) of Abraham,[4] and finally the *saiy* which consists in running seven times between the hills of Safa and Marwa. We hoped to negotiate our way through these rituals together with the vast congregation of *umrah* pilgrims and complete the *umrah* before the sunset prayer and breaking of the fast.

With affection and open eagerness, Amr took my arm and led me through the confusion of the crowd toward the swirling orbit of people moving about the Kaaba in a steady stream of worship and spiritual rapture. "We need to get as close to the Kaaba as possible," he whispered urgently in my ear. No sacramental dictate required us to get as close as possible to the Kaaba, yet custom and tradition suggested proximity to the structure if possible. I also knew that Amr harbored a secret desire to kiss the black stone, said to be a meteorite fallen from Heaven that is lodged in a silver encasement in the east corner of the cubic structure which marks the place of commencement of the *tawaf* or circumambulation.

No Muslim who has made *hajj* or *umrah* will deny that the circumambulation is a physical experience that takes stamina and will power. When you view the scene from the roof of the Grand Mosque or witness the event through TV cameras hoisted on high, it gives every appearance of being a rhythmic stream of humanity flowing in sublime unison around the central axis of the world. However, the reality of being amid this throbbing, densely packed mob is tumultuous and unpredictable and yet all the while nobody seems to care

[3] Indeed, it is a sad legacy that the Jews and the Muslims, who trace their Semitic line back to the great patriarch Abraham through his two sons Ishmael and Isaac and whose symbolic value still conveys a profound meaning to the world's population, are such bitter enemies in today's world.

[4] Inside the Station of Abraham is kept a stone bearing the prints of two human feet. The Prophet Abraham is said to have stood on this stone when building the Kaaba and the marks of his feet are miraculously preserved.

about the tumult around them or complain about the crush of people. Upon entering the throng, you lose your sense of personal identity and personal space and become one with the teeming horde moving about the symbolic vision of the ancient edifice and focusing all your hopes and aspirations on the reality of the Divine Being in a state of ecstatic rapture.

Entering the ritual practice of circumambulation is like entering into the "once upon a time" of myths and folktales, *in illo tempore.* The pilgrim enters into sacred time that is actually the "real" time of the "vertical" or eternal dimension, as opposed to the horizontal, linear, and progressive time that we experience here on earth as a relentless, forward-moving machine. I fell immediate victim to this sublime transcendent state of mind as if by some remote control of heaven and felt at one with the rotating vortex of the crowd. I no longer seemed to matter as an individual entity for I had been swept away in this "first sanctuary" to a primordial time of perfection and heightened consciousness when the truth is there to behold, there to witness, and there to be known as nothing else can be known. As I circumambulate the sacred Kaaba, I make my entreaties, I send my greetings, I pray to Allah and worship the Divinity. Soon enough, beyond all reckoning of time, I am truly swept away by a flood of emotion and higher sentiment as I become one with the wave of worshippers. Indeed, I feel myself giving up and surrendering to this moment of eternity in time and this central place that makes possible the ascent of man beyond the horizon of the rational mind and beyond the dictates of the lower self.

Amr has managed to seize a seven beaded cord resting on the wall by the Station of Ishmael along one side of the Kaaba with which to keep track of the seven circumambulations that are required of the *tawaf* ritual, although how he has managed this feat is anyone's guess as he grins sheepishly at me with the beaded cord. Our arms are locked together for security as we make our way round and round within the circumference of the sacred precinct. I am happy to have this fellow with me as we make the circumambulation in communion with the Spirit of God that overshadows the environment. It feels as though I have known him for a thousand years.

Perhaps it is the writer and natural-born observer in my nature, but I unconsciously take the time to notice the behavior and movement of the people around me. Everyone seems solicitous of the other's safety and comfort, although admittedly the movement around the Kaaba is far from harmonious at ground zero. It takes effort just to keep standing and one is literally carried forward on tiptoes by the mob pressing in on every side. Still, no one exaggerates the hectic quality of the procession and everyone seems to be trying to defer to the person nearby. Of course, there is every size, shape, and color of person to be imagined in this vast horde of humanity. I see the elderly and the young, husbands and wives, fathers, sons, and daughters. There are groups of women clinging together for safely and surprisingly strong as they race past me. There are groups of men, from Iran, from Ethiopia, from Malaysia, from China, arms linked together in a chain for support. People of all races and nationalities are praying aloud, uttering in Arabic the Quranic epithets and litanies that are appropriately noted for the occasion, entreaties to Allah for health, for blessing, for provision, for the *hasanat* or good things of this and the next world. The elderly and the crippled are being carried in litters overhead on the hands of husky black Africans; others are being moved along in wheelchairs by family members or friends. In one shocking instance, I felt a rustle at my feet and upon looking down toward the marble floor of the enclosure, I see to my horror amid the disorder of moving legs a crippled woman crawling along in circumambulation on all fours with a look of determination and joy on her face.

I cling to my Egyptian friend Amr for stamina and support, approaching an age when I can call myself elderly and fearful of falling down and being overrun by this juggernaut of moving humanity. On the sixth round, a way close to the wall of the house suddenly opens, seemingly miraculously, for both Amr and I noticed that the agitated waters of humanity we were among have unexpectedly opened a path to give free passage to the vicinity of the *Hajar al-Aswad* or the beloved black stone. I think to myself that Amr and I are of one accord.

Under normal circumstances, it is well-nigh impossible to get anywhere near this sacred artifact for the crowds that are clambering to touch and kiss the holy object. Amr suddenly sees the opportunity and makes his move, veering toward the black stone and dragging me alongside with him. We are immediately engulfed once again by the teeming throng of people surrounding the stone and only footsteps away from touching the sacred object. I look up and see Amr standing by the silver frame of the black stone grinning broadly with satisfaction. I knew that he has achieved his goal and has touched the stone. I try to lean forward and extend my arm as far as possible in the direction of the blessed object, but I simply cannot move another inch forward. I am about to give up the effort and blend back into the wave when I feel a hand seize my wrist and move it down into the framed enclosure wherein resides the *Hajar al-Aswad.* It is the swift movement of Amr's powerful grip that has made this possible. For a second, I feel the cool, electric presence of the stone run up through my arm and down into my soul and I smell the unearthly fragrance of the Paradise evoking a memory of some primal purity and perfection amid the chaos of the moment. Then, we are both summarily thrown beyond the area of the building containing the black stone by the crowd surging forward around the corner, whence we raise our right hands to greet the Divinity one last time before commencing the final *tawaf* around the Kaaba.

Once this sacred ritual is completed, we ease our way out from the surging mass and make our way over to the Station of Abraham where we find a small area to make the traditional two prostrations. After that, the traditions allude to the ritual of drinking and refreshing oneself with the Zamzam water, spring water that dates back to the time of Abraham. According to the Islamic traditions, Hajar, one of the wives of Abraham, was searching within the area of the Kaaba for water for her son Ishmael. In her desperation, she ran seven times between the two hills of Safa and Marwa[5] adjacent to the precinct of the Kaaba. She eventually discovered the waters of Zamzam flowing from under a rock and began to drink. In commemoration of this hardship, the pilgrims run seven times between the hills of Safa and Marwa[6] and refresh themselves with the Zamzam waters. Indeed, after the ordeal of the *tawaf*, which we undertook in the afternoon under the blazing glare of the relentless desert sun,[7] the waters

[5] The distance between the two hills is about 500 yards.

[6] "Behold! Safa and Marwa are among the symbols of Allah. So if those who visit the House in the season or at other times should compass them round, it is no sin in them. And if any one obeyeth his own impulse to good, be sure that Allah is He Who recognizeth and knoweth" (2:158).

[7] Most notably, the marble floor of the precinct contains special cooling metals to prevent the soles of the feet from being scorched by the intense heat of the sun.

of Zamzam were unbelievably refreshing—not to drink of course because we were still fasting, but to pour over our heads and faces.

The final ritual calls for the pilgrims to run seven times between the Makkah hills of Safa and Marwa in remembrance of the ordeal of Hajar and the infant Ishmael. To that end, the Saudi government has constructed an enclosure between the two hills in the form of a two-storied hallway adjacent to the Grand Mosque proper. It is a magnificent setting of a two-way hallway enclosure with two tracks running down the middle to accommodate wheelchairs and litters. As Amr and I undertake this final ritual of the lesser pilgrimage, we enter once again the vast crowd of pilgrims similarly recommemorating the ordeal of Hajar and her son. It is difficult to recreate within this magisterial setting adjacent to the Kaaba the dry, dusty terrain amid two now famous hills in which the wife of the patriarch experienced her desperation, although anyone who has lived in Saudi Arabia knows just how hot it can get in that country. Even now, several millennia later, it is not an easy task even in this sublime setting. After running a number of times through the concourse of these two hills, both Amr and I are feeling hot and tired and thirsty. Perhaps it was appropriate that we were still fasting and had been fasting from food and drink since before dawn because it added to the rigor and poignancy of the moment. We finally completed the tiring trek back and forth seven times in keeping with the tradition which considers seven a sacred number in the science of numerology associated with the Islamic traditions.

The final act of the pilgrimage upon completion of the *saiy* is the cutting of the hair. The Prophet advised either shaving the head or cutting a part of the hair and to that end there are multiple barbershops ready with straight-edged razors to service the pilgrim community. Both Amr and I decide to trim each other's hair, however, for the sake of convenience. We have both had our heads shaved on the former occasion of the greater *hajj* a number of years ago. Hot, tired, and feeling emotionally drained after the effort of the sacred rites, which have taken us nearly two hours, we obligingly snip off various locks of hair from each side of the head including the crown. We then depart the mosque enclosure in silence and climb the stairs leading up the side of the mountain encroaching upon the back side of the Grand Mosque to make our way to a nearby hotel.

Upon completion of the lesser pilgrimage, the rest of the visit seemed to flow in the wake of its afterglow. Exhausted but exhilarated though we were, Amr and I still had a busy schedule ahead of us. We had only a few minutes until the call of the *adhan* for the sunset prayer (*salat al-maghreb*) and the breaking of the fast and we needed to check into the hotel, change out of the pilgrim cloth (*ihram*), wash and present ourselves at the Grand Mosque once again. Later that evening, after the fifth and final prayer—which occurs at the point of total darkness after the sunset—there occurs the traditional Ramadan prayers called *al-tarawiyah*. At best, many non-Muslims think that the holy month of Ramadan calls for the Muslims to fast from dawn to dusk. What they may not realize is that in addition to the fast, the month involves added austerities including special prayers and night vigils that have been enjoined by the Prophet. The *al-tarawiyah* prayers call for twenty *rakaa'* or prostrations during which a full *juz* or part of the Quran is recited.[8] During the last ten days of Ramadan, additional night vigils take place in the early morning hours before dawn, which are witnessed by the angels.[9]

After a hurried breaking of the fast and a few moments to refresh in the hotel, we made our way back into the Grand Mosque for the night prayers. Lest the reader need reminding, movement in and out of the mosque at any time requires negotiation through vast crowds of people. At the prayer times, it is advised to be well ensconced some-

[8] There are 30 *juz* in the Quran. Each of them is of equal length comprising 20 pages of text in a standard publication. Reciting a *juz* each night during the *al-tarawiyah* ensures that the entire Quran will be recited by the faithful during Ramadan. In addition, many Muslims read a part of the Quran per day on their own as part of their spiritual efforts and to earn the blessings that are associated with Quran recitation during the holy month of Ramadan.

[9] The Night of Power (*al-Laylat al-Qadr*) takes place on one of the nights during the last ten days of Ramadan. It is a night, according to the Quran, that is "better than a thousand months" when the angels and the Spirit of God descend to earth with Allah's permission. The Prophet was not specific about when precisely the blessed night occurs, alluding in his sayings (*hadith*) to an odd numbered day and hinting at possibly the twenty-seventh night of Ramadan. Consequently, the last ten days of Ramadan are traditionally held in reserve for supererogatory prayers and spiritual disciplines.

where within the inside enclosure and inner concourse of the mosque in front of the Kaaba, otherwise it is just about impossible to get inside the mosque itself. Amr and I decide to attend the evening prayers on the roof of the mosque. I have been told that at any one time, the mosque itself can hold over a million people by rough estimates. The mosque enclosure includes the ground floor area of building and open courtyard within, a second floor, and a roof with a capacity for hundreds of thousands of worshippers.

We make our way along the roof of the hallways that connect the hills of Safa and Marwa where we earlier had performed one of the rites of the pilgrimage. As we move forward along the roof through a narrow passageway together with a steady stream of pilgrims with the same intentions that we have, I notice row upon row of people already positioned on carpets laid down on the roof for purposes of the prayer. Amr and I hope to reach a point on the roof close to the open concourse with the vision of the Kaaba in front of us as we recite our prayers. Alas, we find a place close to the edge of the roof where we can say these special prayers—which take nearly two hours—in comfort, but we do not have a direct view of the Kaaba. Instead, from this vantage point on the roof, we have a panoramic view of the entire Grand Mosque, including the rest of the roof, the second and ground floor, and the open plaza in the middle of this ensemble containing the Kaaba and the orbiting mass of humanity that continues day and night with its circumambulation. There must have been a million or more worshippers gathered together at that moment to offer their *tarawiyah* prayers.

The imam of the Grand Mosque leads the prayer and recites the appropriate Quranic verses. At the Quranic injunctions that occur during the movement of bowing and prostration, there is the voice of the imam followed by the voice of a human echo, in keeping with an early tradition before the era of microphones that had a second voice mid-way in the mosque echo the calls of the imam in distant areas of the mosque where the imam could not be heard.

We took our places, heard the call to prayer, and began the ceremony of prayer as the evening passed into night. During this night vigil time itself fades away, together with the individual, just as day eventually fades away into night. You stand, you bow, you prostrate yourself with forehead touching the ground—considered in Islam the position of most profound humility and the moment when a person is closest to Allah—and you no longer understand yourself as you know yourself to be in normal times. As time goes on, there is a stripping away of all the cares of the world, the mind becomes free of the psychological complexes and knots that unceasingly worry it during the course of the day, and the soul takes on the wings of the dove as it soars above the cares of the self and the world. A feeling of attachment develops that springs from the deep well of desire in which everything matters because it reminds you of God, followed by a profound feeling of detachment that enters the higher consciousness of mind like a wind moving through fields of wheat, a detachment in which nothing matters except God.

I look out onto the world momentarily during this spiritual reverie to witness the scene around me. The rugged Makkan hills are clearly visible all around the mosque enclosure. Various hotels and palaces loom from the distance over the sanctuary. I see the bowed heads of a million strong people in front of, in back, indeed all around me, who have come together as one community with one aspiration and one goal. The voice of the imam cuts through the layers of the night like the sound of a reverberating bell, cold and clear and full of latent power. It rocks the surrounding area in a wave of amplification that reverberates outward into the night sky aglitter with distant stars. The imam intones the sacred words of the Quran, what the Muslims believe to be the actual Words of Allah, throughout the mosque enclosure, and their amplification moves through the congregation standing in rows with hands folded and heads bowed, through the rooftops of the city and out into the surrounding hills of this "mother" of cities. An intense, electrifying light floods the mosque and open concourse of the interior. As I look toward this primordial point which houses the Kaaba from my vantage point on the roof, it seems as though an unearthly illumination moves vertically heavenward from this center of the earth, a monumental beacon of light reaching to touch the heavens as a symbolic visual representation of the aspirations of the worshippers.

Through sound and light, there seems to be a visionary outpouring toward the heavens that is matched perhaps only by the psychic and spiritual outpouring of the minds and hearts of the worshippers. This sound and light experience electrifies the worshippers—perhaps I should speak for myself alone—with a feeling of devotional rapture, heightened by the onslaught of the words of revelation that not only echo through the night sky but that reverberate their tonal vibrations down into the very texture and fabric of the human body. Many people may not realize the importance that Quranic recitation has during the prayer ritual. The essence of the prayer is praise and worship of the Divinity and the essence of the worship is the recitation of the sacred sound of the Quran because of its ability to transport the listener through the psalmody of the chanter into another dimension of reality altogether.

The chanted Quran is the prototype of all sacred sound. It is a kind of divine music that overlays a person's soul with a knowledge of origins and provides the guidance that will lead him in the right direction on his way of return to God. "The first words of the Sacred Text revealed by Gabriel surrounded the Prophet like an ocean of sound as the archangel himself filled the whole of the sky. The sound of the Quran penetrates the Muslim's body and soul even before it appeals to his mind. The sacred quality of the psalmody of the Quran can cause spiritual rapture even in a person who knows no Arabic."[10] The Quran contains a majesty, a harmony, and a rhythm that pours out from the sound of the sacred text and cannot be translated without seriously altering the nature of the profound sacredness that emanates from the letters and sounds. There is a majestic projection of sound that is primordial, central, and eternal; primordial in that the sound and meaning resorts back to its original source in the Divine Mind; central because it brings man immediately back from the periphery of his earthly existence to the very center of his being; eternal because it lifts a person out of earthly and horizontal time to the vertical dimension of the eternal now, the sacred present, that neutralizes and ultimately transcends the temporal march of time with its window to eternity.

By the end of the special *al-tarawiyah* prayers several hours later and after this visionary outpouring of sound and light, the inner heart, that inner sanctuary that is the spiritual counterpart to the physical cardiac heart, feels expanded, open, and full to bursting. All of the sacred symbolic images that the traditional literature uses in speaking about the capacity of the heart to contain the Divinity come to mind to describe the feeling upon completion of the *tarawiyah* prayers. If the heart is a cup, it is now filled to brimming; if it is a hidden cave, it

[10] S. H. Nasr (ed.), *Islamic Spirituality*, p. 4.

is now filled with light; if it is a sacred crypt, its secret is now revealed; if it is the seal of the intelligence, it now sees with a clear certainty; if it is a holy niche, it is now cast in the glow of some higher emotion impossible to describe.

As Amr and I gathered up our individual prayer carpets and as the bulk of the dense crowd was beginning to thin out and leave, I suggested that we make our way now to the edge of the roof so that we could look down upon the inner plaza of the Grand Mosque. As we leaned over the railing and gazed down reflectively upon the scene below, I felt a great filling of soul and spirit. I remember the tradition that the sight of the Kaaba is a form of worship; I remind myself by saying the words; I hear Amr telling me the same and the mind registers the fact and concedes its truth. Yet the reality of the experience cannot be contained by words, cannot be fully comprehended by the mind, cannot be actively taken into the soul by the will. It simply happens without cognition or force. The two of us stand there as if hypnotized. We take in the sight; we behold the vision of the Kaaba *in situ*; we meet it face-to-face and in person. And a small miracle happens. We do not enter the house, not literally and not figuratively, instead the Kaaba enters us to become the Kaaba of the mind and heart, a spontaneous outpouring of pure emotion from the human to the Divine, the final emotion if you will from the human soul to the Spirit of God.

It may seem odd to report that I was counting the hours to my departure in the style of those who do not want something to end, this being perhaps a kind of prefiguration of the desire to experience eternity. In fact, there was very little time left in the holy places. My group had arrived in Makkah on Saturday afternoon after having spent two blessed days in Madinah. The *umrah* rituals on Saturday were now complete; I had the full day of Sunday to spend in the Grand Mosque and I was scheduled to leave on Monday after the noon prayer to return to Abu Dhabi in the United Arab Emirates and take up my duties once again as a professor of academic writing. After the early morning prayer on Monday, I took advantage of a lull in the crowd and the protracted dawn, before the onslaught of the harsh desert sun, to make my "farewell" circumambulation (*tawaf*) around the Kaaba, this time alone among the vast multitude without the aid and support of my Egyptian friend Amr. To facilitate freer movement and because I had the leisure of time, I kept to the outer fringes of the circle this time, creating a longer circuit for myself, but far less tumult than the mayhem in the center closer in proximity to the house.

I will not repeat my experience of the *tawaf* again; only to say that it was as intense and personal as before, perhaps more so, now that I was on my own. I experienced the same heightened awareness and the elevated "God consciousness." I witnessed once again the fervid devotion of the worshippers and the intense configuration of multi-national and multi-racial peoples. I noticed a heightened "military" and security presence inside the Grand Mosque and most notably in and around the Kaaba itself. Standing on the wall of Ishmael[11] were three unarmed officers surveying the crowd. In Makkah, the city of peace and security, so identified in the Quran itself, I would have felt this presence incongruous if it weren't for the shattered reality of a very real threat of terrorism in the world today from which no place seems immune, not even the city of peace.

Because of commitments back in Abu Dhabi, about 14 members of our group had scheduled to return "early." Our Saudia flight was to leave on Monday evening at 6:00 pm. The rest of the 60 odd members of the group were to return the following Wednesday. One would not expect to make a commentary about the weather in Makkah, except perhaps to mention the intense heat experienced there for much of the year. On this mild mid-November Monday, however, the weather was notably "strange." According to Arabs in this part of the world, cloudy weather is "good" weather, while rain is considered a blessing. The sky was overcast with an eerie saffron glow and while there were bundles of angry-looking clouds moving quickly across the heavens, they looked as dry as ashes. The air was blustery and full of dust. As I sat in the mosque most of that morning reading the Quran, feeling transfixed by the presence of the Kaaba in my line of sight and melancholy at the thought of leaving the physical presence of the beloved Kaaba behind in a few hours, I could hear the force of

[11] The graves of Ishmael and his mother Hajar are purportedly within this semi-circular wall.

the wind blowing through the vestibules and hallways of the Grand Mosque, shattering the serenity of the place with echoes of slamming doorways and rattling windows. I could see eddies of dust swirling like ghosts through the worshippers; but I did not care. Nothing mattered but the heightened feelings of spirituality I was experiencing at the moment. I would have time enough after the noontime prayer to come back down to earth and negotiate my way back into the ways of the world.

Indeed, the prayer came and went in a flash; its memory lingered and continues to linger in the mind as a sacred remembrance of the timeless and the eternal. I returned at once to the hotel, making my way out the back and up the stairs carved into the hill to the hotel overlooking the sacred enclosure. I needed to get my things and return immediately to the lobby to board the bus arranged for me and my companions scheduled to make our way on the hour's journey to the Jeddah airport in time enough to escape the worst of the weather and meet the heightened security and airport formalities in time enough for our 6:00 pm flight. I quickly gathered up my belongings and gifts: a few bottles of musk oil, a fragrance mentioned specifically in the Quran as a scent of the paradise and beloved by the Muslims especially at prayer time; a few prayer carpets, possibly made in China, but bought here in the holy city of Makkah and thus highly valued by my Muslim friends and colleagues, and some white skull caps, again highly treasured for their "Makkan" quality, for want of a better term.

When I returned to the lobby around 1:30 that afternoon, there was a great hubbub at the entrance of the hotel. Upon closer inspection, I discovered an unbelievable sight: The day had suddenly and paradoxically turned into night. I looked up at the sky disbelievingly, up and down the street, at the well-lit shops across the street, and the same sight greeted me in the form of an uncanny darkness. People were looking up at the sky wondering where the day had gone. It had the feeling of a total eclipse, for suddenly everyone behaved as if the person next to them were a long lost friend. Portentous events such as this have a mysterious way of making brothers out of perfect strangers. Within minutes, all speculation about the peculiar darkness was resolved when the heavens opened their floodgates. It began to rain sheets of streaming water, the lightning shattering the pitch-blackness of the daytime night, and the thunder rolling across the heavens in competition to the resounding roar of the falling rain on the metal rooftops of nearby shops. This was a storm to behold anywhere, not to mention in Makkah, where it nearly never rains and certainly never quite like this.

Porters ran through the rain toward the massive bus awaiting our passage to the Jeddah airport and unceremoniously threw the luggage stuffed with our precious Makkan gifts into the carriage hold. Grateful in this instance to be dressed simply and wearing plastic sandals, I gathered up my Pakistani pantaloons and ran for the security of the bus that promised to provide the perfect vantage point to view the spectacle of the storm. The other Emiratees of my group followed suit, including the *harem* (the women). Within minutes the doors of the bus were sealed shut and we were on our way. The inside of the bus was aglow with excitement; rain in these places is a rarity and the mood within the bus gave testimony to this unexpected downpour.

The querulous Saudi driver ground the massive touring bus into gear and with a lurch forward we began to make our way deeper into the thickening storm. The excitement inside the bus soon died down with the growing realization that we were heading into trouble. The women were sitting together in the back, the rest of us were interspersed randomly throughout the bus, while I was sitting alone with my thoughts. Undoubtedly, everyone was watching the incredible spectacle of the storm through the bay windows of the bus. Makkah is no easy town to negotiate through even under normal conditions. It is hilly with narrow, difficult-to-navigate streets that link up to main arteries leading out of the city. We eventually made our way through the rain up and down the side streets abreast of the Grand Mosque, all the while noticing the flash flood conditions quickly developing along the side streets and alleyways adjacent to the vicinity of the mosque, itself situated in the central valley of the city. We were making our way around the mosque and heading west to Jeddah, the port city situated on the Red Sea. The gathering floodwaters presumably also had the same idea and were following the dictates of the topography of the land in which flowing waters find their natural course to the sea. In this instance, the gathering flood showed no mercy and made no concession to man, animal, or object as it followed its own natural tendencies and the dictates of its own violence. Within its turgid forces, the flood gathered unto itself everything in its path. I watched spellbound through the window of the bus as the cascading floodwaters gathered strength and rushed through the narrow byways and alleyways along the crevices of the hilly terrain down into the center of town.

As we advanced beyond the fringe of the mosque quarter, the cars alongside were coming into increasing difficulty. The main road was unwittingly receiving the floodwaters and becoming itself a raging torrent. I soon realized that this was going to get worse before it got better. I had visions of watching stories of flash floods on CNN in places like Bangladesh or the flood plains of the Amazon; but this was happening to me, now, here in the desert, in the middle of an arid zone, in Makkah of all places! Was I to be swept away a second time in this beloved city, this time literally? I was beginning to wonder as I sat on the edge of my seat looking out and clouding the window with my hot breath as floodwaters crept higher up the side of the bus.

I saw that the cars on the slip road and the side roads perpendicular to the main road were in trouble. Several on the hill above had been compromised and had washed aside into the gutter like abandoned toys. People were milling about on higher ground, standing in doorways with water up to their waists and looking out from second story windows at the cars below inundated with water. The bus itself made a brave attempt to forge its way through the amassing river, unnatural and diabolical as it all seemed. The cars adjacent to the bus, both on the road and off to the side, were becoming inundated by the floodwaters. The flow down from the Makkan hills was simply too much too soon, and the landscape simply could not accommodate the raging waters. This was quickly becoming a flash flood of monumental proportions.

Through it all, the massive bus, like a great ship at sea, coursed its way through the wild current and cresting waves that came crashing down against the side of the bus from the sidelong rush of water running down the cliffs. First one car, then a second, surged perpendicular to the curb out of their normal direction, the one slamming into the other as the torrential current of the waters crashed into the side door and window of the cars. Another came crashing by and stacked itself up against the gathering build up. The people inside were terrorized; it had all happened so quickly, and with no experience with such matters, they had suddenly become trapped. They couldn't very likely stay where they were and survive and they certainly couldn't leave the car at that point, for they would be swept away in the blink of an eye. I have no notion what happened to them. The huge bus passed them by, and the instant became an immediate memory of how destiny and the forces of nature can invade the serenity of the day.

One describes all this as if this flash flood happened in but a momentary flash. On the contrary, several hours had now passed by; we were still on the bus in the thick of the flood; we had only advanced perhaps a kilometer or two west of the Grand Mosque; torrential rains continued to inundate the area, and it seemed at that point that we could as well have been in no-man's land awash in a sea of swelling tide and not still in the heartland of Makkah in the shadow of the Kaaba. Traffic was stalled everywhere and many cars were fully compromised, even the four-wheel drives. At one point, as we slowly made our way forward along a main artery heading out of town, I noticed several police vehicles by the side of the road where a mini avalanche had occurred. Gallons of water had poured into the gap inundating a number of cars to the extent that you could only see the roofs of the cars surfacing above the waves. The subdued faces of those standing around the police car seemed to convey a sad message.

Only the scenic cruiser we were in continued without fail to advance through the encroaching deluge. The bus driver was having none of this trouble. He cursed heaven and earth, in addition to a multitude of drivers and cars that managed to get in the way of his forward movement. If he could not advance the bus, he turned left or right down a side street to find a way through the morass. When that did not work, he simply revved up the engine and careened across the central strip, almost losing an exhaust in the process. When all else failed, he simply drove down the wrong side of the road waving aside whatever vehicles were still left mobile along the way. The water at this point had reached well over the luggage area and was alarmingly approaching mid-way point, not far from the windows. Still, the driver cursed the weather and swore at the drivers in his way. His crude manner bordered on the humorous, while his insolence toward the weather and the road conditions gave the rest of us courage that we would get through this in one piece. Meanwhile, the engines continue to purr like a kitten; the indomitable bus and its spirited driver still continued to make way through the abandoned cars, the sludge, and the debris, not to mention the still raging waters of the flood.

After three more hours of persistent anxiety, the bus finally escaped from the inner confines of the city and made its way toward the outskirts of the town. The foreboding among the group of us inside the bus had died down, together with the floodwaters, and I noticed a developing party atmosphere along the sides of the road, where people were milling about splashing each other with water and dunking themselves. We were approaching the time of the sunset. We had been fasting throughout the entire ordeal and were still attempting to reach the airport in Jeddah, even though the plane was scheduled to leave in another 15 minutes time.

At the call to prayer, we were still marooned on the bus with nothing to eat. People on the roadside however realized our predicament and sprang into action. The door of the bus and several windows were opened and people threw small cartons of juice, bottles of mineral water, and little cartons stuffed with Makkan dates with which to break the fast. This spontaneous display of quick thinking and perception conveyed to me an intense feeling of camaraderie and brotherhood; to think that people by the side of the road had understood our predicament and come to the aid of a passing bus to feed its passengers, an experience comparable to the breaking of the fast in the Prophet's Mosque in Madinah in terms of power and impact.

At 7:30 that night, an hour and a half after the flight departure time, as we slowed down for security checks on the outskirts of the airport, a message came through on one of the cell phones of an Emiratee who I noticed had been making frantic calls to unknown places that the plane was being held for us, yet another example of the fluid nature that events can often take in the Arab world. An airline representative met us with a walkie-talkie in contact with the plane. Porters were on hand to receive the luggage, which was pulled from the hold of the bus along with the water and sludge that had been deposited by the floodwaters. We were rushed through the airport, our passports were unceremoniously stamped, and we were sent on our way without further delay. As I passed through security, a Saudi guard stopped me and asked where I was from. In the rush of it all, I was a little surprised. "America," I hesitatingly replied, unwilling to come out of my incognito status even for a friendly inquiry, for this is an era when the politics of a person's country can get them into trouble. The man surveyed my Pakistani cloth and roped-tired pantaloons and laughed aloud. "If you're American," he replied in Arabic, "then I'm from the other side of China." On that note, he waved me on with an expression of good-humored disbelief spreading generously across his face, and with the words *salaam alaykum* (peace be with you), I was gone.

I wish I could report that from the plane I saw the great beacon of light emanating from the hallowed precinct of the Grand Mosque, rising heavenward as a visionary seal of my Makkan experience as I did when I first arrived in Madinah; but that was not meant to be. In compensation, I felt within my mind a translucent clarity after five days in the two cities of light and peace, while within my heart the smoldering embers continued to burn of this intense, spiritual sojourn that hopefully will linger a while to illuminate the shadows of my life within the latticework of passing time. This account has been written in remembrance of a unique and memorable visit to the two holy places of Islam, when the body, soul, and spirit of a man made a sacred journey to the very center of the earth, were swept away, and came back again to tell the tale.

# EPILOGUE

## The Spiritual Journey of Our Time

Nothing answers to the question: what is it?
—Jili

Most books end on the last page; this one may linger on for a while after the book is closed. Perennial themes emerge within these pages that witness the mystery of nature's beginning and profess the revelation of a universal secret that would not otherwise be known if it weren't for the beneficence and mercy of the Divine Being who created us. These themes will not begin to fade until we finally slip through a crack in the universe to witness the final reckoning on a day that Islam calls the Day of Religion or the dreaded Day of Judgment in Christian parlance. The waves of spiritual yearning that have filled these pages with their sacred sentiments have risen in a crescendo over the millennia like the echoing waves of distant church bells and will continue to fill the minds and hearts of future seekers of truth until the end of time. It is a message of loss and discovery that plays upon the deepest cord of the human being and that calls forth emotions that wash clean the ancient habits of a fallen human race.

We have commenced this work with reflections on the nature of the Divine Mystery. We will conclude, however, with some final thoughts on the mystery of the Truth. As the Sufi mystic Jili has remarked in the quotation opening this chapter, nothing really answers the existential question that faces all individuals within the course of their lifetime, except perhaps the truth that conquers all.[1] Truth is the summit and center of all knowledge and spiritual practice. Its radiance substantiates all spiritual doctrine, while at the heart of all spiritual experience lies truth's comforting reality. "The Truth comes from thy Lord, so be not of those who doubt" (3:60). Truth as the objective Reality encompasses the entire created universe within its cosmic Face

[1] "Truth is good, not because it is opportune or obviously efficacious, but because it is true, not forgetting that truth coincides with reality and that, therefore, *vincit omnia veritas*" (Frithjof Schuon, *Language of the Self* [Madras: Ganesh & Co., 1959], p. 198).

and, through an expressive and fully developed spirituality within the life of man, truth's verity can become imprinted upon the soul to reflect the human face of the Divine Reality. As the Quran repeatedly asserts, truth will abolish all falsehood and conquer all ignorance, and thus will establish with certitude the cosmic balance to the relativity and transience of this world.

The Divine Mystery must be accessible to the mind of man to the extent that human individuals can open their intellects and their hearts to its intriguing question; yet it must remain fundamentally incomprehensible and mysterious to the mind of man because the Transcendent is incapable of total expression in non-transcendental terms, even if humanity is "capable" of transcending its limitations by virtue of the higher faculties and the capacity of the soul. Thus, while the truth is fully available to man and comprehensible, the mystery conveys itself symbolically as a permanent veil between the world of matter and the world of spirit, between the world without and the world within, between the world of knowing and the world of the unknown (*al-ghaib*). The Divine Mystery, however, is not only denoted by a veil. The fundamental mystery at the heart of all existence confronts us nightly in the symbolic image of the night sky, for example, and conveys at a glance the symbolic meaning of infinitude and eternity whose implicit promise belies all that is secular, mundane, and profane in the finitude and temporality of our world. The mystery as cosmic veil is a fundamental key that lies at the heart of the universe, but as far as man is concerned, it can also serve as a fundamental key.

In fact, Truth could be referred to as the open face of the Divine Mystery. But unlike the Divine Mystery, the full range of truth is completely accessible to man because he possesses an intelligence that is capable of understanding the truth in principle and because he possesses a free will that can turn toward the truth with insight and devotion. The mystery of the truth is woven into the very texture and fabric of life itself whose weft is "no" and whose warp is "yes," and this is none other than the message of denial and affirmation that is encoded within the sacred formula of Islam that claims that there is no truth but the Absolute Truth (*la ilaha illa-Llah*). Truth is therefore represented through the choices that are implicit in the duality of the world. Mankind is truth's representative in this world, the human center in contact with the Cosmic Center and the human balance in a world of impersonal contingencies. Individual thoughts and actions strike up reverberations of the "no" and "yes" of truth within a given lifetime in order to create a melody within the human spirit that reflects the truth at every level of a person's being whenever he or she acts in accordance with truth's truth.

Cosmic questions require human responses. Within man's being lies the perennial potential to respond to life's choices with either "yes" or "no" because this challenge is written into the very fabric of existence. Universal questions require definitive answers on the human level in order for humanity to transcend the limits of the human soul and pass beyond to a higher order of experience and consciousness. From the spiritual point of view, the human response to life's mysterious challenge calls for an initial denial of the lasting value of the "world" and "this life" with a committed "no," followed by the affirmation of the Supreme Being and the Truth that validates all of existence. So important is this fundamental truth that the Religion of Islam has made this doctrine the basic testimony of faith in the one God, including the implicit denial of this world through the words "no god" in order to actively affirm the reality of "but God." In Islam, truth's pivotal point forever plays on this earthly polarity of no and yes, a polarity that lies at the heart of the human entity and whose balance must be achieved in order to escape what the Buddhists call the "round" of this existence.

This affirmation can take shape through the spiritual disciplines that are in effect a kind of celestial loom through which the great fabric of a spiritual life is interwoven. These spiritual rites and rituals are preserved intact within the traditions and continue to guarantee the spiritual influences and graces that emanate downward from Heaven to earth. Revelation and prayer, surrender of the human will combined with perennial remembrance, good works as the counterpoint to clear and inspired thinking, charity and fasting all amount to statements of denial of the body, the mind, and the world, for the sake of the other-worldly alternative implicit in the divine promise and the sacred trust. The experiences of the outer, externalized world constitute the weft of a horizontal and worldly life, while the reality of the one God and His profound truth are the warp of man's inner existence, or the vertical perception that intersects the horizontal plane of earthly experience with its promises and implications of a larger, deeper and more profound existence through a higher consciousness of the one Reality.

Contemporary man still does not realize what is happening to the life of his time, but he does seem to realize that the road is getting shorter, the sands of the hourglass are getting thinner, and time is passing more swiftly. People are beginning to feel the pulse of time relentlessly beating out the measure of their lives. The road and its journey are rushing by and the sands of the hourglass are flowing through the isthmus of time with frightening alacrity. The days are growing shorter and the fellow travelers of our time still don't know the object of the search implicit in life or their final destination. The symbol of the road and the hourglass are fundamentally linked on the plane of the absolute. If you ask how far there is still to go, someone will inevitably point to the horizon, and you will feel obliged to move forward, uncertain as to the final outcome and unsure whether you have done everything possible to meet the existential situation with sufficient insight and intelligence. We seem to be fatally adrift on the river of time that flows through our beings with its absolute message of finality and leads us on a current whose destination is unknown and possibly not even desired.

The Islamic traditions insist that the answers to life's fundamental mystery lie both on the horizon and within oneself. A person need only open his mind and heart to these outer and inner messages and develop an affinity for the knowledge implicit in the symbols of the horizon and within nature generally, and to the knowledge that can be uncovered within the experiences of the human soul. "Soon We shall show them Our signs on the horizon and within their own souls until it becomes clear to them that this is the Truth" (41:53*)*. The answer to the cosmic question lies at the center and on the edge, at the center of the human being and on the edge of the known world. The certainty that man desperately desires is never fully at hand, and neither is the happiness and peace that is a latent promise of the human condition as embodied in the symbolic image of the Paradise. The veil that separates man from an absolute solution to his human dilemma is there to be lifted, either as a veil within his own being or through the veil separating the material and spiritual worlds. Once again, the knowledge that we need in order to perfect our entity and fulfill our vocation lies within the inmost depths of our being and on the horizon of the known world.

The objective Reality demands that we acknowledge the reality that permeates all of existence, and that must include the true state of ourselves and the world we live in. We can no longer continue to fool ourselves with numerous illusions of the world and delusions of self that in fact have become the secular myths of the 20th century. We should no longer fool ourselves into thinking, for example, that we can live on our own without the aid and support of the Divine Being and without the aid of Heaven. We should no longer pretend that our ego is anything more than an individual consciousness that is full of pretensions and vain desires, in effect a coagulation of egocentricity that disperses us outward and downward rather than centers us inward and upward. We should start to recognize the ego for what it is in reality, as nothing more than a passing cloud or a candle flame in the wind. We should no longer put all our trust in a rational faculty that systematically fails to recognize the incredible miracle and mystery of life. We should no longer carry on the illusion of our own uniqueness and superiority in the face of an existential loneliness and spiritual inadequacy that we all feel at the root of our beings. And finally, we should no longer ignore the fact that we live in a pretentious and materialistic civilization that has unleashed destructive forces that mark the negation and end of an earlier and superior world, a negation that is not counterbalanced by the affirmation of all that is sacred and holy in life. It is time we abandon the lie that is fostered about man and the world during these secularized times and turn once again to the spiritual practices that the orthodox traditions still preserve, traditions that will lead us out of the quagmire of the human predicament and back to the truth that lies beyond the limits of the individual ego.

The road that leads us through the spiritual journey of our time has become exceedingly narrow. In many ways it could be likened to a tight-rope over the abyss, and yet, for all of that, there are a number of distinct advantages during these times that are worth mentioning as a message of hope for individuals everywhere still interested in crossing earthly boundaries and exploring distant horizons.

The sublime advantage of the modern pathway to the spirit is that it is incredibly straight and leads directly to man's true destination and end. Perhaps for that very reason the Quranic revelation exhorts the faithful to follow the "straight path," for indeed the path of return, once embraced, is without deviation during these times. The spiritual journey of our contemporary time takes us down a road that leads us through the final phase of a four cycle epoch that ends in the Iron Age or more appropriately termed by the Hindus the Dark Age of modern times. We are now coming to the termination of the spiritual journey that began with primordial man, scripturally portrayed through the persona of Adam, who represents the archetypal human being who understood truth without any intermediary veils and whose key was the integrity of his own being and his own self. In fact, Adam needed no key as such, for he was principally himself both humanly and spiritually. The spiritual journey contains elements of this primordial man, who beheld the mystery in all its incomprehensibility and wonder. This was followed by traditional man who held the vision of God in the mirror image of the world, and finally contemporary man, who sees only himself when he looks within the mirror of his own being.

For all of the miseries that result from and must accompany the experience of the Dark Age, many of which we are presently witnessing on a multitude of levels, the dark and tremulous atmosphere of the *Kali Yuga* also creates a climate that is conducive to both spirituality and wisdom. The near termination of an existing cycle can bring about a detachment and a spirituality within the people of these times that would not otherwise be possible in a time period that was relatively normal and unaffected by outward constraints, such as in the traditional times of the past where an ambiance of tradition and thus of spirituality was normal.

Martin Lings has pointed this out in his insightful book *The Eleventh Hour*. "Detachment is an essential feature of the sage, and this virtue, which in better times could only be acquired through great spiritual efforts, can be made more spontaneous by the sight of one's world in chaotic ruins."[2] In this sense, the world is an old man and the people in it are old souls who have available to them the benefits of old age and its blessed compensations, namely a wisdom and a detachment that often comes with the experience of age and the proximity to death. Old men are proverbially wise, and while an old world may not radiate wisdom in its degeneracy, then certainly the compensation of age-old wisdom is available to those who recognize its inscrutable face in the light of impending disaster.

It is small wonder, therefore, that during these times, people the world over are turning back to the traditional forms of spirituality that still contain the essential knowledge concerning the true nature

[2] Martin Lings, *The Eleventh Hour* (Cambridge, UK: Quinta Essentia, 1987), p. 66.

of Reality and the valid means of realizing that knowledge. A new and contemporary wisdom may well be possible in which the ancient and traditional knowledge that comes down to us directly through revelation can become integrated once again within the being of the individual by means of a spirituality that belies the anti-spiritual atmosphere of the contemporary world. The fine line between ignorance and wisdom is the same as the fine line that exists between faith and disbelief. The dark and portentous condition of this time period in many ways makes it easier to return from the edge of the abyss, develop a sincere faith, and become wise.

In addition, spirituality is very often a compensation of the old age of a person, particularly if that person has attempted in some genuine measure to live a life of spirituality, with a consciousness of what is required of the human being and of what is demanded by existence itself. Therefore, by way of extension, direct access to the knowledge and wisdom at the heart of all spirituality is the compensation of the old age of our time and the final "outpouring" of the spirit within this dark cycle. Similarly, if old age enjoys such close proximity to the "other side of death," it may also actually experience a foretaste of the paradise by way of prelude and promise. "The imminence of death should bring with it special graces, such as premonitions and visions, as a foretaste of what is to come. The mellowing of spirituality, which is the highest aspect of old age in itself, is thus crowned with an illumination which belongs more to youth than to age; the nearness of the new Golden Age cannot fail to make itself mysteriously felt before the end of the old cycle."[3] In this way, cycles overlap and merge so that the benefits of the new cycle can serve as compensation to the dying cycle, and can prepare the mentality of mankind for future cyclical offerings.

The spiritual journey of our time is essentially the same journey that has occurred down through cyclical time since the termination of the Golden Age and the fall from the Paradise at the end of the primordial era. Its path proceeds from the inner self and moves outward toward the horizon of man's being, the horizon of the physical world, unto the horizon of the known universe, since it is within the self and on the horizon that man will find the essential knowledge of

[3] *Ibid.*

his meaning and final destiny. It is a journey of man through time and space in search of the greatest truth for which he is capable. The time has now come when we must distinguish between a purely theoretical knowledge that may only intrigue the mind and a spiritual experience that will transform all theoretical knowledge into a realized knowledge within man's being.

We have elected to write about a subject for which we can claim no real authority since all authority must reside with the Divinity, who is both the Cosmic Reality and the Ultimate Truth. Nevertheless, the challenge confronts everyone to come to terms not only with his own mystery, but with the mystery that is implicit in the universe. Every individual must seek the answer to the Divine Mystery through his or her experience here on earth. Everyone has the duty to explore the secret within his or her being, a secret that must be learned through trial and error and cannot be learned from anyone else. Everyone must cultivate a sense of the Sacred that permeates every existing thing with its living, holy quality. Everyone must come to terms with the great and solemn facts that lie sequestered within the souls of people everywhere.

As such, then, the writing of this book has represented a search for a fuller understanding of the truth, a means of expressing that truth through human spirituality, a yearning of the heart for the Beloved, and a cry in the spiritual wilderness of modern life. Therefore let its final statement be a prayer of aspiration and hope; namely, that if we face the Divine Mystery with persistence and courage, then the Face of Truth will be revealed to us in all its clarity and light.

# INDEX

For a glossary of all key foreign words used in books published by World Wisdom, including metaphysical terms in English, consult: www.DictionaryofSpiritualTerms.org.
This on-line Dictionary of Spiritual Terms provides extensive definitions, examples, and related terms in other languages.

# BIOGRAPHICAL NOTE

**John Herlihy** was born into an Irish-American family in Boston, Massachusetts. Upon completion of his studies at a Paulist seminary, he went in search of adventure as a traveler and teacher and has since worked as a lecturer in English in several Near and Far Eastern countries. In the early 1970s, he made the acquaintance of a Kashmiri Indian whom he now fondly remembers as "the laughing Sufi." In his book *The Seeker and the Way* he explains that his conversion to Islam was a raw and unexpected awakening that pulled him back from the abyss and set for him a new direction in coming to terms with the purpose and meaning of his life. Twenty years after his conversion and with a life-long interest in writing, he began to explore through words the complex nature of his relationship with this and the "other" world. In addition to writing for such traditional journals as *Sacred Web* and *Sophia*, his publications include *In Search of the Truth*, *Veils and Keys to Enlightenment*, *Modern Man at the Crossroads*, *Near and Distant Horizons*, and *Borderlands of the Spirit: Reflections on a Sacred Science of Mind*, all of which reflect upon the disparity between modernity and tradition and the pursuit of spirituality in today's anti-spiritual world.

# Titles in the Perennial Philosophy Series by World Wisdom

*A Christian Pilgrim in India: The Spiritual Journey of Swami Abhishiktananda (Henri Le Saux)*, by Harry Oldmeadow, 2008

*The Betrayal of Tradition: Essays on the Spiritual Crisis of Modernity*, edited by Harry Oldmeadow, 2005

*Borderlands of the Spirit: Reflections on a Sacred Science of Mind*, by John Herlihy, 2005

*A Buddhist Spectrum: Contributions to Buddhist-Christian Dialogue*, by Marco Pallis, 2003

*The Essential Ananda K. Coomaraswamy*, edited by Rama P. Coomaraswamy, 2004

*The Essential Martin Lings*, edited by Reza Shah-Kazemi and Emma Clark, 2010

*The Essential René Guénon*, edited by John Herlihy, 2009

*The Essential Seyyed Hossein Nasr*, edited by William C. Chittick, 2007

*The Essential Sophia*, edited by Seyyed Hossein Nasr and Katherine O'Brien, 2006

*The Essential Titus Burckhardt: Reflections on Sacred Art, Faiths, and Civilizations*, edited by William Stoddart, 2003

*Every Branch in Me: Essays on the Meaning of Man*, edited by Barry McDonald, 2002

*Every Man An Artist: Readings in the Traditional Philosophy of Art*, edited by Brian Keeble, 2005

*Figures of Speech or Figures of Thought? The Traditional View of Art*, by Ananda K. Coomaraswamy, 2007

*A Guide to Hindu Spirituality*, by Arvind Sharma, 2006

*Introduction to Traditional Islam, Illustrated: Foundations, Art, and Spirituality*, by Jean-Louis Michon, 2008

*Islam, Fundamentalism, and the Betrayal of Tradition: Essays by Western Muslim Scholars*, edited by Joseph E.B. Lumbard, 2004

*Journeys East: 20th Century Western Encounters with Eastern Religious Traditions*, by Harry Oldmeadow, 2004

*Light From the East: Eastern Wisdom for the Modern West*, edited by Harry Oldmeadow, 2007

*Living in Amida's Universal Vow: Essays in Shin Buddhism*, edited by Alfred Bloom, 2004

*Of the Land and the Spirit: The Essential Lord Northbourne on Ecology and Religion*, edited by Christopher James and Joseph A. Fitzgerald, 2008

*Paths to the Heart: Sufism and the Christian East*, edited by James S. Cutsinger, 2002

*Remembering in a World of Forgetting: Thoughts on Tradition and Postmodernism*, by William Stoddart, 2008

*Returning to the Essential: Selected Writings of Jean Biès*, translated by Deborah Weiss-Dutilh, 2004

*Science and the Myth of Progress*, edited by Mehrdad M. Zarandi, 2003

*Seeing God Everywhere: Essays on Nature and the Sacred*, edited by Barry McDonald, 2003

*Singing the Way: Insights in Poetry and Spiritual Transformation*, by Patrick Laude, 2005

*The Spiritual Legacy of the North American Indian: Commemorative Edition*, by Joseph E. Brown, 2007

*Sufism: Love & Wisdom*, edited by Jean-Louis Michon and Roger Gaetani, 2006

*The Underlying Religion: An Introduction to the Perennial Philosophy*, edited by Martin Lings and Clinton Minnaar, 2007

*Unveiling the Garden of Love: Mystical Symbolism in Layla Majnun and Gita Govinda*, by Lalita Sinha, 2008

*Wisdom's Journey: Living the Spirit of Islam in the Modern World*, by John Herlihy, 2009

*Ye Shall Know the Truth: Christianity and the Perennial Philosophy*, edited by Mateus Soares de Azevedo, 2005

## Titles on Islam by World Wisdom

*Art of Islam, Language and Meaning: Commemorative Edition*, by Titus Burckhardt, 2009

*Christianity/Islam: Perspectives on Esoteric Ecumenism*, by Frithjof Schuon, 2008

*Introduction to Sufi Doctrine*, by Titus Burckhardt, 2008

*Introduction to Traditional Islam, Illustrated: Foundations, Art, and Spirituality*, by Jean-Louis Michon, 2008

*Islam, Fundamentalism, and the Betrayal of Tradition: Essays by Western Muslim Scholars*, edited by Joseph E.B. Lumbard, 2004

*The Mystics of Islam*, by Reynold A. Nicholson, 2002

*The Path of Muhammad: A Book on Islamic Morals and Ethics by Imam Birgivi*, interpreted by Shaykh Tosun Bayrak, 2005

*Paths to the Heart: Sufism and the Christian East*, edited by James S. Cutsinger, 2003

*Paths to Transcendence: According to Shankara, Ibn Arabi, and Meister Eckhart*, by Reza Shah-Kazemi, 2006

*The Sacred Foundations of Justice in Islam: The Teachings of 'Ali ibn Abi Talib*, edited by M. Ali Lakhani, 2006

*The Spirit of Muhammad: From Hadith*, edited by Judith and Michael Oren Fitzgerald, 2010

*A Spirit of Tolerance: The Inspiring Life of Tierno Bokar*, by Amadou Hampaté Bâ, 2008

*The Sufi Doctrine of Rumi: Illustrated Edition* by William C. Chittick, 2005

*Sufism: Love and Wisdom*, edited by Jean-Louis Michon and Roger Gaetani, 2006

*Sufism: Veil and Quintessence*, by Frithjof Schuon, 2007

*Understanding Islam*, by Frithjof Schuon, 1998

*The Universal Spirit of Islam: From the Koran and Hadith*, edited by Judith and Michael Oren Fitzgerald, 2006

*Unveiling the Garden of Love: Mystical Symbolism in Layla Majnun and Gita Govinda*, by Lalita Sinha, 2008

*Wisdom's Journey: Living the Spirit of Islam in the Modern World*, by John Herlihy, 2009